Perspectives of Social Security

Collection of Lectures Delivered

PERSPECTIVES OF SOCIAL SECURITY

Edited by

R.K.A. Subrahmanya

L.D. Mishra

B.N. Som

Under the auspices of

Social Security Association of India

SHIPRA

ISBN: 978-81-7541-551-5

First Published in India in 2011

Perspectives of Social Security

Published by:
SHIPRA PUBLICATIONS
LG 18-19, Pankaj Central Market,
I.P. Ext., Patparganj, Delhi-110092
Ph. 91-11-22235152, 22236152

Br. Off: 4617/18, Ansari Road, Daryaganj,
Delhi-110002; Ph. 65946453, 9810522367

Email: info@shiprapublications.com
www.shiprapublications.com

Contents

PREFACE

The Association arranges seminars/round table conferences every year on the most contemporaneous issues confronting labour. Since its beginning it has also been organizing annual lecture series on the occasion of its annual day to highlight or to initiate debate on the most burning issues confronting the society. It started with the address by Dr. Manmohan Singh, the then Finance Minister who not only inaugurated the Association, but also set the perspective of social security in the context of the new economic order that had emerged in the 1990s across the globe and the economic reforms that had been set in operation in our country having far reaching effects on the governance, on labour and on the society. Then, from year to year, annual lectures have been organized on a wide range of socio economic issues like the effect of social clause in international trade agreement, the question of securing social security for workers of unorganized workers, the need for state support for development of children in poor households, social security for women workers in informal sector, the role of National Human Rights Commission in ensuring the fulfilment of right to social security, social security for migrant workers, right to food, right to medical care, employment guarantee as an instrument of social security, the strategy of ensuring social security in developing countries in Asia, corporate social responsibility for securing social security net for the workers at the workplace and the need for pension reform for securing old age and survival pension for the unorganized workers.

By publishing this anthology of lectures on social security we have endeavoured to project the multidimensional perspectives of social security for study by students, teachers as well as thinkers in the field of social security. Social Security Association of India acknowledges its indebtedness to Oil & Natural Gas Commission (ONGC) for the latter's support of its cause to spread the message of social security far and wide, and create appropriate consciousness among the lawmakers, policy makers and also among the working populace the need for building a decent social security net for all. We are beholden to Chairman, ONGC and especially to Dr. Balyan, the then Director (HR), for his helping hand in approving our project of bringing out this publication.

We do hope that this compilation will stimulate serious thinking among the scholars and researchers on various issues concerning social security.

B.N. SOM
Secretary General
Social Security Association of India

Introduction

'Social Security Association of India' was founded in 1991 with the primary objective of promoting social security in India. The Association holds an annual conference to coincide with its Annual General Meeting when a lecture or a symposium is organised to provide an opportunity to the members to exchange ideas on the emerging issues concerning social security.

It is now nearly twenty years since the founding of the Association. During this period the Association had invited several distinguished personalities to deliver lectures on various aspects of Social Security. Many of these lectures have been published in the *Indian Journal of Social Security*. As, however, the circulation of this journal is somewhat limited it has been felt desirable to bring out a collection of the lectures in the form of a book which may be available to wider sections of the society. Hence this book.

There is no commonly accepted definition of social security. There are, however, a variety of definitions a study of which would indicate that there are two streams of thought on the subject. According to one, represented by the ILO, social security means the "protection which the society provides for its members, through a series of public measures against economic and social distress that otherwise would be caused by the stoppage or substantial reduction of earnings resulting from sickness, maternity, employment injury, unemployment, invalidity, old age and death, the provision of medical care, and the provision of subsidies for families with children. In this view, the scope of social security is limited largely to maintenance of one's income against loss or diminution due to the occurrence of a contingency. According to another view, the object of social security is broader to enable a person to attain a decent standard of life and also to maintain it. It may be preventive or promotional, as the case may be. It is said that in this context social security policies and strategies would need to be addressed as a part of antipoverty policies and that social security should include income support through promotional measures such as employment promotion, food subsidy and child nutrition, as well as income maintenance through protective measures, such as public assistance for old age, maternity disability and death. The lectures included in this book represent both the streams of thought. Hence the book is called 'Perspectives of Social Security'.

As stated above, the Social Security Association of India was founded in the year 1991 in the wake of the introduction of the New Economic Policy because it was felt that social security was necessary for the new policy to succeed. Dr. Manmohan Singh, the then Union Finance Minister, underlined this point in his inaugural address. He said that a credible instrument of social security was necessary to ensure that the process of change would not impose undue burden on the working class. It was reiterated by Sh. Pranab Mukherjee, the then Dy. Chairman of the Planning Commission, while inaugurating a Seminar on Social Security in the context of the New Economic Policy. He said that during the 1970's Government resorted to nationalization of sick units to protect the workers affected by retrenchment or closure of industrial units but that could not be done in the current circumstances due to fiscal stringency. A different strategy would have to worked out, firstly, to bring the population in the unorganized sector within the system of social security and, secondly, to protect the workers threatened with unemployment as a result of the new policy.

According to the Universal Declaration of Human Rights, the Right to Work as well as the Right to Social Security are basic human rights. Many speakers have, therefore, adopted the rights based approach to the subject. Justice Sh. M.N.Venkatachaliah, former Chief Justice of the Supreme Court, spoke about the Right to Life and the Right to Livelihood being the basic elements of the Right to Social Security. Unfortunately, the recording of his speech has been lost and, therefore, we have not been able to reproduce it here. His lecture was in the nature of an exposition of the following rulings of the Supreme Court regarding the right to livelihood being inherent in the right to life:

> "The sweep of the right to life conferred by Article 21 is wide and far reaching. It does not mean merely that life cannot be extinguished or taken away as, for example, by the imposition and execution of the death sentence, except according to procedure established by law. That is but one aspect of the right to life. An equally important facet of that right is the right to livelihood because, no person can live without the means of living, that is, the means of livelihood. If the right to livelihood is not treated as a part of the constitutional right to life, the easiest way of depriving a person of his right to life would be to deprive him of his means of livelihood to the point of abrogation. Such deprivation would not only denude the life of its effective content and meaningfulness but it would make life impossible to live. And yet, such deprivation would not have to be in accordance with the procedure established

by law, if the right to livelihood is not regarded as a part of the right to life. That, which alone makes it possible to live, leave aside what makes like livable, must be deemed to be an Integral component of the right to life. [79 F-H, 80 A-B]

2.2 The principles contained in Articles 39(a) and 41 must be regarded as equally fundamental in the understanding and interpretation of the meaning and content of fundamental rights. If there is an obligation upon the State to secure to the citizens an adequate means of livelihood and the right to work, it would be sheer pedantry to exclude the right to livelihood from the content of the right to life. The State may not, by affirmative action, be compellable to provide adequate means of livelihood or work to the citizens. But, any person who is deprived of his right to livelihood except according to just and fair procedure established by law, can challenge the deprivation as offending the right to life conferred by Article 21. [80 G-H, 81 A]

(Mum v. Illinois [1877] 94 US 113 and Kbarak Singh v. The State of U.P. [1964] 1 S.C.R. 332 referred to.)[1]"

Justice Sh. J.S. Verma has cited several legal provisions to show that social security is a human right and has stated that the framers of the Indian Constitution gave considerable thought to the protection of economic, social and cultural rights and, in particular, the right to social security. He has spoken at length of the initiatives taken by the National Human Rights Commission to enforce the rights of the disabled, the right to health, and the rights of older persons.

Mr. Jean Dreze has spoken about the right to food. The day Mr. Dreze addressed the Association that was Dr. Ambedkar's birthday. His speech was largely an exposition of Dr. Ambedkar's views. He said:

"Dr. Ambedkar had revolutionary vision for India's future which included Participatory Democracy, Social Equality, a Welfare State and the realization of a wide range of economic and social rights including the right to Social Security. We would do well to remember and revive this vision today as we consider the prospects of achieving social security for all in the near future."

"In his vision of India's future, as I understand it, Social Security rested on three pillars-Participatory Democracy, Constitutional Rights and the Welfare State. So I will comment briefly on each of these, because I think they are really still very relevant today."

At the outset Mr. Dreze clarified that his view of social security was much broader than the conventional definitions of the term. He said:

---

1. India — Olga Tellis v. Bombay Municipal Corporation (1985.07.10) (Right to Life and Livelihood for Homeless)

> "Before I proceed, I would like to clarify what I mean by Social Security because it goes a little beyond the standard interpretation you may be used to. I am not thinking of Social Security in the narrow sense of guaranteeing a minimum level of income, or at least not only in that sense, let alone thinking of Social Security in the sense of doing it for a privileged minority of citizens who happen to belong to the organized sector. I am thinking more broadly of Social Security as a set of social arrangements that protect all citizens from poverty, hunger, illness, illiteracy, violence and deprivation of other basic needs. Social Security in this broad sense can be seen as one of the concerns of Dr. Ambedkar's life and thoughts."

He pointed out:

> "that the basic reason why Social Security in the sense in which I have defined it, is still so far from being realized in India today is that it is not much of a political priority. That is the bottom line and in fact this can be seen as one particular example of a more general pattern of massive neglect, if not invisibility of people's basic needs in Indian politics. That itself, in turn, can be seen as a reflection of the continued marginalization of disadvantaged groups in democratic politics, in contrast to the process of gradual expansion of participatory democracy that was envisaged by Dr. Ambedkar. In other words, because people are excluded most of the time from the democratic process and even have limited ability to exercise their right to vote, because they do not have adequate information about the different parties, sometimes may be even physically prevented from voting. Therefore their concerns and basic social issues tend to count for very little."

As regards the right to food he said: "Broadly speaking, the Right to Food can be thought of as a right to be free from hunger. It is a claim of the individual on Society. That means the right to food is an assertion that society has enough resources, both physical and institutional, to prevent hunger and to ensure that nobody goes hungry. The responsibility for protecting this Right is primarily the responsibility of the State, since the State commands the required resources and is generally responsible for the welfare of the citizens." He pointed out that the State had failed in ensuring this right.

He further said: "As you all know, we live in a very strange and shocking situation today in India which may be called hunger amidst plenty, where on the one hand, India is one of the most undernourished countries in the world and on the other hand this is happening under the shadow of enormous food stocks. According to recent data published in the World Development Report and the Human Development Report, no country has higher levels of undernourishment than India except possibly Bangladesh."

"It is in this context that I think it is important to invoke the Right to Food because in an obvious sense the situation is a violation of Right to Food which is a part of the Directive Principles of the Constitution. In fact, the Constitution talks nothing about the Right to Food but about the Right to Nutrition which is an even more interesting and advanced concept. I think it is by highlighting this aspect of the situation-this massive violation of the Right to Food - that we can hope to ensure that the problem receives the attention that it deserves-as has been happening. I think, to some extent, in the last two years."

Ms Aruna (Bunker) Roy spoke about her campaigns for the right to information and employment guarantee. About the right to information she said:

> "Politics is a very large issue for me, which defines any tussle for power between two groups, one which is deprived and one which benefits from power; whether it is a women's issue, whether it is a Dalit issue, there is politics. Electoral politics is really seen as dirty business. Unless we address this issue, there is nothing for us. So how do we do it? One of the fallouts of this big debate, and an important fallout, is the Right to Information campaign. Every time we went to Government and demanded payment of minimum wage, we were told that we were lying. So we had to demand to see the records,. Many of our friends in the IAS and outside, lots of politicians who are honest, lots of lawyers, judges, journalists and all sorts of people joined the campaign because no single group had any claim to an ethical view of life today. NGOs are corrupt, social institutions are corrupt, politicians are corrupt, civil servants are corrupt, wherever you see, there is corruption and I do not think there is any group of people whom you can see today, is corruption-free. So the coming together of all people who wanted ethics in civil society and decent administrative system and who wanted the poor to have the right to know and right to live was important. Because, for us, the right to know is connected to the right to live."

About employment guarantee, Ms Roy said: "the EGA (Employment Guarantee Act) is the only means by which we can have livelihood security, assured future for our children, for education, for health, for access to any of the resources, even to stay in the villages, to mobilize, to fight for our demands. Otherwise, because of lack of employment there will be an increase in migration to cities. They come to Delhi and go to other places as construction workers without any rights; they do not have ration cards, they do not have living rights, they do not have any other rights, adding to their own problems as well as those of the State. So overall, if you look at this country, employment is a vital issue.

Mr. Jan Bremen spoke about the rights of migrant workers. He said:

> "My lecture would address the problems of labour not only as a factor of production and as a commodity but as human beings who have a right to a decent life and a right to life of dignity, a right to get a wage which enables them to care for themselves and also those who live with them." He did not offer technical solutions for providing social security to migrant labour. He said that he wanted to "contextualise migrant labour in society and the economy and then explain why it seems so difficult to include them in programmes of social security".

He pointed out that most of migrant labour belong to the class of agricultural labour and their conditions of life were pitiable. He described the conditions of agricultural labour and explained why they migrate. In this connection he said:

> "People at the bottom of the village are both pushed out and pulled out of the local economy. They are pushed out because the farmers do not need them throughout the year any longer. There is no work for them in the village throughout the year. In that sense, they are pushed out of the village economy. But they are also pulled out because the diversification of the rural economy has made it look both possible and also attractive for them to leave the village economy. They escape from a closed labour market. They escape from a situation where they will be under the rule of the landowners and when they go out they escape the social control and the social power and economic power of the landowners. So to that extent, there is both a pushing out of labour of the village economy and a pulling out of labour of the village economy."

Explaining why employers preferred migrant labour, he said:

> "Why do employers make use of migrant workers? Why do they use them at all? There is a very conventional and a very simple idea which you find in many labour studies. In these studies on labour migration, it is said that people move from one place to the other because there is no work at the place where they live and there is work at the place where they go to. That is a very simple, a very convincing and a very persuasive explanation. But I am afraid it is not so simple; it is a bit more complicated than that."

Nowadays, employers prefer temporary labour to permanent labour. They prefer to hire and also fire labour instantly and not involve themselves in permanent relationship with them. It is very interesting to observe that in places where there are many migrant workers coming from outside, there is no dearth of local labour. Local labour is available but employers prefer outside labour for two reasons because, basically, outside labour, as a rule of thumb, is cheaper than local labour and outside labour is more pliable. Local labourers are not only workers, they also have their social life. They have a house to go back to in the evening. They have dependents around them. A family to care for. They have events in the family like marriage, birth, death. They are not only a commodity, but they are also human beings who have a social life and they cannot be totally and completely controlled by employers in the way that outside labourers can be controlled. Outside labour is a commodity. You do not know them, you have no personal relationship with them, you hire them when there is work, in the fields, in the salt pans, in the brick kilns or you fire them if there is no need for them any more. You cannot do that to local labour. Local labour also has social power. Local labour has also social capital in the village, in the habitat where they live. They have a kind of bargaining power. The bargaining power of migrant workers is next to nil - yes, they can run away and they do that. If you talk to employers, they complain about migrant labour - who are not faithful, who are not loyal; they talk to you, pretending that the migrant labourers are unreliable and irresponsible. They say – "yesterday, they were at work and today they have gone, I do not know where, I do not know why". They do not understand that absconding, running away leaving the worksite is also an expression of protest. Yet, employers prefer outside labour."

About social security, he elaborated: "Then what is the Social Security of these migrant labourers? That is what I am expected to focus on. Let me say at the outset that there is no Social Security for them. The process of migration is itself a form of Social Security for them. Labour migration is denial of Social Security. They go away because locally they do not get enough work throughout the year to make a living and to reproduce their labour power for the next generation. The employer has no interest in investing in Social Security for the migrant workers.

Social Security is meant to help a worker during periods of unemployment, sickness or old age. These basically are the reasons why people require Social Security. Migrant labourers are not able to make any provision for these purposes. They cannot put aside any savings for bad days. Bad days in terms of unemployment, bad days in terms of ill health, bad days when they cannot work anymore because of old age. The wages paid to migrant labourers and the large masses of them are unskilled, poorly educated, the wages paid to migrant labourers are so abominably low that they cannot afford to invest in Social Security. As a matter of fact, on days when they have no income, they have to sell their labour power in advance in order to get some money to buy food or meet any other expenditure they have necessarily to incur. That is the Social Security for them. Social Security is being tied to credit. Very often, migrant labourers are indebted to the Mukaddam, the labour contractor, the employer, the shopkeepers or money lenders in the village.

Mr. Bremen drew attention to three dimensions of migration of workers which keep them in a state of despair:

> "In the first place, they are mobilized from far away, but always time bound; they are not mobilized indefinitely; they are mobilized for a particular period of the year, and they have to get out again. Mobilization is the first dimension.
>
> The second dimension is compensation for their work. The payment for their work, is not based on time rate-is not based on the hours of work say, they do not work for a fixed period of time from 8 O'clock in the morning till 4-5 O'clock in the evening like many of us do so, the modality of payment is different. It is based on piece rate for the job work done. That is why it becomes necessary for a labour migrant to involve other members of his household-wife and children. It is only by involving other members of the household in the labour process that he can make a living. Compensation is the second part.
>
> The third dimension is casualisation. Migrant labour is essentially casual labour. They are not permanent labour. They can be hired and dismissed within a couple of hours and the employer does not accept further obligations. Even the cost of travel has to be borne by the labour migrant himself. The employer does not pay for that. The labourer has to pay for his or her own mobility. The pattern of migration and the income the migrant workers earn does not have a margin which can be used for their protection in times of crisis."

He concluded with the following remarks:

> "All said and done, India is still a society dominated by social inequality and a rather callous, careless, indifferent attitude towards people at the bottom of the economy and society. The idea that they have a right to dignity is basically denied by the powers that be. That is because society is structured in terms of hierarchy and not in terms of equality. If there is no counter veiling power in the society to improve the condition of those who are at the bottom, then all you write on paper will be meaningless and will only be a means for officials to make money at the cost of the poor just as they make

money out of the minimum wage legislation – not by implementing it but by using it for their own purposes, to line their own pockets. This is the economic factor.

The political factor has to do with social inequality. If there is no more countervailing power in society to assert the rights and also the dignity of the labouring pool, then social security co-efficients will not work. They give a lip service by which mainstream politicians and policymakers say that they are doing something for them but in fact, the will to implement it is lacking. There is a stark contrast between the democratic fabric of Indian Society – praise be to that democratic quality of Indian society from Independence onwards – and it is an enormous tool for assertion, for the downtrodden in the society of India, but, in contrast, there is the Government which is not giving to the poor what they have a right to ask for."

Nearly 93 per cent of the Indian workforce are in the unorganized sector characterized by lack of legal protection and social security. The Social Security Association of India has spearheaded the movement to provide social security to the workers in the unorganized sector. The Association organized several seminars and symposia on Social Security for the workers in the unorganized Sector. Lectures delivered at one of the symposia organized during the Annual Conference of the Association are reproduced here.

Mr. John Woodall, Senior Specialist in Social Security in the ILO, spoke in the National Workshop on Social Protection of Women in the informal sector on the "Coverage of contingencies under formal social security schemes and the needs of women workers in the informal sector". Mr. Woodall said: The work of those who participate in the informal economy gives rise to a set of issues which are highly topical in India. He drew attention to two features of the informal economy which are immediately apparent. They are:

(a) The importance of this sector to women's employment reflecting to some extent their relative disadvantage, compared with men in formal employment
(b) The nearly complete absence of institutions (either public or private) of social protection.

He pointed out that the objective of Decent Work cannot be achieved in the absence of appropriate conditions, high amongst which is the type of protection against income loss and for health care. He expressed the view that formal social security schemes offer the most reliable structure within which provision can be made for such protection. He then proceeded to discuss how a social security system can be organized for the informal sector in an optimal manner. He set out a conceptual outline of the system he had in view. In doing so he proposed an alternative definition of social security which would include the following elements:

(a) The provision of benefits to households and individuals
(b) Through public or collective arrangements
(c) To protect against low or declining standards
(d) Arising from a number of basic risks and needs

He stated that a broad definition of this kind would allow the inclusion of education, shelter, food security and crops insurance within the scope of social protection.

Mr. Woodall then offered certain comments on the applicability to the informal sector of the ILO Conventions relating to the various contingencies indicating the need for modification thereof and the need for establishing priorities among the various benefits. He further stated that in countries where the wishes of the people had been surveyed the overwhelming priority was for the provision of effective healthcare; further down the list of priorities was old age benefit, benefits for survivors, and employment injury or invalidity benefit.

Referring to the financial arrangements, Mr. Woodall said that no contributory scheme would be effective if the workers were unable to afford contributions or the demand for contributions from the employers was such as to deter employment altogether.

Mr. Wouter van Ginniken, another specialist in social security from Geneva also spoke about the provision of social security to the workers in the unorganized sector. His talk was in three parts: the first part related to the coverage of the existing schemes and the specific social protection needs of the workers in the informal sector which in his view were different from those of the workers in the formal sector. In the second part, he spoke about the various options available to extend social protection to the informal sector including micro insurance. In the end, he spoke about the activities of the ILO and about the experiments for extension of social protection being carried out. In this connection he stated that the ILO was not sufficiently advanced in its knowledge to have full fledged and integrated policy for the informal sector. He expressed the hope that the experiments being carried out would enable them to develop a more comprehensive policy of social protection for the informal sector in a period of two to three years.

In 1997, three years after the democratic elections in South Africa the South African government introduced a new social security benefit scheme, a modest cash transfer targeted at three million children up to the age of seven years old who live in poor households. The benefit, called the Child Support Grant, came to be means tested, and accompanied the phasing out of the previous State Maintenance Grant. This interesting social intervention came at a time of radical political change accompanied by a relatively conservative macro economic policy. It raised all sorts of interesting issues about social security and social development – issues which are interesting conceptually, politically, and technically. Ms Frances Lund Professor in the University of Natal in South Africa who headed a committee that recommended the introduction of the programme was in India and was invited to speak about it. She explained how the Committee came to make the recommendation "in a climate when the overall policy movement was towards social development, which many would think would be antithetical to the idea of social security."

There is currently an ongoing debate in India about the desirability of introducing a system of cash transfers in preference to the programmes under which social assistance is provided in kind, such as the PDS. The speech of Ms. Lund is topical and relevant in that context.

Till the passage of the Unorganised Workers Social Security Act, 2008 social security legislation in India was concerned mainly with the workers in the organised sector. The Association organized several programmes to educate the workers about social security generally and the social security laws in particular. Some of the lectures included in this collection are those delivered at the inauguration of the training courses. Of these, mention should be made of the lecture delivered by Mr. L.P. Massum, former Director in the office of the ILO in India which is in the form of an introduction to social security as developed globally. The concluding words of his lecture are noteworthy and are reproduced below:

"The lessons for the future are that we must seek to ensure that social security schemes meet the needs of today and tomorrow, rather than yesterday. You are probably aware that other international organizations, such as the World Bank have developed quite radical ideas for the financial development of social security and these need to be evaluated in relation to the social dimension, which is of course ILO's primary concern. There is an almost infinite variety of possible designs for each country's social security system and of the ways in which the responsibilities and benefits due to members may be arranged and shared with their social partners, the employers and the Government."

Mr. Dalmer D. Hoskins, Secretary General of the International Social Security Association (ISSA), spoke about the global crisis in social security. He started with the statement that ISSA was concerned about the current status of social security in the world and that it had found itself increasingly living in a world where social security was under attack and in some countries social security was facing a crisis of confidence. If one picked up a newspaper in Europe, North America or Australia one would find on the front pages comments on social security that it was expensive, it was creating unemployment, it was encouraging people not to work and so forth. It was all because people were living in a time of uncertainties including economic uncertainties and there was a breakdown of the old consensus about social security. Elaborating this point, Mr. Hoskins said that at the end of the World War II people in the ILO, in the ISSA and at national levels fought hard to put in place programmes like the EPF and the ESI. This happened all over the world and country after country put in place some form of social protection based on a consensus between the social partners about the social security needs of the people. It would appear that consensus was breaking down.

"One of the biggest changes that has occurred since then is that institutions such as World Bank, the IMF have suddenly started taking interest in social security. They are going to countries and telling them that they reform their programmes or they would not get loans. They have created a crisis of confidence In many countries coverage of social security is shrinking. There is also the problem of delivery of services and benefits in many parts of the world. Besides, a number of big old time social security schemes have real problems in running the programmes. There is a political blockade in these countries, the partnership between the employers and workers is not working and they are finding it painfully difficult to go forward." He, therefore, felt that people should sit back and try to have a calm and informed debate about the crisis.

He then indicated the issues that needed to be discussed and the possible solutions thereto.

Ms. Corazon de la Paz, President of the International Social Security Association, in her article has spoken about the developments in the field of social security in Asia and the Pacific. She has referred to the issues under discussion at global level. She said:

"Social security discussions in the 1990s were dominated by issues on the advantages and drawbacks of publicly managed defined benefit versus privately managed defined contribution old-age pension schemes. Happily, the discussion of the 1990s have since given way to more balanced and less polarized views on social security reform, especially with the knowledge that reforms must be more adapted and calibrated to a country's unique circumstances.

Thus, from the heated debates of the 1990s, the social security agenda has refocused itself on four of the long-standing challenges confronting it, namely, coverage, programme adequacy, sustainability and governance.

The refocusing of the social security agenda serves as a reminder that the basic purpose of social security is to offer people income security over the course of their lives. I, for one, have always believed that work or a job is the best form of security and that the role of social security is to ensure that if an unexpected occurrence disrupts the income stream provided by employment, then there are mechanisms in place to meet these unforeseen contingencies. (Emphasis supplied)"

She also stated that there were three global factors driving this refocused social security agenda: the globalization of markets and its consequences; the ageing of the population; and the dramatic implications of public health threats such as SARS and HIV/AIDS, particularly in developing countries. She explained the developments in these areas.

One of the major schemes designed primarily for the workers in the organized sector is the ESI Scheme the working of which has come in for great deal of criticism. The Association, therefore, organized a symposium on Revamping of the ESI Scheme in collaboration with the Corporation. The symposium has generated many useful suggestions for improving the working of the Scheme.

Old age benefit is one of the major benefits provided under social security. The former Chairman of the Pension Funds Regulatory and Development Authority spoke about the pension market in India, the genesis and the current status of the New Pension Scheme which was introduced as a measure of reform of the pension system. He said: "The NPS has been mainly designed to fill the gap of old age income security to the unorganized sector. The scheme is envisaged to be a voluntary one for this segment of the population. Given a high savings rate of 35 per cent of GDP, Indian workers are encouraged in respect of their capability to contribute towards a self financed old age income security scheme. In this framework, the New Pension System will provide them with the opportunity to fulfil their needs of old age income support in the most productive way. Further, the system will also be capable of providing a delivery mechanism for the other segments of population viz. Pillar-I (population vide mandatory pension system) and Pillar-II (mandatory occupational pension system). The low cost structure of the architecture will enable Government to utilize this infrastructure to deliver any scheme of old age income support to any segment of the population in the most efficient manner."

The genesis of social security is usually traced to the Declaration of the Rights of Man and the introduction of social insurance by Bismarck in Germany. Justice Rama Jois in his lecture has pointed out that social security was in practice in ancient India and that several Moral Codes like Sukra Niti have laid down the duties of the king for protection of the people in distress. He has highlighted the famous declaration of Raja Rantideva in Mahabharata that his desire and duty was to wipe out the tears of those in distress and has stated that it was one of the fundamental duties of the State to provide social security to those in distress.

"In conformity with the above principle, from ancient times, one of the fundamental duties imposed on the state in this land has been the protection of the people. As part of this, specific directives were incorporated in Rajadharma (Constitutional Law of Ancient India) to provide Social Security in many ways to those who are in distress."

Ordinarily social security is required to be provided by the State or the society as a whole. Lately, however, the concept of social security has been widened to include measures adopted by the employers for the benefit of the employees as well as the community at large. Dr. A.K. Baliyan Director (HR) of the ONGC spoke about the philosophy of Corporate Social Responsibility and what the ONGC has been doing in discharge of that responsibility. He said that:

"In ONGC, our philosophy is to do business and earn enough to give back to the society as much as possible for its sustenance and development. Under the corporate policy, we have developed a highly focused policy, called, Corporate Citizenship Policy (CCP). ... Under this policy, ONGC group of companies shall promote, as a responsible Corporate Citizen, the following:

(i) Education.
(ii) Health Care.
(iii) Entrepreneurship in the community and support.
(iv) Water Management.
(v) Disaster Relief in the country.
(vi) Environment.

He then proceeded to describe the various measures undertaken by the ONGC in discharge of its corporate social responsibility.

R.K.A. SUBRAHMANYA

1.

Social Security in the Context of the New Economic Policy

Dr. Manmohan Singh
The then Union Finance Minister

DECEMBER 1991

I am very happy to associate myself with this inaugural function of Social Security Association. The need for social security is an established reality in all civilized societies to day. Because all modern societies find that traditional ways of coping with the problems of unemployment, the problems of ill health, problems of accident and other misfortunes that come in life of individuals, in the form of premature death, injury, disablement, are not adequate and that these are problems which need to be tackled by the Society as a whole; that a caring society, and any civilized society must aspire to be a caring society, cannot leave those who suffer from these misfortunes to suffer in silence; and that society, therefore, has a responsibility to its unfortunate members by way of coming to their assistance.

All over the world various approaches have been adopted to deal with the problem of providing adequate means of social security. In Britain, for example, in the early 40s the late Lord Beveridge produced a monumental report which laid the foundation of growth of the social security system in Britain in the post war years, out of which was born the National Health Service and other associated components of a comprehensive system of social security. There are several other models also. There are some countries which lay emphasis on taxation as the primary means of financing some of the needs of social security. For example, the British National Health Service is financed out of taxation. In some other countries, the emphasis is on the principle of insurance and on the pooling of risks.

In our own country, since 1948 when the Employees State Insurance Act came into being, considerable advance has been made in providing for social security needs of industrial workers. Also if I may say so today we have about 25 million workers in Government, in the Public as well as in the Private Sector who are the primary beneficiaries of various schemes of social security in our country. The working of these schemes requires constant re-examination so that the benefits that are sought to be provided or in fact provided, over a period of time, are improved. Also taking into account the overall economic situation of the country adequate attention is paid to the financing of these schemes and, I say so for obvious reasons while inaugurating the Association.

All over the world, systems of social security desirable though they might be are under great strains. For example, in the United Kingdom there has been a major controversy about the future role of the National Health Service because modern health care is proving more and more expensive and, therefore, the economics of social security is something which also needs investigation and careful analysis.

Because we are a very poor society we have to cut our coat according to the size of our cloth. At the same time we have to recognize that the bulk of India's labour force is to be found in the unorganized sector. We have millions of people who have nothing but the bare hands to offer. They do not have security of employment. They are mostly casual workers and they have no social security of any kind. No health care facilities, no unemployment insurance or accident insurance.

Then we have the problem of social security of landless workers in agriculture for whom we have minimum wage laws and some States have old age pensions but how effectively they are administered is, a big question. And it is precisely because we lack credible institutions of social security in our country particularly in rural areas that schemes like small family norms have proved very difficult to propagate.

I, therefore, greatly welcome the initiative that you have taken to constitute this high powered body which would study the problems of social security, study the working of existing schemes, to what extent these schemes are achieving their objectives, how, over a period of time, their benefits can be enlarged consistent with the recognition of the underlying economic facts of India's life. Also I do hope that you would pay adequate attention to the needs of the unorganized sector, both the informal sector employees in the urban areas as well as the landless workers in rural areas. Those are the people whose needs of social security have remained unattended thus far, by and large. And while we expand, improve the facilities of social security for our industrial workforce I think we must not forget those millions and millions of our countrymen and women who simply do not come within the ambit of social security legislation that has been devised.

I would also like to say that in all these matters there is need for fresh thinking.

Technical change is a fact of life. A country like India cannot cut itself from the rest of the world and the pace at which science and technology are growing every 5 years there is such a massive explosion of technical and scientific knowledge that it compares with what used to take place 10–15 years ago over a period of 50 years. Now we cannot survive in a world in which knowledge is growing at such a fast pace without making conscious efforts to absorb, to assimilate and adapt this knowledge for improving our living standards. But the process of technical change, howsoever beneficial it might be, is also in some ways disruptive. When you introduced new technologies it hurts those who are using techniques of an earlier vintage. There is the problem or the fear of unemployment, loss of jobs, this cannot be wished away and if we want our society to accept the need for technical change then we need credible instruments of social security to ensure that the process of technical change will not impose undue burden on the working classes. This is in my view today more necessary than ever before, particularly because the pace of technological change has very considerably quickened. The world economy whether we like it or not is being integrated at a pace which was unheard of. Even if we want to isolate ourselves from the rest of the world we cannot do so. The question before our country, therefore, is not whether India can remain cut off from the rest of the world but how to integrate ourselves with the rest of the world in a manner which is consistent with the achievement of basic social and economic objectives enshrined in our Constitution. That is, we must work towards a society where social gain rather than private profit remains the dominant concern. The society which would be a caring society, a society which would ensure that the fruits of economic progress are equitably distributed, the society which would ensure that if technical change is essential for the country as a whole, then the costs of technical change, then the costs of adjustment would not be borne exclusively by the working class and that those who have the least capacity to bear these costs must not be asked to bear them. This is the challenge for social scientists, policy planners and all those who are engaged in research relating to social security. I, therefore, greatly welcome the establishment of this new organization. I hope through your experience, through your knowledge, through our wisdom you will help evolve a pattern of social security which would be appropriate to the needs of our time.

2.

Contribution of Social Security in the Emerging Economic Scenario

Sh. Pranab Mukherjee
Dy. Chairman, Planning Commission

FEBRUARY 1992

I compliment your Association for having organized this seminar on a subject of crucial importance to the economy in the present context of momentous changes that are taking place. I am sure that the deliberations at this seminar and the conclusions and recommendations that may emerge there from would be helpful to all concerned in evolving the relevant policies.

Social Security is basically an instrument of social policy designed to promote social justice. The process of economic development creates imbalances in the society and it is one of the functions of social policy to correct these imbalances. Social Security is one of the means for achieving this objective.

It is said that social security "represents a guarantee by the whole community to all its members of the maintenance of their standard of living or at least of tolerable living conditions by means of a redistribution of income based on national solidarity." (Pierre Larougue in the Bulletin of the SSA 1966 N 3-4). Whenever a contingency occurs which is likely to affect the standard of living of a person due to loss on diminution of income, social security comes in very handy and provides a safety net so that it may not fall too steeply. This is achieved through a mechanism of transferring the resources from the active to the inactive, not directly, but through a community effort so that it also promotes solidarity among the people.

A system of social security so conceived encompasses the entire population. It requires vast sums of money and a large organization to administer. Operations of such magnitude will have profound effect on the economic as well as political life of the country. It cannot therefore, be viewed in isolation. It will have to be built into the national plans.

We in India do not have such a system. Undoubtedly, we have several laws and schemes which provide protection to certain specified groups of people under certain contingencies. They are very much limited in their scope both in terms of coverage as well as the benefits provided. It is high time that some thought is given to the possibility of establishing a national system of social security.

In the meantime, there seems to be no alternative to continue with the practice of preparing separate schemes for different contingencies such as occupational injuries, maternity etc. As your President has rightly pointed out the new industrial policy has thrown up a contingency requiring a social security type of protection for those affected by involuntary unemployment due to retrenchment and closure of sick units. We have yet no idea about the magnitude of the problem and about the number of people who may be affected. Whatever be the number, there can be no doubt that it will cause great hardship to the persons who are affected. If the number is small its impact on the society may not be noticeable but if it is large it may shake the whole society leading to unforeseen consequences. It would, therefore, be prudent to anticipate what is likely to happen and be prepared to meet the unforeseen contingency. Viewed in this perspective the seminar you have organized is both timely and welcome. I would, therefore, look forward to see the report of the seminar.

The problem of unemployment has basically two aspects, the demand aspect and the supply aspect. Any proposal based on the demand aspect only will be incomplete. There are no two opinions about the need for social security for those who may be thrown out of employment. The form in which it should be provided may also not be in question. The question is as to how to provide it. I have seen from the background papers that there are suggestions for introducing a scheme of unemployment insurance. There are also suggestions for introduction of old age pension schemes and for enhancing the benefits under the other existing schemes. You will no doubt discuss all the suggestions on merits.

I would, however, like to place before you an aspect which does not seem to have been discussed in these papers and, that is, how the expenditure involved, if these suggestions are accepted, can be met.

In a system of planning we have been following which accounts for all the sources and uses of funds, given the gross national income, no expenditure can be incurred on any new head of expenditure unless:

(a) there is an increase of revenue; or
(b) there is a saving under any head of expenditure; or
(c) we resort to deficit financing.

When the level of fiscal deficit is already high and the Finance Minister is striving to reduce it any proposal which is likely to increase the deficit will not be acceptable. In the circumstances, if a higher level of expenditure is to be incurred on social security we shall have to find either additional sources of revenue or savings. Whether there is scope for such additional revenue or savings is a matter that would need serious examination.

This is, however, not a matter that can be determined in an adhoc manner. It calls for an application of the techniques of economic planning to the social sector whereby the relative priority of the social programmes are assessed and resources are allocated among them accordingly.

It is in the nature of social welfare programmes that decisions regarding them are taken politically and economic calculations have a limited role. It is only right that it should be so because political decisions are likely to be nearer social reality than those of an economic planner and the rigours of planning do not come in the way of political decisions on mattes which are socially necessary. Even so, integration of the social programmes with the economic plan is unavoidable. This calls for adaptation of the system of economic planning to the social sector. There are examples of several countries who have successfully experimented with it. The Planning Programming and Budgeting System developed in the USA is one such example. The system of Social Budgeting developed in France is another.

3.

Social Clauses – International Trade Agreement

Ms. Josephine Karavasil
Director, ILO, New Delhi

1995

The phrase "social clause" is on everyone's lips and yet there is no definition of it anywhere. It can mean many things to many people. However, the issues involved in it are clear. There are four key ones:

(*i*) First and foremost, there is the general concern about poor labour standards and how to improve these. In the context of international trade this means that working people should have their fair share of the benefits that result from enhanced international trade.

(*ii*) Second, there is the concern about the most discussed "level playing field". Without minimum labour standards workers would be placed in a potentially disastrous competition against each other. In this perspective, international competition could lead to a destructive downward spiral in the conditions of work and life of working people around the world.

(*iii*) A third element is fear of protectionism. The relevant question here is: Are concerns about labour standards being used as a pretext for stopping or reducing imports from low cost producers in an effort to protect capital and workers in the importing country against the cold winds of international competitions? (It should be noted however, that a consumer movement with a strong sense of social justice is also emerging around the world).

(*iv*) The last element is the principle of national autonomy. To what extent should governments (or non-governmental organizations) in a particular country judge the political, economic and social situation in another country, and take actions which may or may not have the desired effects.

These four concerns keep coming up in the debate on respect for minimum labour standards and international trade – or on the "Social Clause" for short.

The outcome of the world-wide discussion on the social clause is by no means certain, as the views of workers, trade unionists, other NGO's, employers, representatives of importing countries and representatives of exporting countries need not, and frequently do not, coincide. In the ILO, we are very much aware of this divergence of views.

Some wonder why this debate should come up at all in the ILO which in any case promotes a coherent body of International Labour Standards and does so in a non-coercive manner. Here, I would refer to the Declaration of Philadelphia, Article II:

(*a*) all human beings, irrespective of race, creed or sex, have the right to pursue both their material well-being and their spiritual development in conditions of freedom and dignity, or economic security and equal opportunity;

(*b*) all national and international policies and measures, in particular those of an economic and financial character, should be judged in this light and accepted only in so far as they may be held to promote and not to hinder the achievement of this fundamental objective;

(*c*) it is the responsibility of the International Labour Organisation to examine and consider all international economic and financial policies and measures in the light of this fundamental objective;

(*d*) in discharging the tasks entrusted to it the ILO, having considered all relevant economic and financial factors, may include in its decisions and recommendations any provisions which it considers appropriate.

Article V adds:

The conference affirms that the principles set forth in this Declaration are fully applicable to all people everywhere and that, while the manner of their application must be determined with due regard to the stage of social and economic development reached by each people, their progressive application to people who are still dependent, as well as to those who have already achieved self government, is a matter of concern to the whole civilized world. The Director-General is concerned to establish ILO as the social conscience of the UN system, counterbalancing the Bretton Woods Institutions.

I will attempt to summarize the steps in the "social clause" debate as far as the ILO is concerned.

First of all, the Director-General, in his report to the International Labour Conference 1994, *Defending values, promoting change: Social justice in a global economy: An ILO Agenda* brought up the whole issue inviting discussion on it at the conference in June. The result of this was two-fold.

(i) There was a broad consensus that the defence and promotion of the fundamental rights of working men and women remain a basic responsibility of he ILO. However, various aspects of the standard-setting activities needed to be improved – speed of adoption; updating and revision; topical needs and the importance of subjects; the need for new standards to retain their universal nature and better use of flexibility clauses. These issues are being addressed by the Governing Body and the Secretariat.

The basic human rights on which there was consensus have since found their place in the Declaration and Programme of Action of the World Summit for Social Development. The Summit undertook to "pursue the goal of ensuring quality jobs and safeguard the basic rights and interests of workers, and to that end, freely promote respect for relevant ILO Conventions, including those on the prohibition of forced and child labour, freedom of association, the right to organize and bargain collectively and the principle of non-discrimination" (Commitment No. 3 of the Declaration). In the Programme of Action, Governments were called on to observe and implement human rights obligations they had assumed, "safeguarding the promoting respect for basic workers' rights, including the prohibition of forced and child labour, freedom of association and the right to organize and bargain collectively, equal remuneration for men and women for work of equal value and non-discrimination in employment".

(ii) A meeting of the Governing Body just following the June Conference mandated the office to set up a Working Party in order to discuss all relevant aspects of the social dimensions of international trade in relating to its ongoing process of liberalization.

When the Office document for the Working Party on the Social Dimensions of the Liberalization of International Trade was discussed at the Session of the following Governing Body in November 1994, it elicited profound debate.

To keep you informed of the contents of this, the Office document started from the generally accepted promise that liberalization of trade is a source of progress and that there should be a certain parallelism between economic progress resulting from trade liberalization and social progress. From this general objective, it focused on two sets of issues.

Firstly, whether it was possible to incorporate into the international trade system a minimum set of standards, which would not seek to establish a common level of social protection and benefits but simply give to workers the possibility to obtain a fair share of the fruits of growth made possible by trade liberalization. Concretely, the problem was whether the international trade systems which guarantees from access to market should also contain a guarantee that conditions of work are determined freely in the internal labour market through a guarantee of freedom from forced labour and freedom of association.

Secondly, whether there could be more specific action on the part of the ILO in fulfillment of the above objective. The document pointed out that the rationale for ILO's involvement in any attempt to set standards for trading partners was derived from its mandate under the Philadelphia Declaration.

In this context, the ratification and implementation of the four basic international labour conventions, dealing with freedom of association, the abolition of forced labour, child labour and discriminatory employment practices respectively, constituted a significant indication of the country's determination to pursue social progress parallel to trade liberalization. But more specifically, the ILO could set up a machinery for conducting a systematic and structures review on the basis of relevant criteria of the member state's efforts to ensure that social progress goes hand in hand with trade liberalization. Towards this end, ILO could also provide technical assistance for setting up the appropriate labour market institutions in member states which would also ensure a fair distribution of the fruits of growth.

This documents elicited profound debate, as I have said — a debate which is currently ongoing.

At the first debate of the topic, a request was made by the Governing Body for the Office to prepare a preliminary outline of an analysis of the broad patterns of the social aspects of trade liberalization in a global perspective. This outline has been presented to the current Session of the Governing Body.

Call for this analysis followed by a debate where even those Members show ere mot pronouncedly opposed to any social dimension being imposed from outside made it quite clear that, since they had chosen to the Members of the ILO, they naturally did not contest the need to pursue social progress in conjunction with trade liberalization (and partially as a result of it).

They believed that there was a need to know how this two-fold objective could be pursued most effectively and most actively in an area where we still have a great deal to learn - state of affairs that only tends to perpetuate a war of ideas, if not of ideology. It would be in keeping with the ILO's vocation if it were to take some of the heat out of the debate by endeavouring to fill the gaps in our knowledge and to promote a better understanding of the interplay between trade liberalization and social progress as actually experienced by all the social partners. Once it had done this, the ILO would be in a better position to embark with a sufficient degree of credibility on the type of action that might further that twin objective. Furthermore, an empirical approach of this nature should mean that possible overlapping with the activities of other organization could be avoided.

The ILO believes that by calling upon the knowledge and experience of this tripartite constituents through out the world, it could, using just limited resources, gain access to certain information that is directly relevant to a genuinely global view of the link between the two objectives.

At the same time, the ILO's structure would allow it to validate, for the purposes of the action to be taken, the conclusions reached on the basis of the data collected.

The preliminary outline proposed that the analysis could look at:

- efforts to define a coherent policy on the issue, and the extent to which the social partners are involved in it;
- the extent to which the guarantee of basic freedoms in the labour market (recognition of freedom of association and freedom from all forms of slavery or forced labour) goes hand in had with trade liberalization;
- efforts to provide support for industrialization and the redeployment of industries: (i) in terms of labour legislation (for example, to deal with safety and health problems resulting from more advanced technology); (ii) in terms of labour administration (by increasing human and financial resources) to ensure better enforcement of the labour legislation;
- the policies and measures adopted to facilitate the adaptation of workers to structural changes resulting from trade liberalization and their reintegration into the employment market – for example, occupational training and retraining, strengthening of employment services, occupational and geographical mobility assistance, etc;
- efforts to extend or, on a more general level, to adapt social protection schemes (bylinking them to adjustment efforts);
- the role of labour relations systems, freedom of association and collective bargaining in the equitable distribution of the benefits of liberalization and in adapting to the changes brought about by trade liberalization.

4.

Social Security in India in the Historical Context

Justice Rama Jois
Former Chief Justice of Haryana and Punjab

1995

Service to Humanity is service to Divinity. The persons who have organized this programme, by devoting considerable time, energy and spending finance, have done so in plain discharge of their duty towards human society of which they are inseparable part on account of their concern for the difficulties, hardship and miseries of fellow human beings. They are gentlemen in the true sense of the term as described in the following Sanskrit verse:

Sajjanasya Hridayam,
navaneetham tadvadanti
kavayastadaleekam
anyadeha vilastparithpat
Sajjno dravati no navaneetham

The description by poets that the heart of a Gentlemen is as soft as butter is not correct. (In fact it is an insult to Gentleman) for, butter (though soft) melts only when the body (vessel) in which it is kept is heated; but the heart of Gentlemen melts when any other body (individual) suffers from the heat of misery.

Therefore, I thank also all those, who are participating in social security activities, who are Gentlemen, in the real sense of the term. Further, I immensely thank the organization for conferring on me the privilege of inaugurating this important Seminar and training course.

The relationship between individual and the society is mutual and inseparable. Every individual is, as long as he has the capacity to work is under a duty to serve the Society. Every profession, employment, avocation, trade, business or power positions, should be used to render service to the Society. In return it is the duty of the society through the instrumentality of the State as also through social organization to come to the rescue of individuals, when they are in difficulty and they are in need of help. In fact the very object and purpose of founding the institution of State was to secure protection and social security for all individuals. This aspect is highlighted in the famous declaration of Raja Rantideva in Mahabharata:

Kamaye dukhataptanam Praneenam artanashanam

(My desire and duty is to wipe out the tears of those in distress)

Thus, it is one of the fundamental duties of the State to provide social security to those in distress.

In conformity with the above principle, from ancient times, one of the fundamental duties imposed on the state in this land has been the protection of the people. As part of this, specific directives were incorporated in Rajadharma (Constitutional law of ancient India) to provide social Security in many ways to those who are in distress.

I shall quote a few of them which at once will indicate the concern shown for social security.

1. Duty to restore stolen property or its value: Katyayana Smriti, Verse 816-817: (Sanskrit sloka)

"The king should cause restoration of stolen property to the owner. If it is not possible to restore the same property he must pay the owner the price of the stolen property".

"If the thief is caught, but the stolen property is not recovered from him, either the thief must be made to pay the price, if possible, or the king himself must pay it".

2. Narada Smriti Vide Dharmakosha, p. 1961: (Sanskrit sloka)

"When thieves are not caught the king must make good the loss from his treasury".

It shows that payment of tax to the king itself was regarded as an insurance against theft and exhibits an excellent sense of Social Security.

There is no corresponding provision in modern law. What happens in several cases is if a person lodges a complaint before the Police that there was a theft in his house, after a few weeks, police would submit a report called 'B' Report which means that "Offence is not Traced". There ends the matter. Some provision should be made to give relief in needy cases, particularly when a man loses all his hard earned moveable property or money and become a destitute overnight on account of theft, and who cannot be expected to insure their house hold articles.

3. Liability to compensate in addition to suffering Punishment:

(a) Yajnavalkya Smriti Ch-II:-222

(Sanskrit sloka)

"He who causes bodily injury to another shall pay the fine imposed and shall also pay the incidental expenses".

Mitaksara states that the offender has to pay medical expenses as well as expenses on diet etc.

(b) Yajnavalkya, 221(2), 223:-

"That if the offender had, in addition to causing injury during the course of assault, also damaged any property of the victim or took away any article during such scuffle, he should pay damages for repair and also restore the property taken away by him".

Justification for such provision is now recognized in Section 357(1) (b) of the Criminal Procedure Code, 1973,which empowers the Court to award compensation to the injured, if in the opinion of the Court it is recoverable through civil suit.

While the above are general provisions concerning all the subjects, there were specific provision for the employees.

1. Treatment of Servants: Dharmakosha P-816:

(Sanskrit sloka)

"While distributing food to all the guests, if there is any shortage of food, the householder may stint(reduce the share to) himself, his wife and children, but by no means the food due to a servant should be reduced".

The rule indicates that utmost kindness and consideration was required to be shown to a house servant. In the matter of food, his requirement was placed above that of the owner and the members of his family.

2. Sick leave with pay:- Sukraniti Ch-II, 819-824:-

(Sanskrit sloka)

(i) No deduction should be made from the wages if an employee is sick upto one week.
(ii) An employee suffering from long illness can however send his nominee to work in his place.
(iii) A highly qualified employee, however, should be paid half the wages for the entire period of his illness.

3. Compulsory savings: Sukraniti Ch-II 834-835:-

(Sanskrit sloka)

$1/6^{th}$ or $1/4^{th}$ part of the wages of an employee should be deducted and the said amount should be paid to him (either in full or half) after 2 or 3 years (according to his retirement).

4. Pension and family allowance: Sukraniti Ch-II 8254-829:-

(Sanskrit sloka)

"An employee who had put in a service of 40 years should, on retirement, be paid a pension throughout his life equal to half of his wages and, after his death, a family allowance equal to half the amount of his pension, i.e., 1/4th of his original salary, should be paid to his wife or daughter, as the case may be, till employee's son becomes a major.

5. Preference for the appointment of a deceased employee's son, Sukraniti-II 832-833:-

(Sanskrit sloka)

"If an employee dies even before retirement, his son becomes automatically entitled to get the employment of his deceased father. After attaining majority his wages should be determined according to his qualifications".

6. Subsistence to wives of soldiers:

Vasista Smriti commences Ch.XIX saying that 'the special duty of a king is the protection of his subjects'. After refereeing to the necessity for the king to engage men as soldiers to fight in defence of the realm it provides vide Ch. IX-20, thus:-

(Sloka)

"Their (Soldier's) wives, who have no other means of livelihood, shall be given subsistence (by the king)."

All the works referred to above give a clear picture of the nature of responsibilities entrusted to a king. The right of a king to collect taxes was coupled with his responsibility to protect the people.

Robert Lingat in his Classical Law at p. 213 observes:

"Numerous texts establish a strict correlation between the duty of protection incumbent upon the king and his objects' payment of tax to which they are assessed".

The genuine and natural human feeling has expressed itself in the Universal Declaration of Human Rights, adopted by the General Assembly of the U.N.O. on 10th December 1948. Article 1 of the declaration reads:

"All human beings are born free and equal in dignity and rights. They are endowed with reason and conscience and should act towards one another in a spirit of brotherhood".

Article 3 declares that every one has the right to life, liberty and security of persons. Article 22, 23 and 24 are the other relevant articles for the Seminar on Social Security. The articles read:-

22. *"Everyone as a member of society, has the right to social security"*

23. (i) "Everyone has the right to work, to free choice of employment, to just and favourable conditions of work and to protection against unemployment".

24. "Everyone has the right to form and to join trade unions for the protection of his interests".

Our Nation is a signatory to the above said declaration, along with other members of the United Nations. Constitution of India which was adopted thereafter has given effect to the above declaration regarding right to equality and right to life and liberty in the Articles 14 and 21 respectively. These articles confer those rights as fundamental rights which are enforceable in a Court of Law. They read:

14."Equality before law:

"The State shall not deny to any person equality before the law or the equal protection of the laws within the territory of India".

21. Protection of life and personal liberty:

"*No person shall be deprived of his life or personal liberty except according to procedure established by law*".

The other declarations are incorporated as Directive Principles of State Policy vide, article 38,39 and 41. They read as follows

38(i) State to secure a social order for the Promotion of welfare of the people:

The State shall strive to promote the welfare of the people by securing and protecting as effectively as it may a social order in which justice, social, economic and political, shall inform all the institutions of the national life".

39. Certain principles of Policy to be followed by the State:

The State shall, in particular, direct its policy towards securing:

(a) that the citizens, men and women equally, have the right to an adequate means to livelihood".

41. Right to work, to education and to public assistance in certain cases:

"*The State shall, within the limits of its economic capacity and development, make effective provision for securing the right to work, to education and to Public assistance in cases of unemployment, old age, sickness and disablement and in other cases of undeserved want*".

These articles are not directly enforceable in a Court of law, but are enforceable only when they are given effect to through appropriate legislation.

Though right to work is not included as a specific fundamental right in Part – III of the Constitution, the fact remains that Article 39(a) read with Article 41 of the Constitution, which are the Directive Principles of State Policy, make it obligatory for the State to secure inter alia the right to work and thereby secure adequate means of livelihood. Expounding the scope of article 21, the Supreme Court of India in the case of Olga Tellis Vs. Bombay Municipal Corporation [A.I.R. 1986 S.C. 180], popularly known as "Pavement dwellers" case said thus:-

> *"In view of the fact that Article 39(a) and 42, requires the State to secure to the citizens an adequate means of livelihood and for the right to work, it would be sheer pedantry to exclude the right to livelihood from the contest of the right to life".*

Therefore, it is one of the fundamental duties of the State to secure one or other employment by which an individual can earn his livelihood. Unfortunately, it is in respect of this fundamental duty, the State has failed miserably.

There are various aspects of providing Social Security by the State. The two most fundamental aspects of Social Security are:

A. To Provide Employment

B. To Provide Dwelling.

In fact after the commencement of the Constitution having regard to Article 39(a) read with Article 41 of the constitution, top priority should have been given to the above aspects.

By nature no individual wants any benefit without doing any work, unless he is physically handicapped or unable to work on account of illness or infirmity, God has provided every individual not only a mouth and a stomach to eat and digest but also two hands and two legs and also intellect and energy to work. All that is needed is to provide proper education, appropriate to his need which would become a means for undertaking any work and earn his livelihood and he would be satisfied with this. In addition to this he needs a dwelling. Unfortunately there has been a failure on the part of the successive Governments to fulfil the aforesaid two requirements.

As a result, today the biggest problem the nation is facing is the problem of unemployment and the problem of want of accommodation for living.

Total number of applications registered with Employment Exchanges all over the country as on February 1994: 3,61,68,000

Total number of applicants registered in Karnataka alone as on February 1994: 16,03,000

These figures obviously exclude the uneducated employees. The figures indicate the magnitude of the problem after the implementation of Seven Five Year Plans and forty four years of functioning under the Constitution. This is a sad commentary on our planning and their implementation.

In fact, for many offences, such as theft, chain snatching and the like, unemployment and consequent want of earning required for living, is the cause. Instead of providing employment it has become necessary to pay unemployment allowance. This and various other problems indicate that the problems are created by acts of omission and commissions and thereafter solution to the problem are thought of. This is the cause for unemployment problem which has now become a social security problem.

Another illustration is whereas Article 47 which is a Directive to the State to prohibit consumption of intoxicating drinks, which was incorporated at the instance of Mahatma Gandhi who was of the view that it was essential for the economic advancement of poorer sections, and also to protect the youth, against moral and material abandonment which again is a directive incorporated in Article 39, are violated by the state itself indulging in supplying liquor to the people and at the same time spending money on advertisement in Doordarshan to impress on the people that the consumption of alcohol is ruinous to family life. This is the type of activities indulged in by the State in many matters.

Problem of Housing

The problem of housing is also enormous and acute. This can be witnessed by any one of the big cities in this Country. We see on both sides of railway lines thousands of persons live in slums under subhuman conditions. There are such slums spread over other places. They have no proper education or employment or adequate means of livelihood and medical care. There are foot path dwellers in several lakhs in various cities and towns. This is national shame. Why is it so after more than four decades and Seven five year plans? If there has been proper planning, and proper spending of the National resources, ear marked for the purpose, it would not have been difficult for the State to provide housing colonies to which all the slum dwellers could have been shifted, where they could have been provided with reasonable dwelling. But unfortunately, it was not our priority in planning. Heavy amounts are invested on *Five Star* hotels and various types of luxurious and wasteful activities without giving top priority to the basic requirements of citizens. Such attitude has created innumerable social security problems.

Similarly having regard to the fact that compared to America, Canada and Australia and the like the size of the Country is small and population is more, all our economic planning should have been labour incentive, which alone could ensure employment to all our people. In fact, this aspect had been stressed by Mahatma Gandhi ji, that we should go in for simple life on Swadeshi Principles in economic planning. These views have been expressed by Mahatma Gandhi ji in the book "My Picture of Free India". Relevant portion reads:

> "Our civilization, our culture, our Swaraj depend not upon multiplying our wants – self indulgence, but upon restricting our wants – self denial".

> "Civilization in the real sense of the term, consists not in the multiplication, but in the deliberate and voluntary restriction of wants. This alone promotes real happiness and contentment.
>
> "A certain degree of physical harmony and comfort is necessary, but above a certain level it becomes a hindrance instead of help. Therefore, the ideal of creating an unlimited number of wants and satisfying them seems to be a delusion and a snare. The satisfaction of one's physical needs, must meet at a certain point a dead stop, before it degenerates into physical voluptuousness. A man must arrange his physical and cultural circumstances so that they do not hinder him in his service of humanity on which all his energies should b concentrated".

Unfortunately we disregarded his advice to give importance to labour oriented economic planning, particularly in the field of textiles and agriculture. Further we disregarded his advice for simple life and opted for increasing the wants and luxurious of life. Therefore we are facing the aforesaid problems.

The want of rationale in priorities is also illustrated by the prescription of half the rate in Indian Air Lines for those who have crossed 65 years and who are called Senior Citizens. It is a matter of common knowledge that those who travel by air irrespective of their age by and large belong to affluent sections of the Society, unless circumstances forces a person to travel by air on account of any emergency. It is, therefore, no social security benefit to the aged who are poor and needy. Assuming that such a concession should be granted to the needy it should have been limited to those whose income is less than a prescribed limit. In view of the general concession mainly the affluent sections of the society get this benefit. If an account is taken, the loss which the Indian Air Lines would suffer per annum would come to several crores, which could have been utilized for Social Security of the needy. This is the type of benefit given to old persons.

There is the latest example of the Life Insurance Corporation's Policy, according to which, the convertible term insurance policy to provide Social Security to individual was restricted to employees of Government or Quasi Government or of reputed commercial firms. Holding that denial of such Social Security to others was discriminatory the Supreme Court in its very recent judgment held thus:

> "It was well settled law that the Preamble Chapter of Fundamental Rights and Directives Principles accord right to livelihood as a meaningful life, social security and disablement benefits are integral schemes of socio-economic justice to the people".

> "Life Insurance coverage is against disablement or in the event of death of the insured, economic support for the dependent/s, social security to livelihood to the insured or the dependents. The appropriate life insurance policy within the paying capacity and means of the insured or the dependents. The appropriate life insurance policy within the paying capacity and means of the insured to pay premia is one of the social security measures envisaged under the Constitution to make right to life meaningful, worth living and right to livelihood a means for sustenance.
>
> "It is seen that term policy under Table 58 is the cheapest and accessible policy to the people and that the life of the policy is 5 to 7 years and the insurable lives are upto 50 years. But the class of employees sought to be covered under the policy would, by and large generally be those already insured under whole life policy or endowment policy. Extending the Table 58 policy again to 10 per cent of such a class from total population may not always be more successful apart, extending this benefit to other people who can afford to take the policy and continue to pay the premium would ensure security".

At last the Judiciary has come to the rescue of those who were denied the aforesaid Social Security measure.

Public opinion should, therefore, be created on the above lines to put pressure on the State to discharge its obligation to Social Security.

The problems which call for Social Security can be divided into two. They are:

A. Inevitable calamities or accidents which are beyond the control of human beings to which individuals are subjected to.
B. Man made problems on account of disregarding age old values of life.

As far as the first is concerned, as human beings are bound to suffer on account of various types of calamities like:

i) Disability or death of the bread earner of the family;
ii) Inability to earn on account of old age or infirmity;
iii) Accidents during the course of employment or otherwise; and
iv) Falling sick in the course of employment.

As far as the aforesaid aspects are concerned, provisions have been made by various legislations: They are:

A) Industrial Disputes Act, which provides for compensation for termination of service or payment of compensation during the period of lay off.

B) The Workmen's Compensation Act which provides for compensation in the event of death or in the event of an employee suffering injury which reduces his capacity to earn.

C) Employees State Insurance Act, which provides for Medical Aid or assistance to the employees and members of the family on contributory basis i.e. Out of the funds contributed periodically by both the employer and employee in the prescribed proportions.

D) Provident Fund and Miscellaneous Provisions Act, in which some amount is made available to an employee at the time of retirement which is contributory in nature.

E) The Payment of Gratuity Act, which provides for payment of some amount at the time of termination of tenure of office, calculated on the basis of years of service put in by the employee.

But all these benefits are available only in the Organized Sectors, i.e., Industries, Factories, Trade or Business to which the above said provisions apply. Compared to the number of persons who are employed in various avocations or works, employees working in the organized sector are far less.

Whereas the estimated work force in the organized sector covered by the aforesaid enactments is 17 million, the total work force is over 330 million. Resultant position is that large section of people work without any Social Security.

This Seminar should address itself to this problem and suggest solutions.

Probably, the only law in which adequate Social Security is being given to all sections of people is under the Motor Vehicles Act. Earlier to the introduction of the provision for awarding compensation to the victims of the motor accidents by the motor accidents claims tribunal by the amendment of the Motor Vehicles Act, 1939, an individual had to file a civil suit in Tort against the owner of the vehicle for getting compensation in the event of death or bodily injury to any individual on payment of ad valorem Court fee which many were unable to do. After the amendment of the Act providing for compulsory insurance of motor vehicles and the Constitution of Special Tribunal many persons who become victims of motor accidents are securing adequate compensation.

Creation of no fault liability in which an amount of Rs. 25,000/- has to be paid forthwith in the case of death and an amount of Rs. 12,500/- in case of permanent disability, without proof of negligence is another important provision which is giving Social Security for those who suffer on account of motor accidents which is increasing day by day in proportion to the increase of motor vehicles.

But there are two aspects which require improvement.

First, in many cases there would be inordinate delay in the grant of compensation. It makes the grant of compensation a mockery. Therefore, a time limit of six months should be fixed before which every accident claim should be settled and, if necessary, more Tribunals should be appointed for the purpose.

Secondly, to cover the cases of hit and run where the vehicle which caused the accident goes unidentified, a separate fund should be constituted and compensation should be awarded from the fund. Otherwise the victims of such family have no remedy or relief at all.

Apart from this, immediate help could also be provided by Social Service Organization.

In fact, Bharat Vikas Parishad, under its "Viklanga Sahyata Yojana" is providing free artificial limbs to thousands of victims of motor accidents and other type of accidents. This is worthy of emulation by other Social Organizations.

Man Made Problems

In fact the modern life style particularly disregarding the values of life is another reason for increase of the number of persons who require Social Security.

Firstly the Joint Family System founded by our ancestors was in fact one of the best method of Social Security. Under that system all the members of the family used to stay under one roof and work together, and share the benefits and enjoy and suffer together. This provided sufficient security to individuals. On account of selfishness of individuals this system was destroyed.

Further, one of the values of life has been the sense of gratitude. For instance, parents looked after their children well, provided them with good education and even after they attained majority, parents looked after them, performed their marriage and even thereafter they continued to look after them so long they were physically and mentally strong, with the expectation that their children would look after them in their old age. The sense of gratitude made sons or daughters as the case may be, to look after the parents or parents-in-law in their old age. But unfortunately this human value of sense of gratitude has been eroded and displaced by a sense of throw away attitude, out of purely selfish a motive. The man has become so selfish that parents are considered as a burden or useless by many once they are not in a position to provide money or useful in term of service. Consequently large, number of parents have to depend upon some Social Security arrangements for spending the evening of their life instead of spending their evening of life along with children and grand children. As a result, we are seeing Vridhashramas (Rescue homes for old persons) coming up everywhere, where old people come and take shelter until they die, though their sons or daughter residing in good houses, enjoying life, which presents a pathetic sight. Such erosion of values have added to the burden of Social Security arrangements whether private or public.

Another instance which gives large number of persons who require Social Security is on account of divorce. About four or five decades before, divorce was of a rare occurrence, at least in our Country. Even in cases where the husband and wife were unable to live together for any reason they would pull on or live separately, in the interest of children and would not think of divorce. But in recent years on account of throw away attitude, displacing the sense of gratitude, wife/husband is thrown away like chattel, just as anyone wants to change an old article for a new one or thing the moment he sees a new and attractive one, and he has the financial resource to have it. This is giving rise to lot of Social Security problems, viz., of divorced wives and children of divorced parents.

It's needless to state that the development of personality of children depends upon the good family life. Good families constitute the foundation of any Nation. If family life is destroyed, and as a result children go astray, it would seriously affect National/Social life and if the magnitude of this problem increases, there will be total crash of Social edifice.

Victims of Terrorist Activities and Onslaught on Women

Increase in Terrorist Activities and offences against women are creating large number of Social Security problems. In Punjab, large number of children were becoming orphans, women were becoming destitute.

Punjab Government, had to make provisions for payment of full salary to the members of the family of killed Government servants upto their prescribed age of retirement apart from family pension thereafter. This coupled with expenses for security, constituted terrible drain and strain on the exchequer.

Terrorist activities and violence against women have become a world phenomenon. Human beings are behaving in an inhuman manner. They are nothing but demons in human form. This is the consequence of development of Science minus moral values of life (dharma); *Vijnana minus jnana*.

Therefore, as far as such man made situations are concerned, the remedy must also be preventive, in that, the values of life should be resurrected and duty towards parents the spouse and the children should be roused. This should be done through National Educational System and audio visual education through mass media.

I have no special knowledge or expertise about the topic of Social Security. I have placed before you some thoughts, which occurred to me.

I am confident that the participants in the seminar and training, who are experts on the topic of Social Security would discuss the matter thoroughly and come out with some concrete suggestions, the implementation of which will provide greater Social Security to larger number of people.

You are all dedicated to the cause of Social Security and determined to achieve the goal.

As the famous poet Kalidasa has said:

Ka ipsitartha sthira nischayam manaha payascha nimnabhimukham pratipayet

Who can reverse the course of the mind determined to achieve its ideal and of the water coming down the mountain: None

With these words, I inaugurate the Seminar and Training Programme and wish it all success.

5.

Introduction to Social Security

Lionel P. Massum
ILO Representative in India

NOVEMBER 1998

The International Labour Organization was set up in 1919 to bring governments, employers and trade unions together for united action in the cause of social justice and better living conditions everywhere. The unique feature of the ILO, shared by no other international body, is its tripartite structure. Employers' and Worker's representatives participate in its work on an equal footing with representatives of governments.

In its Preamble, the ILO Constitution declares that universal and lasting peace can be founded only on the basis of social justice. The Declaration of Philadelphia, which is incorporated into the Constitution, was adopted in 1944 and embodies an even more dynamic concept. It proclaims the right of all human beings irrespective of race, creed, or sex "to pursue their material well being and their spiritual development in conditions of freedom and dignity, of economic security and equal opportunity." It further states that "Poverty anywhere constitutes a danger to prosperity everywhere."

The International Labour Office is the secretariat of the International Labour Organization with the headquarters at Geneva. The ILO is what is known as "Specialized Agency" of the United Nation Systems - the agency concerned with all aspects of the world of work. The ILO is different from other agencies in that it has a tripartite structure – our partners are the government, workers and employers. All the three groups participate actively in all the work of ILO. As for as the ILO's work in India is concerned, our work is guided by country objectives, which are prepared with the full collaboration of our tripartite constituents.

The various means of action the ILO has at its disposal for its work are:

- Standard setting. Primarily through Conventions and recommendations;
- Technical cooperation programmes and projects;
- Advisory services to member states;
- Research, documentation and dissemination of information;
- Promotional activities;
- Meetings and seminars, etc.

Turning to the subject to be discussed at this seminar, social security is an aspect of the world of work in which ILO has taken a strong interest for very many years, and has made good use of all of the different kinds of activity which I have just mentioned. In the present world, a sound system of social security is seen to be indispensable for social progress. It can also contribute in a very significant way to economic stability and development indeed, the state of development of the social security system in a country is considered to be an important measure of the progress made towards the ideal of eliminating poverty for its entire citizenry. Fear of insecurity in the event of sickness, old age, invalidity, maternity and employment has been a source of constant concern since the early days of human civilization.

In Europe, as the pace of industrialization quickened, perhaps two hundred years ago, a large new class of factory workers emerged, completely dependent for their livelihood on the regular payment of the wages. In an attempt to protect the urban labouring classes several systems were evolved. There were, for instance, savings bank facilities sponsored by the government; there were measures laying upon employers some obligation to maintain the ill or injured workman; there was the growth of mutual aid societies organized to provide modest cash aid in sickness and old age; and private insurance developed simple life policies and funeral benefits. Although these measures went some limited way towards meeting the problems, workers were absorbed in survival from one day to the next, and hardly had time to consider distant eventualities. Meeting the expenses of today took precedence over saving for the possibilities of tomorrow, and there was hardly anything to spare against the more immediate risks of sickness or unemployment. Also with the spread of education and the widening of the franchise, there was an awakening of hope and an expectation of better things to come. Gradually, social and political groups made their influence felt at policy making levels. We can recognize similar social changes taking place in the India of today.

Step by step, the industrialized countries put in place systems to cover the different risks, so that eventually it became possible to protect almost the whole population of a country. In addition, the coverage established in many although not all of these countries could be "comprehensive" as to the various contingencies which threaten wages and income, and thus the quality and standard of living of working people. And the new term "social security" was found to describe this new state of affairs. It is not easy to define this expression in a way which fits the different condition of each country. Traditionally, it has been taken to mean the protection which society provides for its members, through a series of public measures against the economic and social distress that otherwise would be used by the stoppage or substantial reduction of earning resulting from sickness, maternity, employment injury, unemployment invalidity, old age, and death. This includes the provision of medical care, and the provision of subsidies for families with children. But in developing countries, there is a growing feeling that the whole concept of social security must now be re-thought, in such a way as to meet the needs not only of organized labour but also the much larger number of those in the so called informal or unorganized sectors.

The term "Social security" was first used in the title of the United States legislation – the Social Security Act of 1935 – even though this Act was rather limited in its coverage, and the United States was by no means the first country to initiate a national programme to meet these risks. That had been achieved by Germany some 50 years earlier, and had been followed by a number of other western countries. Britain, for example, started a scheme in 1911, although the goal of comprehensive coverage was not achieved until 1945.

Although the first systems of social security were created by national governments commonly around one hundred years ago, these built on the experience of mutual societies created and run by the worker members themselves to assist their members by pooling regular, small contributions to build up a fund which could be used to support individuals. And perhaps their families, in times of distress. Rather later in certain countries, local governments started to assist the mutual societies, before the national governments took full responsibility for organizing uniform systems of provision for all workers, or better still all citizens. Again, we see that the early trends of developments of social security in the industrialized countries are being reflected in the current developments here in India, albeit a hundred years or so later. Where India's experience differs from that of the west, of course, in the vast number of those who for all or most of their working lives, work outside the organized sectors. For these workers, their income is irregular and insecure, whether or not they are affected by any of the "risks envisaged under traditional social security arrangements".

Many of the earliest social security schemes were designed to provide for the needs of workers who fell sick and were unable to earn their usual wages. The idea that a fund could be built up from small but regular contributions by each member, and used to provide benefits just to those individuals in need, is basically the principle of insurance. Insurance can be arranged in various ways, but in the context of social security we need to make a distinction between commercial and social insurance. Commercial insurance is of the type which is probably familiar from the policies of the Life and General Insurance Corporations – LIC and GIC – where individuals choose whether to take policies and pay premium calculated by the corporations for each person according to the size of the policy. Social insurance is organized on group basis and members are usually asked to contribute according to their ability to pay. So that the better-off do not escape their responsibilities, contributions usually have to be made compulsory.

In many countries, the national social security schemes have developed on the basis of social insurance, with members paying contributions – usually matched by their employers, and sometimes, in addition, by the governments; the contributions established the right of the members to receive benefits in cash or in kind when these fall due under the rules of the scheme. This type of scheme was introduced in Germany, followed by a member of other European countries, the United States and Canada, and in Latin America; and since the Second World War many countries in Africa, Asia and the Caribbean have created schemes based on similar principles, although in many cases covering relatively limited proportions of their citizens.

Certain countries have followed a rather different approach and have financed the required benefit payment from the general revenue of the country rather than from individual contributions, with statutory scales of benefit adjusted according to a person's means. The Scandinavian countries have tended towards schemes of this type, which are usually described as "social assistance" schemes, rather than social insurance. The first group of people to be covered in this way were the elderly, then the sick, invalids, survivors and unemployed, respectively. In Australia and New Zealand, complete social security systems have been constructed by the amalgamation of a series of social assistance schemes.

Another route to social security has been chosen by a number of countries. This is the direct provision by the State, wholly or largely from general revenue, of standard benefits to each resident in a specified category, these benefits may include a pension to every aged, invalid, orphaned or widowed resident. Several countries in South Asia have begun to provide pension benefits to the elderly on this basis, although to-date the amounts paid have been very small in relation to the cost of living. Similarly, some countries operate a national health service providing medical care for all without a contribution or means test: The cost may be met wholly or mainly from public funds, although nowadays, with government budgets under increasing pressure, there is a growing trend to ask patients to share in the cost of medical services – not just in the traditional charges for dental, ophthalmic or other specialist services.

The type of social security benefits which surveys show to be greatest interest to workers in most developing countries are those provided in the contingencies of:

- Ill health
- Old age
- Employment injury
- Unemployment and, of course for women, maternity.

Most of these are paid as cash benefits. Medical care is rather different, and can be provided largely "in kind", although, increasingly, patients have to find money out of their own pockets for doctors' fees and medicines, and look to the social security schemes for help in the form of cash. Nevertheless, the provision of medical services is the one responsibility in the field of social security, which the government should least escape. Health is the right of all citizens, and the difficulties which this presents for social security schemes relate to the need for provision to be equitable between contributors, who obviously expect a relatively high level of service, and their fellow-citizens. The pioneer country in regard to national health services was Britain, in the 1940s, and most of the countries of South Asia have shown a similar – and commendable – commitment. Of course, the financial resources are in short supply, and in India this and other problems have meant that the service provided to workers in respect of their contributions to ESIC – the Employees State Insurance Corporation – has been disappointing. It is well recognized that this problem needs to be tackled, by the development in the ESIC of a greater sense of commitment to the service of the members who contribute to the scheme.

Equally, there is a sense of disappointment amongst many members (although they may be envied by those who are outside the scheme) as to the old age retirement benefits, which in India are provided through EPF – the Employees' Provident Fund. Provident funds are really personal savings schemes, and have been popular in many developing countries in Africa and Asia, largely because the members themselves understand their entitlements and responsibilities very well. But a scheme which pays a cash benefit just once, when a worker retires at the end of his working life, does not do much to keep that person from destitution in the long term and he or she may live on for twenty years or more. Modern day thinking is that the benefits really needed by the elderly are lifetime pensions. Within the last few years, changes have been made to the EPF – so that a part (although not all) of the benefits are provided in pension form. This change does not seem too popular with the members, who may not understand fully the reasons for which it has been made. The managers of the EPF have a duty here to explain clearly tot heir members the way in which the scheme works and the ways in which they are going about improving their commitment to truly serve the members.

In most countries, including India and the other neighbouring countries, the longest – standing social security benefit has been one that is paid to workers who suffer from accidental injuries, or worse, at their workplace. This is employment injury benefit or-as it was more traditionally called workmens' compensation. It has long since been regarded as the responsibility of the employer to provide for a disabled employee, both medical care and cash payments to make up loss of wages. This is the principle of employers' liability. Unfortunately, with many schemes organized on this basis, it takes a very long time for an injured worker to actually receive any payment. From this point of view it is better to arrange the scheme on a social insurance basis, where the payment of benefits can be made from a central fund, perhaps, on a "no fault" basis, with the whole community of employers paying regular contributions to the fund as a percentage of their respective payrolls. Again, India has recognized the value of the social insurance principle in this regard, although the fact that ESIC has not yet achieved national coverage means that the transition from employers' liability is by no means complete in practice.

The situation with the payment of maternity benefits, as provided for under the law, is rather similar to that concerning employment injury.

The provision of unemployment benefit is a very difficult issue indeed for all developing countries. Obviously, all workers fear to a greater or lesser degree – the consequences of redundancy and the loss of their income. But it can be very hard to decide, in a country such as India, who is truly unemployed. Should we include those who are employed only on a seasonal basis, and what about those who have never had a formal paid job? Clearly those who choose by themselves to leave their jobs should not qualify for unemployment benefits, but it is not always easy to know whether redundancy was truly voluntary or compulsory. Such problems, quite apart from those of finding the resources to pay adequate benefits, have meant that it is almost impossible to devise a workable system of unemployment benefits in a developing country, although one or two countries, such as China, have tried to build up schemes with rather limited benefits and coverage. These are now coming under great strain with the economic and employment problems now afflicting the Asian region.

I would like to say something about the pioneering role which ILO has played in relation to social security development. The prime concern of the ILO is the formulation of international policies and programmes to improve working and living conditions. One of the principal ways in which it does involves the ILO secretariat in extensive study and discussion, and in the examination of existing laws and practices throughout the world. When a convention has been adopted by the annual International Labour Conference, member States of the ILO are required by the Constitution to bring the Convention to the notice of their legislative authorities in due course, if the standards, which have been set, are embodied in national laws, the States concerned will be in a position to ratify the Convention. Not every State, which follows the Convention necessarily proceeds to ratification, but the influence of the ILO in setting standards, is effective regardless of the formal procedures involved.

A landmark in international social security was the adoption by the International Labour Conference of the ILO on 28 June 1952 of the Social Security (Minimum Standards) Convention (No. 102). This brought together in one comprehensive document the policies to which the then member States were prepared to subscribe, and defined the range of benefits which form the core of social security. It laid down minimum requirements as to coverage of the populations and the content and levels of benefits, and covered the protection of the rifts of contributors and beneficiaries and ancillary matters of administration. This convention, therefore, provides a target, to which countries are encouraged to aspire in developing their national social security systems, although of course each country's scheme must reflect its own national priorities.

There are a number of other Conventions and Recommendations on Social Security, relating to various contingencies such as workmens' compensation and maternity benefits, and also to the social security provisions, which are thought to be appropriate for migrant workers.

Of course, the fact that Convention 102 was adopted almost 50 years ago means that in some respects it does not reflect modern conditions very well, and the responsible department at the headquarters in Geneva, assisted by our specialists working in the field, are very actively studying the ways in which the relevant concepts can be updated.

A word about the growth of social security around the world. After the end of the Second World War, the number of countries operating some kind of social security programme rose sharply. Social security was an important part of any reconstruction effort, and a prime interest of newly emerging countries, more than 60 of whom achieved independence around this time. Relatively few countries achieved then or have yet achieved the ideal of comprehensive coverage, and in the industrialized world there is much concern about the cost of the schemes which have built up, particularly as the number of elderly people requiring pensions increase in proportion to the workers who pay contribution into the schemes.

However, social security is universally recognized to be a vital component of the working environment in modern States and most countries have put in place schemes to provide at least for some contingencies. A watch on schemes around the world is maintained by the Social Security Administration of the United States, who publish regular surveys of other countries' systems.

No matter what other form of protection has been organized, nearly every country has some type of employment injury scheme; in some cases in the form of social insurance, in others by placing a legal liability on employers. Occasionally both techniques are found side by side in different sectors of employment, for example, when the transition from an older system to social insurance is not yet complete. Many countries organize their social security systems using a mixture of financing systems. Moreover, the degree to which workers, employers and sometimes governments are expected to share the costs varies widely from one country to another.

Most countries have made provision for old age, invalidity and survivorship, again in different ways through social insurance, social assistance, provident funds or general revenue-financed schemes for residents. More than one half of them cover sickness and maternity, and about the same number supplement family resources through a regular system of allowances. Only about one quarter of them provide unemployment benefit, which for the most part is found only in industrialized market-economy countries.

The lessons for the future are that we must seek to ensure that social security schemes meet the needs of today and tomorrow, rather than yesterday. You are probably aware that other international organizations, such as the World Bank, have developed quite radical ideas for the financial development of social security, and these need to be evaluated in relation to the social dimension, which is of course ILO's primary concern. There is an almost infinite variety of possible designs for each country's social security system, and of the ways in which the responsibilities and benefits due to members may be arranged and shared with their social partners, the employers and the government.

6.

Social Security for Workers in the Unorganised Sector

May 1999

Dr. L.D. Mishra

Former Secretary, Union Ministry of Labour

I commend this timely and splendid initiative of the Social Security Association of India to have this symposium as an integral part of their Annual Conference. There could be cynics and skeptics who could ask the question "are you not making an artificial wall of distinction and discrimination between the workers in different sectors of employment by choosing social security for the workers in the unorganized sector as the theme in the symposium?" Such cynics and skeptics are mistaken and it would not take very long to demolish such doubts and misgivings. The distinction between the workers in the organized versus those in the unorganized sector is as real and life like as it could be. The workers in the unorganized sector have always remained in the twilight zone of our attention. Their contribution to the evolution and growth of civil society through their blood, sweat and tears is invaluable; so also is the story of their sacrifice and suffering in the making of the civil society. I would, therefore, like to congratulate and compliment the Social Security Association of India for according this primacy and centrality to these unfortunate sections of the society whom Gurudev Rabindranath Tagore once described as the 'dumb, mute, expressionless', the withered and forlorn' and who for generations have remained as the exiles of civilization. I have no doubt that this day long symposium will not only help in churning of the critical consciousness of the participants on the plight and predicament of the workers in the unorganized sector but would also send some ripples to arouse and awaken the critical consciousness of the policy formulators and implementers so that they part with a minuscule of their

---

A symposium organised by the Association on 15 May 1999.

time, energy and resources as also attention to the workers of this sector who have been relegated to the background and neglected for a long time for no fault of theirs.

Social security is a basic need of all people regardless of the sector of employment in which they work and live. It is an important form of social protection where we should begin with birth and should continue till date. The urge and inclination for social protection on the part of individuals in general and deprived and disadvantaged cross sections of the society in particular would not have been more tellingly brought out than in the following couplet by Gurudev Rabindranath Tagore in Ebar Phiras More quote:

> 'I look before me a dark world
> A deep dark world
> A world caged and combined by narrow artificial walls
> I want food
> I want life
> I want free open air
> I want health
> I want long life "delight" '

Human life today stands exposed to the risk of infant mortality, child mortality, maternal mortality and numerous other forms of morbidity and malnutrition. As it advances from childhood to youth and youth to manhood it is also exposed to numerous occupational risks and hazards. Some of these risks and hazards are inherent in the nature of work and technology behind the manufacturing process and they cause accidents resulting in injury and disablement. It is well known that such accidents are seldom reported nor is the workmen's compensations which is payable in the event of death or disability, ever paid even though there is a legislative protective framework which is nearly eight decades old.

The problems in the unorganized/informal sector are vast and mind boggling: related to social security and various other forms of social protection they are not amenable to any precise classification and description and, therefore, may appear on the surface to be elusive. The unorganized/informal sector has numerous categories/sub-categories and it is considerable in terms of number. According to 1991 census we have total work force of 314 million. 9.4 per cent of them are employed in the organized sector numbering 28 million, while 90.6 per cent are employed in the unorganized sector numbering 286 million. 15.2 per cent are regular salaried employees numbering 47 million, while 53 per cent are self-employed numbering 166 million.

The unorganized/informal sector could be divided into three parts, namely:

- Workers who are in the traditional unorganized/informal sector.
- Workers who are entering the unorganized/informal sector in large number, consequent on shrinkage of jobs in the organized/ formal sector on the one hand and recourse to outsourcing or contractualisation and casualisation on the other.
- Migrant workers who migrate from one district ot another within a state or from one part of the territory of India to another.

The first category has numerous subcategories and it is not easy to precisely identify and enumerate all the sub-categories, in illustrative terms, however, the following could be listed within the various sub-categories of this sector:

- The small and marginal farmers
- The landless agricultural labourers
- The share croppers
- The rural artisans
- The handloom weavers
- The handcrafts men and women
- The fishermen and women
- The collectors of raw hides and skins
- The flayers and tanners
- The scavengers
- The salt workers
- The hammals (loaders and unloaders)
- The building and construction workers
- The bamboo cutters and toddy tappers
- The brick kiln workers
- The stone quarry workers
- The glass and bangle makers
- The lock makers
- The gem cutters and polishers
- The collectors of minor forest produce

The second category is a recent phenomenon in the wake of liberalization, privatization and globalization and emergence of fiercely aggressive and aggressively competitive market forces. With emergence of these forces there is urgent and imperative need for promoting competitiveness through reduction of costs both administrative as well as wage cost. This is what has prompted the managements of several large and medium enterprises in the organized manufacturing sector to off-load a portion of the jobs, occupations and processes which are hitherto being performed by regular employees and to outsource them in favour of contractor/subcontractors. The production systems and labour markets are witnessing a lot of transformation. There is change in the nature of work resulting in reorganization of the workplace and the work itself. As the regular jobs are off-loaded and parceled out, the number of contract/casual workers keep on increasing. Outsourcing gives rise to a typical employer-employee relationship as against the normal employer-employee relationship in which there is no stability or durability of employment and the workers/ employees stand retrenched and displaced as soon as the work order has been executed. Contract and casual workers would represent about 31 per cent of the total workforce numbering 97 million. They are scattered and fragmented with long hours of work and unsafe working conditions with tremendous vulnerability to exploitation in the absence of any worthwhile organization.

The third category deals with an important cross section of the unorganized/informal sector i.e. migrant workers. Right to move freely from one part of the territory of India to another is a fundamental right guaranteed under Article 19 of the Constitution and, therefore, there should be nothing objectionable about migration per se. Migration, however, becomes objectionable when individuals at the originating point who are landless and assetless, unemployed and underemployed and have nothing to fall back upon are recruited by recruiting agents with a lot of false hopes promises and sometimes with loans/debts/advances. They are lulled to believe that this would liberate them from a situation of helplessness and dependence to a new situation where they could be on their own. Exactly the opposite of this happens. No sooner they have arrived at the destination point than these hopes and promises are belied and they are subjected to a chain of ruthless exploitation of numerous agents and middlemen of the principal employer. Husband, wife and children invariably migrate as a unit and such migration results in a terrible dislocation of home life and family life. The members of the migrant family at the destination point are not assured of the irreducible barest minimum needs as human being i.e. a decent shelter, clean potable water, health, hygiene, environmental sanitation and education for the children. The language/dialect which is spoken at the destination point is quite different from the language/dialect spoken by them landing them in a situation of total alienation. Thirty five million men, women and children are constantly on the move and have been placed in the vertex of exploitation, misery and suffering. Since there is no stability and durability in their employment and they keep on moving from place to place employers and middlemen find it easy not to maintain registers and not to comply with the statutory requirements of Contract Labour (Regulation of Employment and Conditions of Service) Act, Employees Provident Fund and Miscellaneous Provisions Act and so on.

Small and marginal farmers (110 million) and landless agricultural labourers (75 million) together constitute a formidable number and are of the order of 185 million. Additionally there are share croppers who also work as agricultural labourers who are not registered as such. Majority of these share croppers and landless agricultural labourers belong to the community of Scheduled Castes who for generations have been victims of social discrimination and economic exploitation. They suffer from lack of stability and durability of employment, landlessness and assetlessness, low wages, low skills, lack of bargaining power—both individual and collective—due to lack of unionization, a culture of silence and dependence and state of stoic resignation to the harsh ground level realities. Many of them do not have a roof over their head and they work as attached agricultural labourers with the bhumiswami or tenure holder under conditions where they do not have the freedom of choice of employment, freedom of movement and the right to bargain for their labour as well as for the product of labour all or some of which tantamount to existence of bonded labour system.

Successive governments at the central level have been trying to identify and enumerate them to issue them identity cards, to regulate their hours of work and wages, to ensure a semblance of social security (including old age pension) for them and to provide irreducible barest minimum facilities and amenities of life to them through constitution of statutory welfare funds. Even though such efforts started as early as 1945 taking a cue from the Kerala Agriculture Act which was enacted by Government of Kerala under the leadership of late Sh. Achyut Menon, former Chief Minister of that State in 1974, no major breakthrough could be achieved till date. As debates go on in the rarified and highly intellectualized environments (like the current symposium of today), landless agricultural labourers and share croppers go on sliding lower and lower in the ladder of human development.

Next to landless agricultural labourers and share croppers come fishermen and women whose plight and predicament is even worse. While the fishermen go to the deep sea for fishing and many of them disappear in the process never to return, the fisherwoman carry head loads of fish for sale in markets by traveling long distances on foot and with all the attendant hazards of dealing with a perishable commodity in the absence of any storage facility. The fishermen who go to the deep sea for fishing under adverse weather conditions are not assured of any accident insurance in the event of their falling victims of cyclones and tidal bores. The fishermen and women live in extremely unclean and unhygienic surroundings without assured clean potable water and basic environmental sanitation on account of which they contact skin diseases and other communicable diseases. In the absence of any country-side survey in general and survey in the coastal states of Andhra Pradesh, Orissa, West Bengal, Tamil Nadu, Karnataka, Maharashtra, Gujarat and Kerala no accurate, authentic and upto date data about the fishermen is available on the basis of which some social security measures like accident insurance, health insurance, old age protection etc could be planned for them. Majority of the fishermen and women are victims of both social discrimination and economic exploitation. Despite successive years of planned efforts we have not succeeded in ameliorating their plight. The mechanized trawler owners who are well organized, who have access to credit and all other resources and who are progressively invading the sea year after year are robbing and expropriating them from their basic aqua rights.

Next in order of magnitude as also in order of intensity of exploitation are the leather workers. This is a broad category which comprises of collectors of raw hides and skins, tanners and flayers engaged in numerous tanneries of Tamil Nadu, West Bengal, Orissa, Karnataka, Andhra Pradesh and Uttar Pradesh. They remove the skin from the carcasses, douche them in chemicals and in the process have to inhale the most pungent and nauseating stench of putrid flesh. These unfortunate sections of humanity work is the most unclean, unhygienic and unsafe surroundings. In course of interaction with chemicals their fingers get corroded. They are also victims of several skin diseases and other communicable diseases. While several such tanneries functioning in unclean and unhygienic conditions have closed down at the direction of the apex Court in Tamil Nadu, West Bengal and Uttar Pradesh throwing thousands out of employment many continue to operate in a clandestine manner and are least concerned about the conservation of environment.

The salt workers of Gujarat, Maharashtra, Karnataka and Orissa constitute yet another most deprived and vulnerable sections of the workforce in the unorganized sector. They prepare the salt fields, pump brine into the fields at a particular temperature and climatic condition and as the water evaporates leaving the raw salt in the fields, they have to scrape them and collect heaps of salt and arrange its transportation. Because of the continuous interaction with chemicals their fingers and feet get corroded and they also become victims of many communicable diseases.

The beedi workers constitute one of the most deprived and disadvantaged sections of the workforce in the unorganized sector. We have nearly 5 million beedi workers who roll beedies, label them, pack them and dispatch them for sale. Majority of these workers are home workers. Home work usually connotes a situation where husband, wife and children work at residential premises. They receive raw materials (tendu leaf and tobacco) from middlemen and hand over the end products to them for a pittance i.e. at the rate of Rs. 20 to Rs. 30 for 1000 beedies. The mal-functional middlemen reject 15 to 20 per cent of the end products on the ground that they do not conform to specification. But ironically enough they sell these so called substandard products in the market and appropriate the sale proceeds to themselves. Like leather workers and fishermen and women the beedi workers also live in unclean, unhygienic, poorly lit and ill ventilated surroundings and often fall victims to pulmonary and respiratory diseases like asthma, TB etc. Beedi is a scheduled industry both under the Minimum Wages Act as well as under the Employees' Provident Fund and Miscellaneous Provisions Act. Minimum wages have been notified for rolling, labeling and packaging beedies on piece rate basis but because of malfunctional and dysfunctional middleman the minimum rates of wages are seldom enforced. Because of low wages it is difficult to conceive of a Social Security Scheme which rests on deduction from wages by way of contribution to PF and ESI schemes. Beedi industry and beedi workers have been brought within the purview of Employees Provident Fund and Miscellaneous Provisions Act since 1977. The constitutional validity of the notification was challenged before the Supreme Court and the latter granted a stay. The stay remained in force for over five years. Even after the stay was vacated barely 1.5 million beedi workers have been covered under the Act as against 5 million workers. There have been enormous problems in issue of identity cards to beedi workers although it is the statutory duty of the employers under rule 41 of the Beedi Workers Welfare Fund Rules. But even 23 years after the Beedi Workers Welfare Fund Act came into existence all identity cards could not be issued till date. The beedi workers live in premises which are scattered and fragmented, many of them do not have a proper shelter and are not assured of the barest minimum facilities and amenities such as access to clean potable water, health care and environmental sanitation. They also migrate on account of disparity in minimum wages prevailing in different states and are subjected to the same exploitation as other migrant workers. Even though under the Beedi Workers Welfare Fund, governments have set up nearly 200 dispensaries yet the health infrastructure continues to be inadequate and ineffective in terms of dealing with the pulmonary/respiratory diseases afflicting the beedi workers.

We have many other sub-categories of workers in the unorganized sector such as hammals or loaders and unloaders, collectors of tendu leaves and sal seeds and other minor forest products and scavengers who even today have to carry night soil on their head—a practice which is repugnant to any civilized human conscience. There is no accurate and upto date data about their number, working and living conditions as also about their preferences and felt needs. A beginning was made during the tenure of

Sh. H.D. Deve Gowda, former Prime Minister to conduct a survey to identify and enumerate the hammals or the loaders and unloaders in different places with a view to ascertaining the state of their houselessness and to formulate a scheme under which a minimum shelter could be assured to them. We wrote to all States/UTs to conduct such a survey but despite best efforts no such survey could yet be conducted or completed. A pilot project could at best be launched in two States i.e. Madhya Pradesh and Karnataka on the basis of positive response from these two states. Hammals are there everywhere i.e. at bus stops, railway stations, mandis, market yards, FCI depots and in practically each and every state. A project, therefore, to provide a basic human need i.e. a roof over their head could not be confined only to two states; this could at best be a beginning which needs to be extended and replicated all over. This, however, has not happened due to lack of positive response from the States/UTs.

- The collectors of minor forest produce as also the bamboo workers and other forest labourers have to work in dense forests and suffer enormous occupational risks and hazards of snake bites, stinging bites of insects as also the hazards of extreme sun, rain and storm. Many of them cry agonizingly in course of their unbearable suffering but their cry remains lost in the wilderness. They do fall victims of accidents in course of their long sojourn to forests and back but such accidents are never reported and workmen's compensation is seldom deposited and paid on the ground that there is no employer-employee relationship.
- Some of the major factors which contribute to the plight and predicament of the workers in the unorganized sector including denial of social security are:
  - Absence of survey to scientifically identify and enumerate the actual number of such workers.
  - Absence of accurate, authentic and up-to-date data about their preferences and felt needs.
  - Employers invariably contesting the employer-employee relationship and disowning responsibility to do anything for these workers.
  - Lack of visibility due to scattered and fragmented nature of the workforce, pervasive illiteracy, lack of numerals, lack of awareness, low level of aspirations and absence of any worthwhile mechanism to impart legal as well as programme literacy to them and to bring them to the mainstream of development.

It is indeed, an irony that while we have been telling about problems and constraints encountered by numerous categories and sub-categories of workers in the unorganized sector for several years we have not been able to provide any worthwhile mechanism to give them the minimum relief and succour in the context of both their day-to-day working under normal conditions as also in the context of accidents invalidating them for life.

Viewed in the above context social security for the workers in the numerous sub-categories in the unorganized sector cannot be viewed in isolation. Social Security for them is a multi-dimensional composite concept and has to be related to the policy of the State, density of population, per capita income, rates of literacy and level of aspirations, level of skills, existence of migration, lack of administrative infrastructure, lack of professionally educated and trained manpower and overall mindsets of employers which are invariably negative. In the context of women, there are severe disadvantages, discrimination and denial of any worthwhile social security scheme for them on account of the following:

- More women are in rural areas and below poverty line.
- More women are contract and casual workers engaged in series of activities in the informal sector.
- Women's rate of literacy and numeracy is invariably lower.
- More women than men are unskilled.
- Women face much greater seasonal fluctuations in employment and earnings than men.

The above problems and constrains have been compounded further by certain other visitations adversely affecting the workers in the unorganized sector in a striking manner. These are:

- Decline in real wages corresponding to increase in cost of living and decline in purchasing power of the rupee.
- Steady accruals to the informal sector-burgeoning size 286 million of workers in the unorganized informal sector according to the 1991 census would be in the vicinity of 315 to 320 million today.
- Informal sector entrepreneurs unwilling to transfer substantive benefits of support programmes to hired workers.

Jobs which are parceled out by the formal manufacturing sector in favour of entrepreneurs in the unorganized and informal sector will have to be executed in less time and cost with very little concern for providing social protection and labour rights.

- Inadequate skill upgradation and technological paradigm shift

- Low productivity
- Lack of capital for modernization
- High mortality rate in informal sector enterprises
- Linkage of the informal sector with the formal sector is exploitative.

Any strategy for providing social security or various forms of social protection to the numerous sub-categories of workers in the unorganized/ informal sector would have to be closely viewed in the context of the situational analysis as has been presented in the preceding paragraphs. In outlining this strategy children would necessarily have to be the starting point as also the focal point of attention. Children are like flowers of home, of the community and the society and childhood represents the most tender, formative and impressionable stage of human development. It is stage of singing and dancing, playing and learning through the process of socialization and not a stage for subjecting children to harsh, rigorous, hazardous and exploitative work. If children are subjected to such work and are denied normal and natural access to educational opportunity, and are denied through such access their evolution, and growth as human beings, it would tantamount to carrying our succeeding generation to the brink of near destruction. Education for all should be the first and most important goal and the State as the agent of the society has to create a climate and environment where not only education is valued and prized by all but basic education becomes a tool of empowerment. Since child labour and educational deprivation are co-termitus, elimination of child labour and free compulsory universal primary and elementary education must also be coterminus and synonymous. Elimination of child labour does not mean mere release of children from work, but opening avenues, facilities and opportunities for access to meaningful education. All children are not eligible or endowed to enter higher education stream or university stream of education. We must therefore, draw a dividing line between children who have crossed the ten plus two stage in education and who can be sent for vocational education, while the rest who have the aptitude and the endowment can enter the higher form of education and harness the same to their advantage. This was the recommendation of the Education Commission under the Chairmanship of Prof. D.S. Kothari way back in 1964-66 and even though more than three decades have passed nothing substantial has been done in the field of vacationalisation of education. Vocational education should be treated with the same dignity and respect as the formal system of education. It is only through vocational education that necessary and desirable links could be established between education, skill formation and upgradation, employment, wages, productivity, savings and investment.

Education for all should be accompanied by health and hygiene for all, nutrition for all, immunization for all, and environmental sanitation for all. Cuba provides one of the best examples of public health and linkage of education with health, nutrition and sanitation. This model needs to be widely circulated.

Gender sensitization must permeate all the layers and levels of education. Just as there should be no discrimination between boys and girls in terms of education, health, medical care and skill training, there should be no discrimination between men and women in terms of adequate opportunities and avenues of employment, wages and working conditions. This ethos and culture of equality regardless of sexes must permeate to all layers of development.

There must be a national wages policy which should lay down the norms and parameters for fixation, review, revision and enforcement of living wages or need based wage below which no employer of an industry should pay. The norms and parameters of that policy should be:

(a) disparities in wages across regions and states should be minimal as disparities in wages give rise to migration.

(b) A major portion of the wages should be paid in cash to enable the recipient of wages to defray their day to day expenses on account of electricity, water and water and various other family obligations contrary to the existing provision of law which permits payment of wages fully or partly in cash of kind which is totally untenable.

(c) Like the age of entry to employment, there should be clear and scientific rationale behind hours of work and this was the central message behind May Day or International Labour Day. regardless of the sectors of employment, employers of enterprises have no moral right or authority to subject the employees/workers to unduly long hours of work without spread over and without payment of overtime.

(d) Minimum Wages Act should be amended to remove the provisions related to employment of adults, adolescents and children and also to remove the differential provisions in terms of hours of work and wages between adults, adolescents and children.

In order that there is a clear linkage between wages and skills and social security, the enforcement machinery must ensure that whatever wages are payable are actually paid on the 7th of the month succeeding the month to which the wages relate without any deduction on account of middlemen's commission or any other form of deduction which is arbitrary and unauthorized. If wages are diluted so will be social security. The workplace has to be clean, safe, healthy and congenial so that employees/ workers contribute their very best to the enterprise and its prosperity. It is futile to talk of production, productivity and high GDP rate of growth without creating a safe, clean and congenial work place. The number of accidents must be minimized by taking recourse to a clear cut strategy on risk sharing and risk communication on the one hand and guidelines on observance of industrial and mining safety on the other. If despite best of efforts accidents do take place in factories or mines due to factors, beyond either of the management or of the workers, accidents must be reported and compensation as payable under the Workmen's Compensation Act must be deposited with the Statutory Authority.

In the event of injuries caused by accidents result in death workmen's compensation should be disbursed to the legal heirs of the deceased after proper verification. Similarly, provisions of the Maternity Benefit Act must be implemented in letter and spirit and there should be no occasion for discrimination or sexual harassment of women at the workplace merely because the employers are required to discharge maternity benefits.

Social Assistance and Social Insurance in a poor and developing country like India is relevant against a number of contingencies such as:

- Unemployment
- Sickness
- Old age
- Widowhood
- Maternity
- Disability
- Employment injury

We must attempt to progressively introduce all the above elements of social security and extend the above elements of social security to the un-organize/informal sector. It should be administratively feasible and financially affordable keeping in view the present stage of country's economic development.

While it may not be possible to provide unemployment allowance in the foreseeable future in view of the magnitude of the problem of unemployment and the problem of resource constraints, efforts must be made to minimize the severely harsh impact of unemployment and under employment through training, retraining, career counseling and redeployment of those workers who have been retrenched and displaced.

In designing any package of social security the basic question to be asked are:

- Is the package deliverable?
- Is it measurable?
- Is the impact assessable?

The number of workers in the unorganized sector is large and is growing in the vicinity of 300 million plus. A beginning must be made to build up an accurate, authentic and up to date data base as a tool of planning. There must be accurate and authentic documentation of whatever developments take place on the ground in the unorganized/informal sector with a view to harnessing its relevance to the field of social security. Coverage under both EPF and ESI Schemes must be progressively increased to cover all categories and sub-categories of workers in the unorganized and informal sector. The administration of the scheme in relation to workers of unorganized sector must be efficient, innovative, positive, responsible, sensitive and accountable. The personnel manning the social security schemes must be professionally capable, empathic, responsible and sensitive.

They must have the patience to register grievances (which are inevitable in the large organization handling problems of millions of subscriber members and insured persons) and redress them with the right attitude, right approach, right perception and right insight. They must look upon the subscriber members and insured persons as their presiding deities as venerable as the deities inside a temple. They must look upon themselves as the custodians of a sacred trust and must not do anything which will forfeit that trust.

This brings out the importance of the State in the context of conceptualizing, planning, formulating and implementing schemes of social security for the workers in the numerous sub-categories of the unorganized/informal sector. The role of the state is extremely important and cannot be wished away. The ardent votaries of advocates of liberalization, privatization and globalization (LPG) advocate that the state's intervention in basic education, primary health care, immunization, nutrition and environmental situation should be minimal. They are mistaken as a matter of fact, as we proceed further in the direction of globalization and privatization, this role will have to be reinforced. This is for the simple reason that market forces can not shoulder the responsibility for basic education, primary health care and so on. While Central Government will have to play an important role in policy formulation, coordination and programme design, monitoring and evaluation of the impact of delivery should be done in close coordination with State Governments. Local authorities must be involved in the delivery of social assistance in the unorganized/informal sector.

In the context of the primacy and centrality of the role of the State, it is a matter of deep regret that the total expenditure on social security over the years in a minuscule in terms of the total GDP in many countries such as:

- Less than 0.5 per cent of GDP in 10 countries of Africa
- Less than 0.5 per cent of GDP in countries of Asia
- Less than 0.5 per cent of GDP in 1 country of Latin America
- 0.6 to 0.9 per cent of GDP in 4 countries of Asia
- 1 to 4 per cent of GDP in 10 countries of Africa
- 1 to 4 per cent of GDP in 7 countries of Asia
- 1 to 4 per cent of GDP in 15 countries of Latin America
- above 10 per cent in 2 countries of Latin America
- above 10 per cent in 2 countries of America
- above 10 per cent in 26 countries.

The total cost of social security as a percentage of GDP is less than 1 per cent in 28 developing countries. It is between 1 to 4 per cent in 32 developing countries.

Since workers in the numerous sub-categories of unorganized/informal sector are scattered and fragmented across the length and breadth of the country, their employment and number of persons employed are also undergoing rapid change year after year organization of the unorganized is absolutely urgent and imperative; this indeed is the key to provision of any form of social protection. Organization does not merely mean a collectivity, an assembly of men and women in shape of trade unions, associations and cooperatives. It also refers to various indigenous groups, thrift and credit groups, DWCRA group, groups of neo-literates etc. They, however, represent only the form. But much more important than the form is the objective, strategy and methodology thereof. I would like to refer to the example of Pudukottai district of Tamil Nadu where it was possible and feasible to provide a semblance of social security to the workers in the unorganized sector through organization of the workers into cooperatives. Pudukottai is a small and backward district on the southern coast of Tamil Nadu where a campaign for total literacy was undertaken in the year 1990. This was an attempt to mobilize all sections of the society for the difficult task of imparting literacy and numeracy in a State where the literacy rate was around 30 per cent. Along with imparting of instructional lessons, an attempt was made to weave several other economic activities, such as mobilizing the workers, and forming cooperative societies of quarry workers, gem cutters, gem polishers etc. This was a bold and imaginative initiative which was possible because of the dynamic leadership of Ms. Sheila Rani Chunkath. Stone quarries which were leased out hitherto to the contractors of Salem district of Tamil Nadu were now given on lease to cooperatives of quarry workers and some of these quarries were manned by women workers. Hitherto-workers, they were made owners and managers of quarries. This was a remarkable transformation which paved the way for extending several forms of protection to these otherwise deprived and disadvantage sections of the society. This experiment, however, died out after some time when the policy of grant of these of stone quarries was revised and resumed in favour of contractors as against cooperatives of men and women workers. The example of co-operatization of beedi workers by late Sh.. C.K. Panickar of Dinesh Beedi of Cannanore (Kerala) is yet another pioneering example. They became the managers and owners of beedi units and had complete control over the affairs of the enterprise. They had a voice in the entire decision making process starting from procurement of tendu leaves, procurement of tobacco, rolling, labeling and packaging of beedies and disposal of the end product. They decided the rates; they also identified their welfare needs and proceeded to implement them in a totally participative manner. Starting with identification and enumeration of workers through survey both household survey as well as enterprise level survey as well as enterprise level survey, the strategy and methodology of organization can stretch this to identification of preferences, felt needs and interests and constitution of welfare funds through which a host of facilities and amenities can be provided. Imparting of skills could be one of the major objectives and activity as a part of the organization process. Imparting of skills should be viewed as important as housing, drinking water, education as it is only through such skills, entrepreneurial and managerial skills that education becomes meaningful and can contribute to the making of a complete man or a complete woman.

Organization of the unorganized for justice and equity cannot be a one day or one night affair; it is a distant goal; it has to be preceded by an intensive process of mobilization, education, conscientisation, orientation and training. This also cannot be the mandate of one Ministry, Department of agency, the Government must enlist the involvement and support of all sections of the society, notably central employers and trade union organizations and NGOs in achieving the seemingly impossible and mind boggling task of organization of millions of workers who are continuing for generations in the traditional unorganized/informal sector and who continue to slide lower and lower in the ladder of development. It is only when the state, as the agent of the society accepts with all humility that it cannot undertake this responsibility all by itself on its shoulders, but can make an humble attempt to do so by soliciting the involvement, cooperation and collaboration of employers, trade union organizations and NGOs, make the seemingly impossible task possible, feasible and achievable. They must think together, plan together and work together to make this a reality.

Sahdev K. Wadhawan

Former Regional Director, ISSA

Social Security for workers in the unorganized sector of economy and, more particularly, for those employed in agricultural occupation in rural areas, has become a topical subject today, both nationally as also internationally.

While industrialized countries usually have schemes of social security extended to the entire population (for the simple reason that there is hardly any distinction between the rural areas and urban areas as regards systems of communication, transport, education and administration), the situation is not so in the less developed and developing countries. Most countries in South America have, for many years, been trying to identify ways and means to extended to the informal sector with or without modification, traditional institutional schemes of social security/social insurance, but have not succeeded. Practically every country, therefore, is searching for models which would meet the need for providing a safety net or social protection to the unorganized sector.

Internationally, the International Labour Organisation and the International Social Security Association are addressing this problem time and again and trying to find a workable solution. While every country has its own cultural, social and economical background, the search is for a broad framework within which the individual countries may formulate their own policies and programmes.

Nationally, the matter has assumed serious concern. At every forum where social security is discussed, attention is invariably drawn to the need for providing satisfactory social protection for workers on the margin of economic security and those multitudes of people working on their own, be they engaged in handicraft, beedi rolling, taxi/scooter driving or carrying load etc. It is not surprising that so much emphasis has suddenly emerged in this area. There is a little more than 300 million workforce in the country. While 11 per cent of this workforce is engaged in economic activity in the organized urban sector, 89 per cent are either in the unorganized urban sector or in rural areas working on agricultural or other allied occupations.

In 1990, ILO Conference Report of the Director General International Labour Office, had as its main theme "the lemma of informal sector". Evidently, the whole work is pre-occupied with this important but so far intractable subject.

In 1989, with a view to providing technical input, the ILO commissioned a study, which I was asked to undertake on social security for the workers in the informal sector in India. The study was confined to four major States – Maharashtra, Gujarat, Kerala and Tamil Nadu. The idea was to make an inventory of what, if at all, was being done in the nature of provision of social protection to workers engaged in unorganized sector of economy.

For the purpose of the study, I defined the term "informal sector" as referring to small scale activities typically operating within a low level of organization and technology and which are likely to fall outside the scope of statutory social security schemes like the Employees Provident Fund; State Insurance; the Maternity Benefit Act; the Payment of Gratuity Act etc.

Most surprisingly, I was able to identify in those four States, as many as 65 statutory and non-statutory schemes providing social protection, social welfare, economic security and allied benefits. The schemes were largely confined to agricultural workers in the rural areas and to individuals belonging to indigent families in the urban areas particularly widows, women with very low level of family income, disabled and handicapped.

Practically every State has a system of old age pension payable at ages varying from 60 to 70 years, the amount of pension ranging between Rs. 50 and Rs. 100. The eligibility for benefits was, however, based on a stringent "means test". In most cases, the family income for the grant of benefit may not exceed Rs. 3,000 or so p.a. More importantly not all old people who were entitled to old age pension knew about the existence of such scheme and, therefore, were deprived of the benefit.

The Life Insurance Corporation of India had introduced a variety of Group Insurance Schemes and Saving Schemes to cover members of co-operative society and trade or occupational association.

The study, though basically factual, did attempt to draw some conclusion and to address the subject of formulation of appropriate models to provide social protection measures to different categories of the workforce in the unorganized sector. It was noticed that the inherent diversities and the federal structure of the country did not permit of any unilateral approach to socio-economic programmes: on the contrary, it involved massive readjustment and review of priorities so that benefits of economic development and consequential gains in other spheres, including social security, accrued in a substantial measure to the poor, the destitutes and the disadvantaged, small marginal farmers, landless labourers, self-employed and low grade artisans and unskilled workers. The report said that in actual implementation, development in most fields, to which social security measures were no exception, had been somewhat tilted to the advantage of the organized urban workforce to the relative neglect of the rural poor and the informal sector. The inadequate flow of social security benefits to the informal sector had thus accentuated the very inequities which the Constitution of India purports to remove. In the result, the social security measures and public assistance programmes had been somewhat restrictive, minimal or cosmetic in their impact and approach, circumscribed as they were by a variety of limitations and constraints.

The imbalance resulting from relatively less attention paid in the past to the informal sector as compared to the formal (Organized) sector had aroused considerable thinking both at the Central as also at the State Governments level. Even this truncated study, confined only to four States, revealed that the Indian social security programmes were now a mixture of a variety of schemes. Besides, the institutional social security schemes in urban areas, there were Central Welfare funds constituted mainly for health care, housing and education; public assistance schemes of the destitutes, the old and the handicapped; unemployment relief schemes for the educated unemployed; employment/self-employment generating schemes, including the Employment Guarantee Scheme in operation in Maharashtra; voluntary medical services, assistance for children and destitutes; and collaborative LIC and GIC Schemes for life insurance and other risks.

While the workers in the organized sector were protected through contributory social insurance schemes, the vast majority of the working population in the informal and rural sector were denied any systematic protection through effective programmes of social security. the study revealed that most of the programmes received funds allocated on an ad-hoc basis, outside the plan. The amount of cash assistance was usually too small to enable the beneficiary to eke out a living even at the minimum needs level and was generally hedged by unduly harsh eligibility conditions. This apart, there was no evidence found that all those eligible have been brought within the fold of assistance or were aware of their entitlement. Different State Governments had evolved different strategies and measures, as the need arose, to quicken implementation of poverty alleviation programmes or responding to the pressures and demands from disadvantaged sectors of the population.

Thus, though a framework of a consistent pattern of assistance was discernible, proliferated formulation of schemes was all too evident. At times, funds allocated fell short of the needed amount for beneficiaries. Instead of a well-knit integrated programme, there was a conglomeration of various centrally sponsored and State Government Schemes, each operating on a splinter basis, though the common focus naturally was on the economically weakest sections.

The ILO report conceded that institutional social security measures were not suited to the informal sector, particularly because of irregular employment, difficulty in assessment of earnings, incapacity to contribute and inadequacy of infrastructural facilities. So, it was necessary to devise other means of providing social protection to large masses of the workforce, which were outside the ambit of the institutional social security systems. (The report said that though a single unified agency coalescing together various social security and welfare programmes was highly desirable, this might not, perhaps, be feasible until a plateau in social security measures had been reached.) a viable alternative would be the coordination and rationalization of all activities oriented towards social security at the state level in the first place and on a national level at a later stage.

What was imperative was an ideologically coherent, financially viable, organizationally compact and neatly orchestrated effort at various levels, i.e. Central Government, State Government, voluntary bodies, village bodies, co-operatives etc., to nurse and expand the present schemes through well designed policy directions at the national level, so that current programmes, however thin their spread, were made beneficial, more protective and effective progressively. The existing piecemeal programmes had to give way to a well-knit more coherent approach.

The Report concluded, "The problem does not certainly admit of a ready solution nor can it be wished away indefinitely. An objective and detailed study in the nature of stock taking needs to be made of the existing laws and institutions in all States which provide some form of social protection in order to assess whether these can possibly be substituted by or enlarged into a more elaborate programme. Despite the vast size of the country and the large diversity of socio-economic conditions in the less organized or the informal sector, it should be possible to size up the present endeavours, including private efforts and to formulate a dynamic mechanism which could lead up to the ultimate goal of near comprehensive coverage, however long drawn the time-frame."

As a follow up of the recommendations of the study on social security for workers in the informal sector in India, the ILO drew up an action oriented project on the evaluation of selected social security and benefit schemes with a view to gauging the extent to which they had accomplished the purpose for which the schemes were instituted and whether their administration was cost effective.

The project proposal was sent to the Central Government which, in turn, referred the proposal to the four States concerned. However, the Central Government was of the view that the project might be confined to only those schemes which were administered by the Central Government itself. Most of the schemes included in the ILO project were being administered by Social Welfare Department of the State Government.

Considering the importance of the subject, the ILO then examined the matter with a view to evolving an alternative approach. Meanwhile, the ILO had established South Asian Multi Disciplinary Team which considered the whole question of social security for the unorganized sector afresh and based on the report of the national experts, prepared a document on social protection for the Unorganized Sector under an ILO/UNDP Project. The project was discussed at a national workshop organized by the ILO in New Delhi on 1-2 November 1995. The workshop concluded with a broad recommendation to follow up the matter with a pilot study in one or two districts in two States. the underlying premise was to consider the possibility of evolving area-wise social security schemes for the unorganized sector. The pilot study is reported to have been completed and it is understood that it has responded positively to the possibility of introducing area-wise social protection schemes providing for health care benefits financed by contributions made by the population covered and other sources; and death and disability lump sum insurance through group insurance policies from Life Insurance Corporation. The recommendations of the pilot study are reportedly under the consideration of the ILO for further action.

My personal view, however, is that while health care and death and disability benefits are important, I feel that there is urgent need for evolving, in addition, a mechanism (not necessarily centralized), which, in the course of next 20-30 years, ensured every person who has been economically active during his/her working life, to receive, as a matter of right, social security pension at a certain age at a flat rate of reasonable amount. The pension should be available also in the event of permanent disablement (Reference here is to the informal and not formal sector, whose ranks will, in any case, swell as existing social security institutional schemes shed off the present artificial and unnecessary constraint of an employment threshold and wage ceiling for coverage).

There has been a lot of interest in the area of promotion of social insurance through government sponsored schemes with LIC; Group Insurance Schemes for weaker sections; insurance schemes for poor rural households; and government sponsored schemes with General Insurance Corporation. These Schemes, financed largely by government, are in the nature of a public assistance programme and do not necessarily require the intervention of the LIC or GIC because there is no insurance element involved. I believe that the country cannot rest content with having only public assistance programmes however widely spread. The problem of providing a universal old age pension to all those wage earners and those who are otherwise economically active but not covered by the statutory institutional social security schemes, needs to be addressed. These schemes have necessarily to have an element of contribution by the wage earner and his/her employer so that the person concerned gets the benefits as a matter of right and not by way of benevolence by the State.

The contribution may be on a flat rate basis low enough to be affordable even for those who have low earnings. The funds so collected may be supplemented from other specified sources e.g. a cess on production or on sale, agricultural or otherwise, marketed by the employers; social security surcharge on sale of alcohol and tobacco; social security surcharge on electricity bills etc., In the rural areas marketing cooperatives can be nodal agencies for collection of social security cess on agricultural products.

What is necessary is to work out appropriate modalities and to design target specific models, both for short term and long term benefits. While short term benefits viz., medical care for all morbid conditions, whether due to sickness, maternity or injury, and wherever possible, cash assistance for such contingencies that prevent normal economic activity can be provided through a network of mutual benefit societies or health cooperatives (approved/regulated by government). The long term benefits viz., old age, invalidity and survivorship benefit will need intervention of the government for the administration of the Trust fund created through review, cess and other taxes levied especially for the provision of social security, besides the workers' own contribution and that of the employers.

State Government should encourage formation of occupational or geographical (area-wise) self-governing mutual benefit societies/health cooperatives. In order to hasten this process, the existing cooperatives may add to their economic activities, the provision of health care facility, for outpatient or domiciliary medical care, these societies/cooperatives may enter into contractual arrangements with general practitioners and chemists conveniently located in the area. Doctors may be paid a pre-determined capitation fee by the society/cooperative; the chemists may enter into rate contract with the society, the beneficiary paying 20-25 per cent of the cost of medicines in order to discourage misuse of medication and keeping the cost of treatment low.

Facilities for specialist services; indoor treatment and diagnostic investigations may be had at government hospitals at subsidized fees payable directly by the society/cooperative. The rationale is that the hospital would not only get substantial relief in their outpatient department would also increase their revenue through fees received from such societies. In rural areas, Primary Health Centres may be upgraded to provide outpatient medical care on payment of capitation fee by the society/cooperatives.

This has been the process of development of social security in most countries in Europe, where the initiative for social security originally came from the people themselves joining together in mutual benefit societies; friendly societies; sick funds; or occupational guilds, to provide their members against contingencies which caused need for medical care or financial assistance. For provision of outdoor medical care, these institutions, which were self-governing and were run on 'no profit no loss' basis, made contractual arrangements with private doctors. For technical assistance, specialist advice and inpatient treatment, the public hospitals provided to such approved institutions facilities at nominal charge. It was considered as 'Help to Self-help'.

Being in the nature of an insurance scheme administered on 'no profit no loss' basis, the rate of contribution is not likely to be high. A mutual benefit society, with surplus funds, can provide benefits to their members in the event of morbid conditions affecting their normal economic activity. Our course, technical assistance will be needed to put the mechanism in place and to fix appropriate contribution rates.

I would like to make a small observation on the attempt at many fore to expand the definition of social security. While food, housing and employment are, broadly speaking, social security measures and should form an important element in an attempt to provide adequate social protection to the population, they must, for practical reasons, be the responsibility of different agencies. Social Security Agency needs only to administer the traditional social security benefits like old age pension, medical care and cash assistance during disability to engage in economic activity. The provision of food security (involving production, efficient distribution or issue of food stamps in deserving cases) housing, shelter and employment should be the responsibility of different specialized bodies or organizations, government, semi-government or NGOs.

Har Mander Singh

Former DG-ESIC and Former Regional Director, ISSA

While considering the issue of Social Security for the workers in the Unorganized sector, it could be pertinent to refer to the remarks made by the Secretary General of the ISSA, Mr. Dalmer Hoskins, at the General Assembly of the ISSA held in Marrakesh in October, last year

He mentioned that the biggest task of the Social security Administrators at the moment was to redefine the role and functions of Social Security in the next century. He pointed out that there was serious global problem of unemployment and risk of poverty and the hard lesson was that economic growth and increasing globalization did not necessarily reduce poverty or increase Social Security Protection. He stated that our rapidly changing societies together, promoted social peace and ensured a degree of social justice. He added that the debate on social security had one beyond the issues of solvency and fiscal sustainability, to reforming and adopting social security to make it conform to the core values of solidarity and social cohesion.

In the context of these remarks by a leading authority on social security, the continued focus by the Social Security Association of India on the need for social security for the unorganized sector is fully justified.

Social Security Needs of the Unorganized Sector

The Social Security needs of the unorganized sector are extensive and varied, whereas the funds available for the purpose are necessarily limited.

Firstly, these are the uncovered wage earners who work for very small employers. Their needs and characteristics are identical to those of the covered workers in the organized sector. They can, therefore, be covered without much difficulty under the traditional social security schemes.

Secondly, there are self-employed persons following regular trades in the non-agricultural sector. They are largely urbanized and can also be brought under the protective cloak of the traditional social security schemes.

Thirdly, there is the vast rural population. They have continued to maintain their links with the family and other social groups, despite the trend towards the gradual breakup of the social cohesion.

These links enable them to cope up with certain social security contingencies with a minimum degree of external intervention and assistance. The rural communities are rarely required to face the contingency of loss of income on account of work interruption in the normal circumstances for there is usually a close relative to look after the land or the livestock in the absence of the principal.

It is essentially the risks affecting the productive functions that can turn into a predominant source of insecurity for the rural population.

Consequently the social security measures for them should begin with their basic need of protection of their means of livelihood against the ravages of bad weather, floods, drought, crop failures, epidemic diseases and other hazards such as loss of livestock.

Social assistance in such cases may include development of a network of positive earnings related programmes in the fields of agriculture, animal husbandry, dairy development, fishery and poultry farming and assistance in the provision of seeds, pesticides and irrigation facilities.

The other basic social security need in the rural areas is health care. The social security health care programmes should be integrated with other health care and medical delivery programmes including programmes of family welfare.

The health care programmes reduce the costs on maternity care and child-bearing, health problems and those arising from absenteeism of the economically active populations.

Obstacles in the Extension of Social Security to the Excluded Population

The main obstacle in the coverage of wage earners in tiny establishments, is the formidable task of their identification and registration. This is more so in the cases of small artisans, the unorganized work force and other unprotected groups.

The high costs involved in their coverage impel the social security administration to shrink from the challenge.

There is also a lack of any vocal demand from the deprived population. They are so engrossed in problems of their immediate survival that any motivation to strive for a social security coverage for a "distant" contingency gets obliterated.

There are also other special problems in providing coverage to the rural areas. Some of these are:

- Weak economic capacity of the rural communities;
- Lack of adequate infrastructure and deficient communication;
- Low educational levels and widespread illiteracy;
- Lack of understanding and acceptance of the social security concept;
- Varied occupational status of the rural population and seasonal work;
- Difficulty in determining wages and income;
- Scattered population; and
- Lack of essential records.

Strategies for the Extension of Social Security

To start with, it has to be understood that for countries such as ours, the goal is not so much one of income maintenance as of raising the income of the poor above the poverty line.

With this view, moderate measures of social protection for the poor and the deprived can be provided through a combination of measures including the expansion of the current social security schemes, and the government-funded social assistance programmes and the enlargement of the employment-generation and poverty alleviation programmes.

In this process a segmented approach is unavoidable, since a comprehensive approach on a rapid expansion may not yet be feasible.

Outside the area of conventional social security, crop and livestock insurance schemes are a priority area of protection. Ideally, these should cover all crops and livestock universally, on actually worked out insurance premia.

The institutions of mutual benefit funds and fraternal groups, which have proved successful in many industrialized countries as a prelude to the development of the present day social security programmes, can provide an alternative system of social security for the unorganized sector, particularly for the self employed persons, through co-operatives and decentralized administrative blocks in the rural areas.

In the Indian situation, the Panchayats and the Nagarpalikas can be involved to administer social security programme. However, these bodies would need to be strengthened for this purpose. Their involvement would achieve effective targeting and transparent, responsive and accountable delivery of benefits, reduce overheads, mobilize local resources and create a basis for community solidarity.

Solutions can be found to take social security to remote areas, provided it is accepted that a start needs to be made.

For example, a decision was taken in 1967 in Brazil to improve the availability of basic health care in the rural areas, an agreement was made with the trade unions to manage the operations on behalf of the Central Body. Equipment and ambulances were dispatched to run mobile units and out-patient clinics and thus a start was made which was later built upon.

Further more, for the unorganized sector, frustration over excessive bureaucracy can be avoided by providing for flexible rules concerning, for example, evidence of births, marriages, employment injury, invalidity, death etc., while at the same time avoiding laxity in the management of funds.

The needs of people engaged in barley subsistence level activities such as semiskilled craftsmen and vendors in urban areas and marginal farmers, fishermen, forestry workers and craftsmen in rural areas require to be considered, specifically with reference to their meager incomes and the distinct social security measures that may have to be devised for them.

In the event that social insurance is preferred as a form of protection, it would need to be considered whether it should be based entirely on a contributory pattern or should have an element of government subsidy to make it sustainable.

Social assistance schemes have necessarily to be selective in their coverage. Nevertheless the needs of those who are in distress and are in dire poverty cannot be overlooked. Such people include non-earning elderly without family support, the unemployable handicapped persons, the deserted women encumbered by young children and the destitutes.

For such categories, social assistance measures are inevitable to provide shelter, clothing and food.

It is worthwhile to involve social workers in social assistance programmes, to determine eligibility, to deliver benefit and eventually to reduce dependence.

A final word: In any Social Security Scheme for the unorganized sector, the comparatively less indigent will be willing to contribute, if they are assured value for their money, the benefits meet their priority needs and the system that administers the benefits is trustworthy.

D.C. Gupta

Director General-ESIC

Provision of an effective social security net to the unorganized and informal sectors in the developing countries is a challenge facing these countries world wide. It is estimated that nearly 80 per cent of the world's population (workers and their dependents) are excluded from any type of formal social security protection. With the opening of the economies due to the recent upsurge in technological development, there has been a noticeable trend of more and more workers in less secured employment such as, self-employed, casual and home workers. According to one definition (ILO 1994); in principle informal sector workers are employed in a (micro) enterprise that has the following characteristics:

a) The owner is personally responsible for gains and losses (the enterprise is unincorporated).
b) Absence of full and written accounts: the enterprise has fewer than ten continuous employees.

Many of such employees have no written labour contracts and usually live in poverty and large proportion of them are women. The informal sectors also may include some population groups such as widows, orphans and older people who are protected neither by the employment income of their family nor by any other family support. Specifically, therefore, informal sector is understood to include self-employed persons, persons engaged in agriculture and allied activities, skilled workers, artisans, professions, workers of very small factories and establishments, casual workers, home workers, petty traders, hawkers, etc.

In India out of a total population of 934.2 million (1996), 314.10 million are workers. Of these, 28.24 million are in the organized sector and the rest in the unorganized or informal sector. The break-up of the workers in the organized sector for whom formal social security is available is under:

a) Public sector employees (Employees of Central Government/ State Government/ Quasi-Government and Local Bodies—19.56 million
b) Private Sector—8.68 million

Social security priorities of Informal Sector

According to Wouter Van Ginneken, principal social security priorities for the informal sector were as follows:

a) Improving the effectiveness in the health care expenditure
b) Death, survivorship and disability benefits
c) Regularizing expenditure on basic education
d) Maternity and child care benefits.

Access to Social Security

However, the workers in the informal sector are not totally out of security net, as at present, self employed persons and skilled workers while performing duties in the premises of the covered units for the purpose of the trade of the principal/immediate employer are covered by the existing social security laws such as the ESI Scheme, Workmen's Compensation Act, etc. In addition, a number of State Government provide social security through State funded insurance schemes, such as Crop Insurance Scheme, Insurance Scheme against drought, old-age Pension provided by the Government etc. In addition, several employment generation and poverty alleviation programmes are also provided by the Government. Several NGOs also provide self-financing schemes such as the Scheme provided by Self-Employed Women's Association (SEWA), Health Insurance Scheme in India, which concentrates on hospital cost insurance and is part of a comprehensive social security scheme covering contingencies of death, disablement and maternity as well as loss of work-tools, house, property, etc.

The formal social insurance schemes are, however, not suited to the needs of the workers in the informal sector because of several factors, some of which are:

(a) Inability of the workers in informal sector to contribute to the social insurance schemes due to low level and irregular pattern of earnings.
(b) Seasonal and intermittent character of work.
(c) Problem in identifying the potential insured persons and their registration. A large number of small land holders are workers as well.
(d) The dominance of self-employed workers over the wage earners among the farming population.
(e) Inadequacy of proper institutional framework for administrative functions and for disbursing benefits.

Even the risk perception of workers in the informal sector is different from those in the formal sector who have the regular employment and the earnings. The informal sector workers on the other hand are generally engrossed in their problems of minimum survival and live from one day to the next and are faced with catastrophes such as natural calamities, loss of earnings due to disability, ill-health or loss of tools etc., sudden and huge expenditure on hospitalization and social occasions. The social security needs are different, as the types of informal sector workers also vary in accordance with the various risks they are exposed to. Further, while the formal sector workers share contributions with the employers, in case of most of the workers in the informal sector they are self-employed or even if they are employed, the employers may not be in a position to pay contributions at par with those in organized sector. In the formal social security insurance scheme, each new employer and employee has to be identified, registered, educated and persuaded to comply with the rules and procedures of the schemes. However, in case of casual workers and other informal sector workers, it is not possible to collect contribution and maintain up to date and correct records as these persons work intermittently and irregularly for different employers. As the social security benefits are generally a replacement of the previous wage, the worker was getting, in case of informal sector workers it is not always possible to determine his wage loss as there are no records of his earning/wage.

In view of above difficulties, the package of benefits provided to workers in the organized sector are not suited for workers in the informal sector. The main requirements of workers in the informal sector are; medical care and cash benefits in the contingencies of sickness, maternity and disability. So far as medical care is concerned, the Central and State Governments do provide free medical care to all citizens as a matter of right. The existing medical care system comprising of primary health centers and other government dispensaries and hospitals are accessible only to about 50 per cent of the population. Further, the poor and under-privileged workers cannot afford to approach these Government institutions for minor ailments in view of distances involved and therefore, there is a tendency to go on working even if they are ill. Otherwise, they are generally forced to go to private clinics. Therefore, instead of organizing fresh infrastructure for providing medical care for the workers in the informal sector, the already existing medical facilities need to be strengthened particularly for providing minimum out-patient care and free supply of essential medicines for minor ailment closer to the places where the workers live so that they do not have to incur expenses on transportation etc.

So far as cash benefits are concerned, the main requirements of workers in the informal sector are not the replacement of their previous earnings, but a small amount is necessary for sustaining them during periods when they are unable to work or to carry on their trade during sickness, maternity or disablement. However, even in case of workers in the organized sector covered under social insurance schemes, many workers tend to misuse the benefits, though to a large extent the social insurance institutions are able to keep control over the medical certification. In case of the workers in informal sector it may not be possible to keep a check on medical certification and, therefore, cash benefits might be liable to abuse. Any cash benefit scheme will, therefore, have to take into account this aspect.

Extending Social Security to Informal Sector some issues:

i. ESI provides multiple benefits to an Insured Person with single contribution and is entirely contributory. Further the scheme is extended on geographical basis related to the group of industries and establishments in an area, mainly because of the necessity of providing medical infrastructure beforehand. Therefore, it appears for the reasons indicated above, that it may not be possible to extend ESI in its present form to informal sector. New social insurance packages might have to be devised which will have to be mostly State funded to provide social security coverage to informal sector.

ii. With the changing socio-economic environment resulting in increasing polarization of society and increasing exclusion of certain sections of society, it appears essential to have an integrated approach to provision of the social security in informal sector which should not only concentrate on the economic security but socio-cultural initiatives also imperative in view of the emergence of nuclear families and the reduced role of joint family system. An integrated approach becomes particularly essential for certain sections of the people, in informal sector like widows, older people, orphans, etc. It pre-supposes a multi pronged integrated strategy to be launched by the State in collaboration with active social partners and NGOs, fully involving them into their effort.

iii. As far as health insurance is concerned which is one of the primary social security needs as brought out earlier, their existing health care system provided by the Government will have to be strengthened and access to these facilities to the poor people enhanced by undertaking several effective measures. However, some special packages will have to be developed and part of the contribution upto a limit could be provided to be met by the employers, wherever the employee-employers' relationship exists in informal sector by amending existing legislation like Shop and

Establishment Act. If the insurance scheme is opened up, it can be expected that targeted packages to tap the informal sectors in rural areas may be for the coming.

iv. For a very large sector of population in the informal sector, particularly for the agricultural worker, rural artisans and others, the most possible and desirable alternative appears to be an effective social assistance programme in the shape of poverty alleviation and employment generation programmes for the targeted population. Over a period of time a fairly credible system of identifying the below poverty line population in the rural areas has been developed. The problem is that of an effective implementation of these programmes in an efficient and convergent manner to derive optimal benefits to ensure the up-liftment of the economic status of family unit. There has been lot of criticism about misdirection of resources in this regard as a result of poor implementation. The silver lining is emergence of Panchayati Raj Institutions at the grass root level, through regular elections. What is, however, needed is greater participation of people in the administrative designing and implementation of these programmes. Multiplicity of the schemes might have to be reduced to provide a convergent approach, so that the BPL family unit is taken as the base for ensuring that it gets a better economic and social status as a result of these efforts over a period of time. Already efforts are under way to redesign some of the main schemes like IRDP etc. to achieve these objectives.

v. Any insurance scheme is based on risk pooling. There may, however, be some target groups which are working as employees in informal sector in special groups like domestic servants, family workers and casual workers where the existing social security schemes could be extended by suitable amendment in the legislation for extending their coverage. Some revision of the existing schemes would take place to facilitate partial membership by the self-employed, agricultural workers, domestic workers and those with regular income in informal sector. It may be very difficult to enforce compulsory insurance schemes in view of the difficulties in identification of the workers, their registration, collection of contribution, determination of their previous wages, etc. apart from frequent shifts in employment. It may, however, be possible to have such compulsory social insurance scheme in case of informal sector workers confined to a particular area or to particular occupation, such as fisherman.

vi. The studies done by Mr. Ginneken have disclosed that the number of public social security schemes is being carefully replaced by private social security arrangements in many developing countries. The latter are mainly mutual schemes or collective arrangements set up by the people to provide social protection for themselves. The analysis of such schemes has shown that there are two fundamental requirements for setting of such self-financed social insurance schemes:

a) the existence of an association based on trust;
b) an administration that is capable of collecting contribution and paying benefits.

In the organization of such schemes the employers-employees organizations, trade unions, NGOs can play an important role. An interesting example is that as on rural health insurance in China which combines the elements of hospitals and primary health care cost insurance financed by a combination of private and public contributions of hospitals and primary health care cost insurance financed by a combination of private and public contributions. In rural areas, about 10 per cent of population is covered by the so called cooperative medical care system, which is mainly financed by rural residents supplemented by the collective economy and supported by the Government. Similar experiments have been done in Tanzania.

vii. For the life insurance, one of the examples is that of rural group life insurance scheme introduced on 15.08.1995 in India as a part of social security package, in which insurance is available between ages 20-60 years for an assured amount of Rs. 5000/-, only premium being around Rs. 60/-. As stated earlier, the progress in this scheme, has not been very satisfactory all over the country and may require revamping by undertaking effective publicity and persuasion and involving community in particular.

viii. Ginneken has brought out that widening of the social security concept implies the broadening of the social security partnership. While in the formal sector, it is logical to use the national tripartite formula to employers, workers and governments, this partnership has to be broadened to make social security work for informal sector workers. A larger role has to be played by the local government by association that directly represent informal sector workers, such as cooperatives, mutual benefit societies and communities and intermediary organizations that work on behalf of informal sector workers such as workers and employers organizations as well as NGOs. There is a room for greater participation of private insurance companies as and when they can, subject to their being properly regulated and supervised.

7.

Social Security for the Unorganised Sector

Wouter van Ginniken
Director, Social Security Coverage, ILO

April 2000

In 1994, when I had just joined the Social Security department, I was not at all an expert in social security and probably am still not. A request came from Mrs. Shashi Jain who, at that time, was Joint Secretary in the Ministry of Labour to the ILO for a study and report on the extension of Social Security to the Unorganised Sector. When I told my colleagues about it they cautioned me "Wouter, do not get into this, you will fall flat upon your face—this is an intractable problem that we have already been coping with for years and years and years, and we just do not know what to do about it." I did not take their advice. I thought that it was a great opportunity and a challenge. I took up the study and came to India. Shashi Jain was highly supportive of the project and she has also contributed a lot towards the thinking about it, particularly on the area-based approach to health insurance schemes. That is a concept which was developed by her and later on I joined her in the further development of the idea. I also met three persons whom I consider as my Gurus. My three Gurus in India are Mr. Subrahmanya, late Mr. Guhan and Mr. Sankaran. I sat at their feet for about two years and listened to what they had to tell me before I could speak with any kind of knowledge about India. The knowledge that I have acquired is basically the knowledge which has been imparted to me by my friends in India.

There is another reason for my attachment to India and that is that my wife is of Indian origin. She is from a Parsi family. She was born and brought up in London but both her parents come from the area of Bombay and therefore I have an Indian family both in Bombay and Delhi. I have always identified myself with India. It has become something of my own blood. I would like to see something done, about this issue of 'Social Protection of the Informal Sector in India'.

My talk will be divided into three parts. First I would like to say something about the coverage of the existing Social Protection schemes, who is covered and who is not. in the international setting with the relevant figures. Then I shall say something about the specific social protection needs of the workers in the informal sector which are somewhat different from the social protection needs of the workers in the formal sector.

In the second part, I shall say something about the three complementary options to extend social protection to the people in the informal sector constituting about 90 per cent of the population which is, at the moment, not covered. In the context I shall first speak about the possibility of extending EPF and ESI schemes, the principal statutory social insurance schemes. I shall then say something about promoting Micro-Insurance, which is meant primarily for the intermediate group of workers constituting about 60 per cent of the workers who are above the poverty line and have some capacity for making contribution to an Insurance Scheme. It is a new coined for the schemes to cover such persons which means insurance for the people in small communities and sectoral groups. Then I shall speak about the overage of the lowest 30 per cent of the population who are below the poverty line for whom the more appropriate strategy is social assistance. You would be familiar with the National Social Assistance Programme which was developed with the help of late Mr. Guhan in 1995 That will be the third option.

In the end, I shall say a few words about the activities of the ILO and about the experiments for extension of Social Protection to the informal sector proposed by ILO. We are not, as far as I can see, sufficiently advanced in our knowledge to have a full-fledged and integrated policy for the informal sector. We, therefore, propose to introduce a few schemes on an experimental basis. We feel that the lessons that we can draw from these projects would help us, let us say, in a period of two to three years, to develop a more comprehensive policy of Social Protection for the Informal Sector.

Coverage: At present the coverage in India under social security schemes is something like 10 per cent of the population The persons covered are mainly the civil servants and the industrial workers. They represent the organized sector which is shrinking as a proportion of the Indian labour Force. For example, in 1985, the percentage of the people in the organised sector was 13 per cent and in 1995 it was 10 per cent. This trend contradicts the classical development theory that economic growth would lead to growth of the organized sector. In India the economy has been growing at the rate of about 5 per cent per year but there has not been a corresponding growth of the organized sector. Instead, we see that the proportion of the organised sector is decreasing. This is a phenomenon which is not peculiar to India. It is a world wide phenomenon and particularly common to countries in South Asia, Sub-Saharan Africa, and also some of the Latin American countries where most of the employment creation has been taking place in the informal sector. This shrinkage of the organized sector and growth of the informal sector has had an impact on the coverage of social protection. Coverage is also shrinking corresponding to the shrinkage of the organized sector.

Social Protection Needs: Informal sector workers have a different perspective of social protection from that of formal sector workers. They have irregular incomes, they normally have a short-term planning horizon, contrary to the formal sector workers who get their salary every month and, therefore, can also have a long-term planning horizon. For formal sector workers it is also quite clear what a retirement decision is – they know when it is going to happen – it may be 60, it may be 65, they can plan for it, and so for them, the issue of retirement is a normal thing. This is not so for the informal sector because most of these people are self-employed. In rural areas, they may be working on land; in urban areas they may have their shop, and for them retirement is not a predetermined event. They will work as long as possible, and if they have savings, they may prefer to put them into their own business or in constructing a house rather than putting them in pension funds. Besides, since their life expectancy is very low they may not even reach what we call the retirement age. In addition, they may feel that in retirement, they should be supported by their children. So for them, the need for pension and its priority is lower than that of formal sector workers.

What is their priority? We have seen in India and in many other countries that health care is of higher priority for them. As a result of structural adjustment, the Government expenditure on health has gone down. For example, the access to primary health care is no longer free. I have seen in some places like Andhra Pradesh, where there may be some healthcare services, but they are under-staffed, doctors are not there. So when people are ill, they have to pay out of their own pocket. Even the poor, the people who are under the poverty line, may spend up to 5-10 per cent of their budget on meeting the cost of health care. So they would be interested in being covered by some kind of a collective scheme which enables them to face the doctors and to negotiate on the price and quality of the services. If there is a collective arrangement they may also do something to promote health care by means of preventive measures. What is important is that if they contribute regularly to a health insurance scheme, they will be able to avoid peaks in expenditure. Without such a scheme, if one gets ill, his expenditure on health will rise to a peak and he will get into debt. On the other hand, if one is covered under a social security scheme one will be able to cope with the shocks much better. Many informal sector associations such as SEWA in Ahmedabad, and many other women's organisations have, therefore, set up health insurance schemes to protect their members against such contingencies.

The other needs of social security for the informal sector are: survivorship benefit in case of death of the breadwinner and disability insurance which, in my view, are of higher priority to them than old age pension. They also attach a higher priority to the financing of the education of their children.

So the priorities of the people in the unorganised sector could be quite different from those of the workers in the formal sector.

Now, I come to the second part of my talk, which is about the various options that are available to extend social protection to the people in the unorganized sector.

I would first like to talk about the possibility of extending the Statutory Social Insurance schemes to that Sector. In India that means the extension of the EPF and ESI Schemes. What are the obstacles to the extension of these schemes to the informal sector workers?

First of all, the rates of contributions are high. In the handout, I have mentioned that the total amount of contribution would work out about 15-20 per cent. I have looked at it again and I find that the total amount of contribution to social security schemes, by the employers and employees together, comes to 28 ½ per cent. This kind of contribution, no informal worker would be able to pay. It would be unthinkable for him to pay out so much for social security and that is a very important barrier to the extension of the existing schemes to the informal sector.

The second barrier is that, as I have already said, the health care is of much higher priority to them than old age security. They would be interested in joining a scheme of health insurance like the ESI. I have found in my talks with the representatives of the medium and small scale entrepreneurs, that they are in principle very much interested in joining the ESI particularly the health insurance aspect of the ESI Scheme with a view to reducing the cost of healthcare for their employees, but because of various obstacles, the quality of services and other things, they may not join it. There may be many reasons for their not wanting to join the schemes although they find it advantageous to do so. One of our proposals, which I shall explain later, is to see that ESI covers enterprises with less than 10 employees in small areas.

Now the other obstacles to extension are the lack of trust in the management of the social security schemes. This is also a very widespread phenomenon particularly in Latin America. Ceilings on contribution, both at the lower level and higher level the enterprise non-compliance, of course, by the employers, particularly in small enterprises contribute to such lack of trust. The role of labour inspectors is a very tricky thing. There is a feeling that the inspectors harass small enterprises and they are discouraged. There are allegations of malpractices on their part. I donot know how widespread it is. It is for you to judge. For me in the ILO it is totally surprising that such things happen. If they do happen they affect the growth of the statutory schemes.

Yet many of the domestic workers, certain classes of employees in the informal sector or in small scale sector, might want to join statutory social security schemes. EPF, for example, has done a good job in covering about 400,000 beedi workers although their contributions are mainly financed by the beedi workers' welfare fund. and there are various ways in which EPF & ESI can bring a number of workers within their ambit.

Another possibility would be to look at disability or death insurance which, in my view, is of high priority for the informal sector. At the moment, these risks are covered by the LIC. I must admit that if LIC gets privatised, they might be less interested in the informal sector. In that case there is the possibility of the EPF stepping into the gap which the LIC may leave behind.

Now the second option for extending social protection to the informal sector is micro-insurance. It could cover, let us say, 60 per cent of the population which is below the 10 per cent that is covered by statutory social insurance but which is above the 30 per cent that is below the poverty line, and this is of course the majority of the Indian workforce. We now call this micro-insurance which means a financing arrangement which is linked to small scale enterprises. Similarly you could think of small scale insurance schemes which might not be, strictly speaking, based on insurance principles; you could also call it social financing of certain basic social protection needs.

Such schemes exist in SEWA, and certain co-operatives in Andhra Pradesh. If there is an association based on trust, capable of collecting contributions and administering benefits it could also provide social protection benefits and that is indeed what has happened. Such groupings may be of different types: They may be Government organisations, Trade Unions, NGOs, co-operatives or credit associations serving the informal sector; they could be used as carriers of a variety of social protection initiatives.

We have a number of successful examples like SEWA in Ahmedabad, Co-operative Development Federation. and ASSEFA. There is a whole gamut of such groups which are listed in a book by Mr. Gupta published in 1994, called "NGO Experiences in Social Security". One can learn from the experience of such schemes.

Even though these schemes have been successful in many respects, they are also subject to certain limitations; for example, many of these schemes are dependent on the commitment and dedication of certain individuals. In some cases they are also dependent on foreign money; when donor support is withdrawn they stop working. They will be economical when the schemes operate at a low level. When they grow big the rise in the administrative cost would have to be factored in. They have many such problems but the good thing about them is that they are able to meet the needs of the informal sector and have found ways of helping them.

There is a feeling among certain sections of people that the poor people in the informal sector do not want to make any contribution to the schemes But I think that such apprehensions are unfounded. If they see that the schemes cater to their priority needs, they are prepared to contribute to them.

The big problem however is whether such micro-insurance schemes can be replicated on a large scale. Most of such schemes cover a small number of persons, 2 to 10 thousand; in the case of SEWA it may be about 50,000 people. Considering the size of the population of the country they are totally inadequate. If larger number of the population is to be covered the Government at the local State or Central level would have to be involved. One cannot extend social security to a large population without contribution from the Government one way or the other.

The third option to extend social protection to the people below the poverty line is social assistance. We all know about the National Social Assistance programme and the schemes framed thereunder, the old age pension scheme, the family benefit scheme and the maternity benefit scheme. These schemes do reach quite a few people. I think that the NSAP reaches 10 million people but still there is a lot of problem in the delivery of benefits under the programme. There are all sorts of irregularities hanky-panky in the delivery of the benefits. Mr. Sankaran has conducted a detailed study of the delivery of old age pension benefits in Gujarat, Uttar Pradesh and Orissa. His findings confirm the allegations of malpractices. The sarpanch demands payment for determining whether a person satisfies the means test for qualifying for the benefit; once this is done, the postman demands a little cut at the stage of payment. These practices need to be exposed and measures taken to prevent them.

One of the conditions for payment of the old age pension is that the person – the widow or widower – should have no son who can support him. It is not a proper criterion but it does help to limit the size of the target group. The problem is that the rights of old people are not well recognised and, therefore, if they have an independent source of income, they would also have a better place in the family.

An interesting form of social assistance is the welfare fund. You are familiar with the welfare funds for beedi workers and mine workers and now a new fund has been created for building and construction workers. It is a very interesting kind of experience.

One of the important issues relating to social assistance concerns the linkage with other social policies. It is necessary to see to what extent social assistance integrated with other policies such as the social safety net, food security or PDS and also the whole question of the employment guarantee. I think it is necessary to integrate all such programmes and to ensure their cost-effectiveness.

Conclusions

During the past 50 years, the ILO has concentrated its activities in the formal sector. The position has now radically changed. We have now a new D.G. whose name is Mr. Somavia. He is a Chilean and he is the man who initiated the Social Summit in Copenhagen. This high level U.N. Summit meeting took place in 1995, Mr. Somavia was the convener of this Summit meeting. He became our D.G. at the beginning of this year, in March 1999, to be precise. He has reorganised the office of the ILO. It has now four pillars. The first pillar is about human rights and the fundamental principles of workers – concerning freedom of association, equality, abolition of child labour, etc. The second pillar is about employment promotion, employment strategies, small and medium size enterprises, and training policies. The third pillar is about social protection. It includes social security and occupational safety and health. The fourth is about social dialogue with Trade Unions and other labour groups that constitute the informal sector. Now each of these four pillars has its own objectives. The major objective of the pillar relating to social protection is to enhance the effectiveness and coverage of social protection. So it is very explicit in the mandate of the ILO that we take all workers on board. So we should make sure that all workers are covered in all our activities. We have, therefore, developed a number of technical co-operation projects and research projects. One such project relates to the extension of social protection to the informal sector. It is in the form of a pilot project It consists of four experiments. The first experiment – that is an idea of Shashi Jain – is to set up an area based social protection scheme at the district level or below with the help of the social partners and other local groups like co-operatives. Government would also be party to the experiment. It will cater to the priority needs of social protection needs of the informal sector of which probably health insurance is of primary importance. It may also deal with certain needs social protection needs. The experiment will aim at forming some sort of Social Security partnership within that area including the local Government, and to build some sort of a contributive structure so as to meet all the social protection needs of the entire population of the area. I have proposed to carry out the experiment in some districts of Gujarat and Andhra Pradesh, I have also made proposals, feasibility studies also in Nizamabad district in Andhra Pradesh. The experiments will rune for about two or three years. John and I are now trying raise funds for the experiment and to identify the districts where the experiments may be carried out. I believe that if such an area-based scheme were to work well and it is properly documented, it would have a terrific impact and the experiment may be extended to other districts in India and it will catch up fast benefiting large number of people who are at the moment not covered by any scheme. If there are about two or three well targeted successful pilot projects well documented, we may have a national conference at which the salient features of the experiments would be explained and it could lead to a tremendous expansion of social protection in India.

The second experiment would be to monitor in a particular area, the same or a different area, the implementation of the National Social Assistance Scheme and the other social safety net measures, namely Food Security through the Public Distribution System, and job security through the Employment Guarantee Scheme, to see the cost-effectiveness of these various measures to reach the poor and to see what improvements are necessary to deliver these benefits to widows and to old age pensioners, in different areas.

The third experiment I propose is to see within the context of the Building and other Construction Workers' Welfare Fund, what types of benefits would be most appropriate for the workers and the best way to utilize the Fund. For example it could be examined whether crèches could be run for the benefit of women workers by using the resources of the Welfare Fund. The effectiveness of the tripartite mechanism for administering such schemes could also be studied. I propose to carry out the experiment in a State say Tamil Nadu where there is a lot of interest in such matters among the people at the local level generally and the trade unions in particular. After the experiment is concluded an analysis may be made of the results and appropriate conclusions draw about he best way to use the welfare funds so as to fit in with the priorities of the social protection of the workers.

The last experiment I would propose, is that within the context of the ESI Scheme to select one or two regions where the ESI is already in force and to see whether it can be extended to establishments employing less than 10 workers, what are the problems and how they can be resolved. In thus extending the ESI Scheme one should, I think, exclude the sickness benefits because it is not an appropriate kind of benefit for the informal sector and the small scale enterprises and it is also liable to misuse. One should focus it on the health insurance part of the scheme and to see what would be the problem from the ESI side, and from the point of view of the health providers, the employers and workers and to see how these could work together. So that would be a fourth kind of experiment. So this is basically what I would like to say, and so I have talked about the three main things.

I have first given you an introduction about what the coverage problem is, it is a huge problem. 90 per cent of the population is not covered. This is not only an Indian problem but is widespread in most developing countries.

We have talked about the social protection needs. We have said that old age pension is definitely a priority need for the workers in the organized sector but for the informal sector it is not of such priority. For them, health and may be education and certainly death benefits are greater priority.

Then I have reviewed three kinds of options for extending social protection. Firstly extension of statutory social insurance, although I think that the impact of such extension will be limited, may be another 5 per cent, on top of the 10 per cent already covered. Secondly, introduction of new schemes on experimental basis to cover the big group in the middle where there is some contributory capacity which have greater chances for replicability on area basis The third option is for the people below the poverty line with social assistance as a major element in conjunction with food security and the employment guarantee scheme.

I would like to carry out certain experiments with these proposals to find out how they will work on the ground because in the final analysis, the schemes should work and not stay on paper and should benefit the people. So I need your help and cooperation in undertaking the experiments.

8.

STEP Programme

Ms. Tsushima
ILO

APRIL 2000

It was an enriching experience for me to listen to the responses of the participating organizations from different backgrounds to the problems of the poor and unorganized women workers. I have been thinking hard on how international organizations can support their efforts. One thing that struck me forcefully during the workshop was the need for a strong partnership among the actors involved. By this I mean that we must look for a way to build a concrete delivery mechanism of social protection on the basis of shared responsibility between people's organizations, national Governments and international organizations. I believe that ILO–STEP can do much in this area and I look forward to some guidance from the SSAI to that end.

On this note I would like to say a few words about STEP by using the OHP.

STEP stands for Strategies and Tools against Exclusion and Poverty. It is part of the Social Security Department of the ILO. It takes an integrated view of social protection. One element of the strategy is to extend the coverage of the statutory schemes. This part of the activity is undertaken by the Social Security Department through research and a programme called 'In Focus'. Another element is to promote participatory micro insurance schemes and this is the main focus of STEP. The Social Security Department and STEP work together with strong linkages between the programmes of the two organizations.

STEP is a global programme. The definition of the informal sector used by STEP is different from that used by others. STEP includes all the excluded and vulnerable sections of the people in the non formal sector. Ethnic minorities, children, refugees, and displaced persons are our target groups. We have a strong focus on women and empowerment of women. We are asked to work in countries in post crisis situations.

We have identified the needs of the excluded populations we are working with. Access to basic health care is one of them. Our focus on women brings us to focus on reproductive health care, income security and food security. We hope to extend these services by using participatory approach of micro insurance.

Micro insurance is a new concept. It is decentralised and it requires the active participation of civil society. It is highly innovative, complex and at the moment poorly documented. Few tools are available for its implementation. Given these factors, especially the last two points we need first to develop our knowledge of the micro insurance schemes The way they function are as follows:

We first identify the innovative schemes and experiences at the community level We then select a few schemes for case study. After carrying out five or six case studies we synthesise them highlighting the similarities and differences and see whether and if so how they may be replicated.

At the same time we hold workshops with a view to developing our knowledge and to discuss the ways of extending social protection and other services. Based on the recommendations of the workshops we carry out pilot projects.

One of our aims is to study how international organisations and development agencies conduct their development work and if we feel that they should change we suggest the changes. We put all our strength to get the changes carried out by advocacy.

We operate through our partners and we try to expand our network of partnership so that we have a bigger boat to sail the uncharted oceans.

STEP started its activities in 1998 first in Africa and then we extended our operations to Latin America. Asia is our priority for this year and we are working in Bangladesh and other counties in South Asia. In future we hope to step up our activities in Asia in collaboration with SSAI and other similar organisations.

9.

State Support for Children in Poor Households as a Measure of Development

The Experience of South Africa

Ms. Francie Lund

Professor, University of Natal, South Africa

APRIL 2000

I am grateful to you for the invitation to address the Social Security Association on the occasion of its 8th Annual Conference. Coming to India has been my dream for over thirty years. I feel very happy to be here on this occasion.

I am going to talk to day about the Commission of Enquiry that was appointed by the Government of South Africa within a few months of the new democratic Government came to power which I was asked to chair. I have drawn the material for my address from a document which I am preparing with the grant from John and Catherine Mac Arthur research network on poverty and inequality. The paper contains lot of technical details about means testing, targeting, etc. which may be of interest to the audience.

I shall concentrate on why we chose cash transfer in preference to programmes which are seen as more developmental such as nutrition for children, mainstream welfare services, employment programmes for unemployed women etc. The decision in favour of cash transfer reflects the tensions and the crises in social security administration to day. The international financial institutions with the exception of the ILO have started saying that "State support should be replaced by public-private partnership; public transfers crowd out private savings, cash transfers create dependency among the poor; the poor should learn to be more thrifty and learn to save etc."

The Commission was set up at a very interesting time historically because our new Government, of the African National Congress, came to power carrying the hopes and aspirations which were expressed in the freedom charter of the 1950s to deliver everything for free health care, free education, land reforms, and everything. But suddenly the government was faced with fiscal constraints on the one hand and the influence of the World Bank on the other.

Poverty and Inequality

South Africa has one of the highest rates of measured inequality in the world. The significant variable is racial. Poverty is concentrated in the African population, followed by the coloured people and Indians. Wealth is concentrated in the minority white population.

There is also significant regional variation in poverty patterns.

Women are specially disadvantaged. Households headed by young women in rural areas are amongst the poorest of all households.

The rate of unemployment is exceptionally high being around 30 per cent.

A high proportion of children live in poor households.

Family life was severely affected by the policies adopted by the previous governments which pulled the families apart. Poor families remained in reserved areas while black men went to towns under the migrant labour system to work. Generations were brought up without father figures, without access to education, creating a social problem of no mean proportion.

There is little reliable information about the problem of child labour. But we do know that it is not a severe problem in South Africa as in other Asian countries. It has mainly affected coloured and African children whose parents work on white owned farms where it is hidden and invisible. Our new legislation takes a firm stand towards total prohibition of child labour. We have exceptionally high primary school enrolment rates both for boy and girl children, probably of the order of 90 per cent. We have introduced a policy of free compulsory nine years of education, free primary health care.

On the other hand the child mortality rate is very high. It is largely due to the epidemic HIV/AIDS which has been spreading.

Social Security in South Africa

The former government had introduced a variety of social security measures to shore up and protect people in poverty with a combination of private and public measures. Those in formal employment contribute to insurance based funds to cover retirement sickness, invalidity, unemployment and maternity.

We have an uneven programme of land reforms and we are looking obviously with anxious eyes at Zimbabwe at the moment.

There are some housing subsidies for poor households.

A state social assistance scheme was administered through the National Department of Welfare and delivered through provincial departments. In 1997/98 pensions and grants were awarded to some 2.54 million beneficiaries and social security spending comprised 2 per cent of GDP. In 1995, when the Commission was appointed, about 85 per cent of welfare expenditure was allocated to social security of which two thirds went to old age pension, (1.74 million beneficiaries) about one quarter to disability grants, (754,800 beneficiaries). The allocation to child and family care constituted a small portion of the budget being less than 12 per cent. The State Maintenance Grant comprised the largest portion of the social security spending on child and family care. The State Social Assistance Scheme is non-contributory.

Old age pension goes to women at age of 60 and men at age of 65. It is payable from general revenues and is means tested. Because of poverty particularly among the African population, about 80 per cent of black elderly people get State old age pension. Of the total population, of about 40 million South Africans which is considerably less than the elderly population in India, State assistance in the form of pensions and grants goes to about 2.7 million people. Altogether, the State cash transfer goes probably to 10-12 million people and it gets pooled as household income.

The State Maintenance Grant was established to support poor women and children. It was a means tested grant payable to a south African woman if she was divorced, deserted by the husband or by the father of her children, or if she was not married or if her husband or the father of her children was in a specified institution such as a jail or psychiatric institution for six months or more. To apply for the SMG the woman had to show that she had been deserted or left alone for six months, and that an attempt had been made to obtain maintenance through the judicial system. The amount payable was Rand 430 per month (US$ 1=Rand 6 officially but Rand 6.8 in the market) per woman and Rand. 135 per child per month. (Multiply the figures by 6 to 7 and you will get the comparable figures in terms of rupees). By the early 1990s the SMG was being awarded to about 200,000 women and about an equal number of children. Exact number was impossible to determine as the information system was defective. The grants were largely paid to coloured and Indian people. Large number of African women and children were excluded from access to these grants. To award the grant to all women and children who qualified at existing levels of the grant would have cost about R.12 billion per annum. The Lund Committee was set up to address this problem.

The urban industrial wage is about 1200 rands a month. Compare it with the rates of allowance paid to women and children and you will get an idea of the replacement rate.

The social assistance scheme was started for whites only and was gradually expanded to cover all citizens though the levels were racially discriminatory. In the 1980s a commitment was appointed to remove the discrimination in the levels of benefits awarded, by enhancing the amounts payable to the African coloured and the Indian people. Racial parity in the awards to the elderly and the disabled people was achieved by 1993. In the field of child and family care the parity was achieved by 1997/98.

Inequity remained in the State maintenance Grant, not in the level of benefit but in its racial and spatial distribution.

The Tasks before the Committee

Whatever be the merits of these grants, it was extremely skewed racially. White people had been means tested out of the grant largely. Indians and coloured were receiving disproportionately major portion of the grants and the African people were receiving almost nothing at all. Of every 1000 children, aged 0-17, Indians were receiving by far the most and African children were at the bottom, receiving almost nothing at all although majority of the people were African and they were the poorest.

When the Committee was appointed, the amount of State Maintenance Grant was about Rand 1.3 billion; old age pensions amounted to about R.8 billion. To equalize the grants upwards would have cost R.12 billion, more than the health budget alone. It does not matter where you stand ideologically in terms of cash transfer, here is a point at which you will have to say that it is not affordable, not even in the New South Africa. The Commission was appointed to address this problem.

The Committee had to undertake an appraisal of the existing system of State support in all departments to children and families. We had to investigate the possibility of increasing parental financial support through the private maintenance system. In other words, we had to investigate whether more fathers could be got at, identified through the court system and financial support extracted through the court system. We had to explore alternative policy options in relation to social security for children and families as well as other anti-poverty economic empowerment and capacity building strategies and to develop approaches for effective targeting of programmes for children and families.

Four key concerns guided the Commission:

1. There was a broad agreement that, in a society of such high inequality, the State had an important and active redistributive role to play There was awareness of the negative effects of structural adjustment policies.
2. All committee members shared a deep concern about disruption of family life in south Africa.
3. The committee members agreed that social security was only one of a number of paths in development, that development should be inter-sectoral and that there are limits to what welfare can do.
4. The committee were conscious of the fiscal constraints. The Committee decided to carry out some reforms realistically with due regard to the need to be economical instead of attempting a radical transformation of the social programme which might cost billions and not get through the budget council. We have been criticized by the human rights lobby for this.

We went to the Minister of Finance for tips and he advised reform within the existing budgetary limitations. He said that the cost of the reform should not exceed the current budget of R.1.3 billions and that the government might be able to allocate an additional plus 10 or 15 per cent of that amount if the recommendations were truly innovative. He also suggested to use the population figures cautiously and not to inflate the demographic figures, not to say that disabled people were 20 per cent while the actual numbers were just 5 per cent.

We, however, had the support of the then Minister of Welfare and D.G. Welfare, Ms. Leila Patel. Both, especially the latter, had a very long history of progressive social welfare advocacy and they understood theoretically the importance of social security and that it was not anti-developmental.

Reform of Private Maintenance System

The Committee considered the various alternatives and decided in favour of cash transfers. The committee first took up the reform of private maintenance system.

The private parental maintenance system operates through the law courts. The system had been established to enable mothers to seek financial support for themselves and for their children from men with whom they were no longer in a relationship. The system made the women who were seeking support very vulnerable. A mother has had to seek out the father, establish his employment status and financial situation and essentially do the detective work needed to make a claim against him. The system has worked so poorly that many women, often with the collaboration of social workers, seek support from the state directly, rather than as a last resort.

In the chaos and turbulence of the New-south Africa, the new Minister of Justice had made a promise to reform the private judicial maintenance system in one of his statements as the new Minister and then he got so completely overburdened with work that he could not initiate any action on his promise.

The Committee got the major stake holders together and put forward a reform proposal based on parental responsibility. We recommended a garnishy order whereby if a woman herself cannot get the husband or the father of the children to voluntarily contribute, it can be recovered from his pay packet. That was a social security mechanism that was in vogue prior to 1962, but it had been phased out since then. It has now been reintroduced. It has not yet been taken to the constitutional court as an invasion of privacy which it might well do, if we watch with interest.

Programme for Unemployed Women

The new Government in South Africa was strongly influenced by India and its public works programmes and the major programmes of social intervention in Kerala and other States. It was, therefore, imbued with ideas of big social programmes.

The committee's work on reform ran parallel to a paradigm shift towards developmental welfare that was being promoted by the Department of Welfare. It signified an important change away from curative, bandaid welfare, towards an emphasis on human capital development, signifying an acknowledgement that economic growth and development are important and that economic and social development have to go hand in hand.

The Welfare Department of the Government had started a small programme for unemployed women with children of the age group 0-5. It aimed at providing women with young children with training and employment opportunity. It targeted women who were receiving the SMG and those who had no access to SMG. The committee decided to put more money into it with a view to supporting women with unemployed children. In doing so we had to combine idealism with pragmatism.

Support for Mainstream Welfare Services

The mainstream social services in South Africa are seriously under funded with a bias in favour of white elderly people being cared for in expensive institutions. There is complete lack of institutional care for severely disabled black children and community based psychiatric services for elderly people. Many countries provide welfare services in support of children and in many it costs more to provide that support outside the family.

The level of the Child Grant component of the SMG at the time when the Committee was appointed was R.135 per month. If the parents are unable to continue caring for the child and the latter is placed in foster care, the Foster Care Grant is more than twice as much, R. 288 per month. A child for whom no home environment can be found and /or who offends the law can be found to be in need of care and is placed in subsidised residential care – at a cost to the State of R.850 a month. Homes for the orphans, for the homeless, and for juvenile offenders are meant to be kept apart but there are too few facilities and young offenders are frequently placed in a temporary children's section of a jail for adults. This is the most inappropriate place for a young person to be; child sexual abuse is prevalent. The cost of keeping children in this wrong place is R. 2040 a month.

The problem is accentuated in the case of those who could care for the children were themselves affected by HIV/AIDS or the children themselves were infected and dying.

The committee did not, however, consider the question of providing for better residential facilities for children in trouble because it felt that it would be a wrong policy though the need for such facilities was acute.

An alternative to cash transfers was to support the NGOs for the development of community based models for the care of children but they were not in a position to take charge of a large new budget.

The Government subsidises NGOs to provide support for children. The South African funded NGOs, as distinguished from internationally funded NGOs are under-funded. Had the Commission been meeting now rather in 1996 it might have decided on major financial programmatic support for new models of child care. We are seeing childheaded households; day care centres which are turning into hostels for children because children have no home to go to. We still do have a thriving family system but especially in urban areas the situation is worrying. It is going to take some money to deal with child care problem. It cannot all be left entirely to the voluntary spirit. Any new organisation created for the purpose would not have gone to scale and absorbed the money that was being offered by international organisations like the UNICEF. It was not a problem of money but one of organisation.

Support for Nutrition Programme

There is a clear association in South Africa between poverty levels and malnutrition. The committee was well disposed to supporting nutrition programmes.

We have some community based initiatives which are trying to combine comprehensive maternal, child care and nutrition programmes with income generation programmes. The problem is that the small programmes tend to have a charismatic leadership, a very special relationship with the community that they are serving. They might have a religious basis also. The moment they try to go to scale they lose something. There appears to be an eternal contradiction between achieving real excellence and vibrance on the ground and going to scale.

The nutrition programme that the new Government started was based on one of Nelson Mandela's inaugural statements to start a nutrition programme for primary school children. That programme was faltering. It had been introduced too early. It had a lot of political appeal but did not make much sense in terms of children's nutritional needs starting at the age of 7 when children mostly go to school. The money (R. 450 million) allocated to the Primary School. Nutrition Programme in the previous year had remained unspent. Much of what was spent went to the wrong people. Advice from those involved in nutrition policy was that it was not more money that was needed but more clarity and consistent national guidelines about policy and the development of local level capacity in community organizations to cooperate with the programme.

However, it is now beginning to show results. If any alternative nutrition programmes had been developed we would have said divert the funds there. But there again the problem was that the programmes were not able to absorb the money they were being given. So the final alternative considered was support for early childhood development programmes.

Early Childhood Development Programme

When the Government came to power early childhood development and adult basic education were very high on the Government's list of priorities. Early Childhood development in South Africa has been defined to include children from birth through their ninth year. It acknowledges that children's developmental processes—physical, cognitive, mental, emotional and social—are continuous regardless of when they are deemed ready for school. ECD incorporates a range of services from creches with little emphasis on learning and development, for safe care for children of working mothers, to highly sophisticated centres with tightly designed curricula. In the face of increasing evidence about the importance of the earliest years of the development of the brains of young children, early childhood intervention programmes had received policy attention in the 1990s.

At the time of political transition, about 90 per cent of South Africa's children had no access to ECD services. Past Government support showed the typical racial bias. The ECD lobby had got it high on the agenda of the new government. But faced with an overall crisis in the field of education, the Government downgraded the importance of this programme.

Once people saw what it was going to take to deracialise the education budget the early childhood and adult basic education lost its importance and all effort went into supporting primary education. All universities suffered cutbacks in favour of a nine years of compulsory and free education. One could not argue with that policy. But when children of six or seven years have not had complete vaccination, they are undernourished, the mothers are having their third child which they do not wish to they have not been offered choice over their reproductive behaviour. There are so many things which warrant higher priority than primary education. On the other hand the programme has helped to build primary schools with nutrition programme.

Decision on Cash Transfer

SMG had been designed to respond to a model of the family which had disappeared. It was built on the Beveridge like assumption of a nuclear family with father in employment, with his employment as the primary source of household income, in a labour market with full or nearly full employment where the mother is likely to have the primary role of home maker and child rearer. The SMG was designed to respond to the unlikely event of widowhood, divorce or abandonment. Change in family norms and in household structure, in unemployment patterns and in women's labour market participation, have fundamentally shifted the ground on which these assumptions were made. There has been a steep increase in single parenting; household boundaries are fluid and porous; many men are in long term unemployment, many women move in and out of the formal and informal parts of the economy and are more likely to be the breadwinners; and households have multiple and often erratic small sources of income.

All of these socio-economic characteristics led the committee to question whether the idea of a family based benefit had become an anachronism.

However, given the serious need to provide some support to children in poor households there was a need to concentrate on children The Committee reached the formulation: "Follow the child" with a form of cash transfer The corollary to this formulation was to recommend that the grant be payable via the primary care giver rather than looking for its parents. Since the cash grant could not go directly into the hands of the child we had to identify the person in the child's immediate environment who was most likely to have the interests of the child a heart and to pay the grant to that person.

In these circumstances, the Committee decided in favour of cash transfers in the form of Child Support Grants to the primary care giver. The Government has accepted the recommendation. The Grant has been introduced as a flat rate benefit, means tested to reach 50 per cent of children upto the age of seven years. It was introduced at R.100 per month and has not been raised since introduction Take up rates have been slow though they are now rising rapidly.

We are still disposed towards that policy and we are fighting a courageous battle with the World Bank to keep the State Social Assistance in place. We are fighting this battle for over four years.

I donot wish to demonise the World Bank. It is not a hegemonic institution. There are different parts of the Bank some of which are more intelligent and sympathetic than others. The part which was advising us on social security was not the most progressive part of the World Bank.

We had really good empirical data to prove what a concrete and positive contribution cash transfers would make to the situation of the elderly people but also to development programmes generally in south Africa. The World Bank itself had funded a survey of income and expenditure and living standards.

The redistributive mechanism involved is that an individual, an elderly person, will apply for old age pension, receive it as an individual. But it gets pooled as household income because poor people live in three generational families. An elderly person gets R.520 in a month equal to about US$80 He brings it home, keeps a part for himself for payment to the burial society, for purchase of meat for the monthly family treat which he gives. The balance is paid into the family income and used for payment for children's education, health care etc. The old age pension is well targeted for poorer households so as to keep the second, third and fourth bottom of levels society above poverty. The rights are demographically driven.

We donot have a very high life expectancy. We donot know demographically what the HIV/AIDS epidemic is going to do to life expectancy figures. But social assistance spending is not out of control any more. We have firm empirical evidence to suggest that cash benefits to households were a good way to cutting out middle people, avoiding corruption in the system and going straight to the pockets of the poor people.

The decision of cash transfers did not mean that we were not in favour of other programmes. We were saying that it is a modest thing that government could do to support children in poor households.

It is going to take sometime to get over the effect of over 100 years of our labour policy which kept men and women separate. We could not, therefore, design a family transfer. We have designed a system under which the cash transfer goes to the households of poorer children not necessarily via the biological parents but via the primary care giver. Preferably via the biological parents but if not through the next of kin starting from primary relatives through secondary relatives. This was an unusual decision.

The committee wanted the grant to be universal for all children i.e., of the age group 0-12. The budget council did not agree. We came down to 0-9. The South African cabinet approved 0-6. The NGO community have got it raised to 0-7.

The grant stands at present at R100 per month. At maturity it is given to 50 per cent of children aged 0-7 in their households via the primary care giver.

We have tried to introduce conditionalities which would ensure that you can only get the grant if you have complete immunisation and that you have to be a registered citizen.

To get the grant you have to go through the whole process of identification which is very important in South Africa for collecting proper information. In the past, the oppressed people were so frightened of the then government that one could make up any name, any number, any identification. Altogether we had a very corrupt civil identification system because people wanted to cheat us for dishonest purposes but for survival purposes. So we have introduced a child support grant.

The take up rate is yet low. It is taking time for people to get identity documents with a new national system of citizens' ID. We had modelled a very cautious take up and introduction rate for the grant, partly because the welfare administrators are weakest in the very parts of the country where we want the grants to go, the rural areas where poverty rates are the highest.

The second election presented itself and the then Minister imposed an unreasonably high take up rate so that she could say, by the next elections, half a million children were helped. She fought so hard to get the thing through and then nearly brought the whole thing to standstill because of the political imperative.

There is a general lack of capacity in overall social security administration. I have no doubt at all that some of the social security personnel are wilfully trying not to introduce the child support grant. There are people in the social security offices who feel that it is morally a bad thing to give money in the form of cash transfers, to children whereas there is a broad national acceptance of the old age pension, a less broad acceptance of the disability grant. There is no doubt that there are people in both the welfare administration and social security who would rather that this grant went away. It is too early to say how robust it is going to be.

It was a great privilege to be involved in this pioneering attempt to do some social policy reform in south Africa. It was also a great experience.

I would not want to withdraw State Maintenance Grant in favour of Child Support Grant. State Maintenance Grant was going to only 300000 women compared to three million children that the new grant is aimed at. It is an enormous redistributive factor that we are introducing. We tried to get the Government to let those receiving the State Maintenance Grant roll off the system over time. However, the senior politicians felt that it was unconstitutional and they insisted on a very rapid phasing out of the grant. It has been reduced by one third each of the last three years. April 2000 is the last month the State Maintenance Grant will be awarded in South Africa. None of the beneficiaries will receive it any more. A small proportion of them will be eligible for the new Child Support Grant because they are poor but not poor enough.

The Department of Welfare takes credit for the change in policy. It has put aside a substantial amount of money to phase out the State Maintenance Grant and to introduce the Child support Grant. It is a very interesting crucible a very interesting laboratory to find out the best way of providing support to people who are poor and at the same time to ensure the basic means of livelihood.

The old age pension and the disability grant are very well targeted in rural areas. The delivery of these cash transfers has been outsourced to private delivery firms who have developed a very sophisticated mobile technology.

Historically the rural areas were under resourced except for some pockets near the cities where black people were meant to govern themselves. Three things did not go to rural areas: the pension system, the primary school system, and the system of clinics. The child support system had also the same problem. The last month's figures show that the urban centres have taken up the scheme well but it is lagging behind in rural areas. But we are not worried because we have estimated that it will take seven years to mature. By that time the urban people who are not eligible for the benefit may be phased out as the social security systems get more robust and administration get strengthened.

Some doubts about the cash transfer system. How effective it is in achieving the goal for which it is set up? The scheme is for under nourished children from poor families who are not looked after well. You transfer cash to them What is the guarantee that the money will be spent on the essential items and on drugs and non essential items?

There is no guarantee, you can state the purpose of a benefit, you can wrap it up and package it as best as you can but there is no guarantee. We know that the bulk of the old age pensions is spent on household gods and very little of it on alcohol. We know that more of our State Maintenance grant was being spent on alcohol. We do not know about drugs. It is the governments that decide whether they are going to award money or not. You can make it conditional or get into food vouchers. We considered your fair price shops and food voucher schemes. We have no history of such schemes It has taken years for you to build up the kind of institutional and social wiring in which they are working. Yet it cannot be said that the system is entirely effective. It is partly effective and partly not. Universally there is lot of waste of money and corruption in developmental schemes. It is a national as well as an international problem causing worry.

Some one in the audience asked a Question: It is intriguing to hear from Ms. Lund that payment in cash has less chances of corruption than payment in kind and therefore the Committee chose that option. How was that worked out?

Ans: It is an interesting experiment that we are trying. There is corruption in the payment of pensions. The new government is trying to eliminate corruption. We have assessed that there is leakage of old age pensions to the extent of 8 per cent. The World Bank says that is one of the best records internationally according to their findings bulk of the money does go to the people for whom it is meant. Out of the 2.5 million people getting the old age pension 100000 or 200000 may not be eligible for it and should not be getting it. But on the whole pension is going out to the pockets of the elderly people may be with small cuts of 20 or 30 rands by way of tips. We should prevent those cuts also.

10.

Coverage of Contingencies Under Formal Social Security Schemes and the Needs of Women Workers in the Informal Sector

John Woodall

Sr. Security Specialist ILO, New Delhi

April 2000

The work of those who participate in the "informal economy" gives rise to a set of issues which are highly topical in both India and the neighbouring countries of South Asia, in part at least because of the importance of this economic sector in providing jobs for the growing number of workers. It is not easy to set down a precise definition of the "informal economy", which embraces a highly diverse range of activities in the manufacturing and service sectors. However, the sector can be conceptualized in some detail on the basis of a number of particular features, mostly "negative" in character, including the lack of regular contact with officialdom and the lack of fixed or well-equipped work-sites; there is a large degree of overlap with the statistical concept of the "unorganized" sector, in India and elsewhere. On a positive note, the informal economy is seen, increasingly, as a reservoir of diverse skills and entrepreneurship, which has a significant role to play alongside the more formal or organized economic agents.

Two features of the informal economy, which are immediately apparent, are:

- The importance of this sector to women's employment, reflecting to some extent their relative disadvantage, compared with men, in formal sector employment; and
- The nearly-complete absence of institutions (either public or private) of social protection.

The present workshop brings together these themes, which are of major importance for ILO, especially in the long-term pursuit of Decent Work for all who seek it.

The objective of Decent Work cannot be achieved in the absence of appropriate working conditions to which there are many aspects. High amongst these is the type of protection, providing against income loss and for health care, which is the "traditional" domain of social security schemes.

Formal social security schemes do not represent the only means of affording such protection to workers and their families. In particular, individuals have relied on family and kinship networks for centuries past, and still do so today. However, social security schemes do-at least in principle-offer the most reliable structure within which provision can be organized in an efficient and sustainable manner. The issue, then, is to organize the social security system in an optimal manner, that is, in the way which, within the prevailing financial constraints, offers the benefits which most nearly meet the needs of the potential beneficiaries.

The provision regarding financial constraints is (obviously) of critical importance. In virtually all countries of the world today, but particularly in the less developed nations, the scarcity of resources which can be allocated to social protection (or to social objectives generally) is such that very difficult choices have to be made regarding benefits and coverage. This, in turn, means that it is crucial that the relevant decisions are made on the basis of a rational and appropriate set of priorities. These priorities must reflect the particular needs of each individual country and its people, and those will themselves reflect the prevailing economic conditions at any particular time.

This paper is intended to provide a fairly basic conceptual outline within which the necessary process of establishing the priorities amongst the parameters for a national social security system may begin, taking as a starting point the "traditional" model for a formal social security scheme of the kind most often operated on the basis of social insurance. The extent to which the various features of such a scheme may or may not meet the real needs of contemporary workers (both men and women) should provide a guide to the design of an appropriate scheme for the present and future. In this commentary, the focus is on technical aspects, but it should be borne in mind that the effectiveness of a system of social protection depends on a broad range of factors, not least those which may be classified as governance, and these aspects are themselves worthy of extensive discussion at another time.

The material set out in the paper reflects the work of the author with ILO, but should not be taken as an expression of the official policy of the

Organization; responsibility for the opinions expressed rests with the author alone.

Questioning the Axioms

A Social Security scheme is intended to provide for the long-term, and may be amongst the most abiding institutions within a government's portfolio. Stability is an important feature of such institutions, and those responsible for their management and administration are almost always-for good reasons-wary of change. Nevertheless, it is equally important that these institutions meet the real needs of their "stakeholders" not only government but also the workers who stand to benefit from schemes and who, together with (in most cases) the employers, pay the contributions from which the benefits are, ultimately, financed. It is, therefore, necessary for the supervisors of any scheme to make a regular assessment of the effectiveness with which it is meeting its objectives.

In the broadest terms, the need is to answer a set of questions, the most important of which may be posed as follows:

Are the right contingencies covered?
Are the contingencies covered in an appropriate way?
Are the right people covered?
Are the benefits administered properly?
Are the finances administered efficiently?
Is there proper accountability?

The first group of questions relates to the design of the social security scheme in question, which will in most cases be specified in the relevant legal code or statute. The second group is concerned with the practical implementation of a scheme. While both are naturally important, this paper focuses on the first groups of issues.

The Choice of Contingencies

The model for a "comprehensive" social security scheme as conceived in what might be called the "traditional" manner is expressed in a series of International Labour Conventions, notably the Social Security (Minimum Standards) Convention No. 102 of 1952. A list of nine specific contingencies is set out, as follows:

- Sickness
- Maternity
- Employment injury
- Unemployment
- Invalidity
- Old age

- Death
- The provision of medical care
- The provision of subsidies for families with children

In present-day conditions, awareness has grown of the needs of informal sector workers, who are rarely included as members of formal social security schemes organized at the national level. The needs of those who may be employed on a very irregular or casual basis, and the manner in which they may be related to individual worker's wage or salary, clearly differ from those of workers who attend their workplace for regular hours throughout the year and earn wages or salaries uniformly month by month. Moreover, the scope of protection which is appropriate is often expressed in terms of the basic necessities of life (such as shelter and nutrition), rather than protection against loss of income when earning capacity is interrupted. For this reason, there has been considerable discussion as to whether an alternative definition of "social security" can be devised which will more accurately reflect up-to-date needs. One such definition which has been proposed is as follows:

(a) the provision of benefits to households and individuals;
(b) through public or collective arrangements;
(c) arising from a number of basic risks and needs.

A broader definition of this kind would allow for the inclusion in "Social protection" of coverage outside the confines of the "traditional" contingencies, including:

- education
- shelter
- food security
- crop insurance

Some commentators have classified the functional objectives of social security schemes into two distinct groups, described as protective and promotional. The inclusion of the latter implies that the scope of operation of a scheme would be very wide indeed, and might include, for example, the provision of means to upgrade the accommodation of workers or the nutritional status of their families.

Although each of these reforms of coverage reflects the expressed needs of workers (and others) who may be regarded as being "at risk", it is clear that sufficient resources are not, and will not be for many years to come, available to meet all contingencies, particularly those in the broader list set out in 3.3. In the contention of the author, it is necessary for any scheme or system of social protection to focus the application of available resources, and that despite their imperfections, social security schemes of the traditional type do provide a framework for doing so which is likely to be more effective, on a national scale, than alternatives organized on a narrower basis.

The Traditional Contingencies

The following comments relate to each of the "traditional" social security contingencies, as listed in Convention No. 102, in turn, noting the features which may impact differently on men and women workers. That convention, in common with many others of course, is drafted in such a manner that its provisions relate much more naturally to the formal sector working environment than to the informal economy, and the comments also attempt to detail a number of specific implications.

Sickness Benefits

Sickness benefits of the kind envisaged in convention 102 are paid in respect of interruption of earnings; in general such earnings would be clearly defined in terms of both amount and regularity. For those who work in less formal settings, commonly employed on a casual or piecework basis, neither aspect of their work can readily be quantified in these terms. If these workers fall sick, their urgent need is to restore their health and ability to carry out their work without delay. For such workers, therefore, it would seem much more important that the social protection system provides effective health services (both preventive and curative). It is arguable that this is even more critical for women workers than for men, since the vast majority will have daily responsibilities for family care in addition to their paid employment. Nevertheless, for those who do work in a fixed workplace, there are important reasons to provide at least some level of sickness benefit, if only to discourage those suffering infectious illnesses from mixing needlessly with fellow employees.

Maternity Benefits

This contingency, obviously, relates specifically to women workers, and its place in the standard list in Convention No. 102 and elsewhere recognizes the importance, for any nation, of providing at least some degree of protection for its future human capital. Social protection in this regard is expected to form the subject of a major discussion at the International Labour Conference of 2000, and may result in the adoption of a revision of the Convention on Maternity Protection No.103 of 1952. The protection described in the Conventions (existing Convention 103 or the proposed draft for a new Convention) relates to the protection of a woman's right to return to her job after confinement, the right to a period of maternity leave around the time of confinement the continuation of an appropriate level of pay during such leave, and the provision of relevant medical care. Each of these items, except for the last, relate fairly specifically to women employed in a more or less formal setting, and it is difficult to envisage the extension of effective protection in this style to the large number of those working in the informal economy.

Employment Injury

It is probably the case that more countries have legislated for protection in this branch of social security than any other. Typically, this is arranged in one of two ways either (a) through the placing of legal liability on employees, or (b) through a national scheme of social insurance. Neither system is able to provide in a satisfactory way for those workers who lack properly, written contracts of employment, either because liability is unenforceable on individual employers or because contributions are not paid to enrol such workers in the social insurance systems. These problems apply equally to both men and women workers. However, the type of work typically undertaken by women working in the informal or unorganized economy, working for long hours in conditions which may be poorly ventilated, generally insanitary, or without even the kind of basic furniture which would allow for proper working postures, does tend to expose them to a wide variety of chronic and debilitating ailments, for example, backache and various kinds of muscular injury which are rather rarely diagnosed (or even categorized) as specifically occupational illnesses.

Unemployment

Protection against this contingency is found in the social security systems of only a minority of countries. as in the case of Employment Injury, protection might be provided through a system of employers' liability or through social insurance; in either case the needs of informal sector workers tend to be overlooked for similar reasons. Again, it is not always easy to define very precisely the circumstances in which benefit should be provided, especially in countries where casual and seasonal modes of employment prevail, and underemployment is as much of an issue as is overt unemployment. In a similar manner, the need to give special consideration to the needs of women workers arises simply from their pre-dominance in the less regulated sectors of the labour market.

Invalidity, Old-age and Survivors' (Death) Benefits

In many national social security schemes, these contingencies are commonly administered under a single branch, and benefits are calculated according to formulae which are more or less similar for the three different types of benefit. Where schemes are organized on the basis of social insurance, all of the difficulties in relation to workers in the informal economy, and hence the differential impact on women workers, apply as noted above. However, in this branch there are two specific issues to which specific attention should be given:

- The tradition in many countries (with little obvious justification in logic) that women should retire from employment at a younger age than men in the same occupations;
- The tradition, also prevalent in many countries and also illogical, that while benefits may be paid to the (dependant) widow of a male worker after his death, corresponding benefits are rarely paid to the widower, however dependant, of a deceased women worker.

Medical Care

The needs of workers of health care cover a very wide variety of aspects. A comprehensive system of care includes, for example, both preventive and curative components, consultation and referral, out-patient and in-patient treatment, the supply of drugs and other medical and surgical aids. The particular need of workers is to maintain their health, or in case of illness to have it fully restored, so as to be able to return to work with the minimum possible delay, and this applies as much to those working in the formal or informal sectors of the economy, men as much as women. The way in which such needs stand to be met by a national system of social security for workers is very much dependant on the effectiveness and accessibility of the more general systems of health care available in any particular country. In one aspect, perhaps, women have a special need, to the extent of their day to day responsibilities for family care, for access to efficient health services not only for themselves but also for their children (and perhaps other dependants).

Family Benefits

Benefits of this kind are provided by relatively few national social security schemes. The variety of possible benefit structures is wide, and may reflect quite heavily the cultural norms of different countries. It is difficult, therefore, to set out specific aspects in which women are generally disadvantaged (or perhaps advantaged) by comparison with their male colleagues.

The Beneficiaries

The model of a social security scheme envisaged in Convention No. 102 and elsewhere includes the concept of a "Standard beneficiary". This "person" is defined separately for each branch of coverage, but a typical formulation is as follows: "man with wife and two children". Elsewhere, the Convention envisages that certain aspects of social security benefit be determined in relation to "the wage of a skilled manual male employee". Very clearly, this model was conceptualized in terms of modes of employment, which, even if typical at that time, no longer reflects present-day realities in most countries of the world.

The existing Conventions, such as No. 102, do not deny the protection of social security schemes to other categories of workers, but it is evident that, henceforth, the way in which such instruments are formulated should begin with concepts and definitions (where necessary) which place all workers on an equal footing, whether women or men, and (as far as possible) whether employed on a formal or informal basis. The overall objective is to extend the relevant coverage, in "the real world" and within an appropriate time-frame, to as many workers as is practicable.

There will always, nevertheless, remain diverse groups of workers who do not fit readily into the standardized categories, which can be defined in Conventions. Those whose needs would be difficult to address adequately in any practicable scheme might include, for example, those who remain in active employment are at advanced age, and as a sub-section of this group, in many countries the number of extremely elderly and very poor widows is growing quite quickly. In the (many) countries whose social security systems omit family benefits, there are no means to meet the social security needs of children who are working-even today, despite the best efforts of ILO's Programme for the Elimination of Child Labour (IPEC).

Observations and Comments

It is impossible within the constraints of a short paper to cover even a small fraction of the important aspects surrounding this topic. The notes which follow are intended only to indicate a few of those aspects which are relevant and which would merit deeper discussion.

The commentary on the different branches of social security schemes, dealing with the range of contingencies, is intended to provide a focus for discussion of the manner in which schemes may provide in a more equitable and relevant way than hitherto for the needs of both men and women workers. However, the fact that financial and human resources are more or less universally limited necessitates means also that choices, which may be very difficult, must be made between the different contingencies against which coverage may be provided.

This aspect of choice is not the central topic of this paper, but it is important to understand that a rational basis is needed to establish the priorities which are appropriate in a given country and circumstances. Those priorities should reflect the expressed needs of the potential beneficiaries themselves, preferably through their representation as equal participants in the Board of trustees or manager, which supervises the scheme. Such an approach to the governance of a scheme would seem to be essential, if the scheme itself is to command the trust, on a long-term and sustained basis, of the members.

In most countries where the wishes of actual or potential scheme members have been surveyed, it is clear that the overwhelming priority is for the provision of effective health care. Further down the list of priorities come provision of benefits on old age retirement, benefits for the dependant survivors of deceased members and injury or disablement. However, it is necessary to analyse the priorities carefully and rationally according to the circumstances of place and time.

Finally, this paper has said nothing about the crucial issues of finance and affordability. While vehicles such as social insurance and social assistance provide the framework in which schemes may operate, whether on a funded or unfunded (pay as you go) basis, they can hardly be effective if workers – as will be the case for many in the informal sector – are unable to afford contributions or the burden of contributions demanded of employers is such as to deter employment altogether.

This brief survey of contextual issues should be sufficient to indicate the range of aspects which must be addressed. The kind of dialogue between the different stakeholders – government, workers and employers – which would enable these to be addressed most effectively is particularly difficult to achieve in regard to the participants in the informal economy, but ways must be found to disseminate relevant information and concepts, with a view to long term progress rather than instant solutions to the problems.

11.

Global Crisis in Social Security

Dalmer D. Hoskins

Secretary General, International Social Security Association

November 2000

We, in the ISSA, are concerned about the current status of social security in the world. You heard the word 'crisis' pronounced frequently here today. May be, that is too strong a word. I am not sure, but as far as Social Security is concerned, and as far as many Government policies, including Social Protection Policies are concerned, we find ourselves at a very uncertain moment in history. I wish, I could stand here and say to you, "oh, we could see this coming. We knew it was round the corner". But that would be a lie. When the Wall in Berlin fell, it changed the world in a very significant way that very few of us could have ever anticipated. The old communist model was thrown out of the window and many Socialist approaches also became tarnished. We are now living at a time when capitalism, and market economy are really dictating the way Row Governments should be run. They are also influencing the way people are thinking about the future and this of course has tremendous implications for national Social Security programmes. We find ourselves increasingly living in a world where Social Security is under attack, and I think, if we are honest we should admit that in many countries we are facing a true crisis of public confidence in the future of these schemes.

One of the very disappointing things which distinguishes the period which we are in right now is the fact that we have rather left the debate – I am saying this because we are here, in Social Security Association of India and I feel like I am among friends and I can be candid and can give a very different kind of speech from what I would give perhaps under some other circumstances – I am saying this among friends and colleagues – that we have rather allowed the debate to be very much dominated by the economists, by the fiscal policy people, almost to the exclusion of people who have really been interested in developing Social Protection Policies and this is reflected in what you see in newspapers. If you pick up a news paper in Europe or north America or Australia, what you often find in the front page of these newspapers are very critical comments about Social Security; it is too expensive, it is creating unemployment, it is encouraging people not to work and so forth. I have even heard the criticism that Social Security is responsible for the breakdown in traditional family relations. So you get a lot of these criticisms.

Where is the defence? Where is the vision about where Social Security is going in the future? And that, ladies and gentlemen, I think is the biggest challenge we are facing today. Let us not be entirely too hard on ourselves. We also have to take into account that we are living in a time when we are experiencing many uncertainties, including economic uncertainties. I hardly need to tell you about these uncertainties to People in Asia, where there have been successive crises in the past decade and they are very familiar with these uncertainties and we have also seen the Russian economy shaken to its roots. Those of us who live in Europe, look everyday at CNN and wonder how far the new Euro can possibly sink against the U.S. Dollar. These are all very destabilizing conditions which obviously do not help us plan for the future.

I was very glad to hear it being said, here today over and over again, that health issues are important and now we have a book to prove that and Ms. Swaroop also echoed the fact that health protection for the informal sector is high on the agenda. But I would have to be very honest and tell you that health gets very little attention at the International level and often even at the National level, where the debate is increasingly dominated by Pension Policy. If we pick up newspapers around the country, you will not find too much discussion about health and if you listen to the debate that occurred between the two Presidential candidates in the U.S., you would notice that they hardly ever mentioned healthcare issues in spite of the fact that the U.S. has a major healthcare crisis on its hands. Instead, they talked about pensions, pensions and pensions. So we are not getting a balanced picture either here or elsewhere. What is behind this, probably, we have to admit now, as we begin the new century, is a kind of breakdown of the old consensus.

At the end of World War II, people in the ILO, in the ISSA, and at the national level, fought very hard to put in place programmes like the ESI and the EPF. You saw this happening all over the world. In Germany, in Italy, in Latin America, where country after country put in place some form of Social Protection, either for health or for pension, based on a consensus that developed between the social partners, between the workers, the employers, and the Government about the social security needs of the people and the way those needs could be met. It would appear that that consensus is now beginning to break down, as we enter this new, rather uncertain world.

One of the biggest changes that have occurred, since then, of course, is that institutions such as the World Bank, the IMF, have suddenly started taking interest in Social Security. Years ago, when I first started working in the field of Social Security, the World Bank was more interested in building bridges and dams, agricultural policy, and such other economic issues. They almost never looked at Social Security issues. Their staff in Washington, D.C. or here in the regions, Latin America, Africa, or Asia included had practically no expertise at all on Social Security Policy but that, ladies and gentlemen, has changed. The situation is very different today. If you go to Washington, among the 14,000 officials of the World Bank, which is incredible to think about, it is, one of the biggest bureaucracies in existence, I can tell you that there are now several Social Security experts sitting on pension policy, on health policy, on unemployment insurance, family allowance, disability and so forth; They have armed themselves with expertise which they did not have many years ago and they are now active players, not only at the international level, but also at the national level. It is now a familiar sight to see officials of the World bank and the IMF going to countries and telling the Governments that they reform their programmes or they would not get the loans they need. So we have new players in this field. And they have created a crisis of confidence, particularly in the developing countries. This problem is particularly grave and serious in some parts of Africa and Asia, and more so in Latin America where the crisis is the most serious of all. We can talk perhaps during the tea break if we have time for discussion about why the Latin American situation has become much more serious. We have to recognize that fact and be honest about it.

Behind this crisis in developing countries with regard to Social Security is the fact that coverage has been low and it has not been extended as we thought it was going to be. In fact, in many parts of the world, coverage of Social Security is shrinking. We are going backwards, rather than forwards and that is because of a complicated situation that arises as a result of privatization. Many public corporations in cement, steel, electricity, telephone, water and such basic industries and public utilities, have been privatized or are being privatized and as that occurs, the workers, who were once employed under the State programmes and public programmes have either disappeared into the informal sector, or are not really contributing to the schemes as they did in the past. So there is a deterioration in the coverage levels.

There is also, I think, to be quite honest with you, a problem in the delivery of services and benefits in many parts of the world. The consumer, the citizen, has become more sophisticated and more demanding. They have more contact with banks and insurance companies and they are saying to the social Security organizations, "Why can not you deliver the same level of services as the private sector companies? Why can not find out about my account? Why can not I get my payment on time, rapidly and in the right amount, just as the private sector does"? No satisfactory answers are forthcoming to these questions in many parts of the world, where there are severe problems in the level of staffing, and the quality of staffing and that is contributing to the crisis of confidence. We have to admit it, and we have to address it.

Another problem that is behind this crisis of confidence is the fact that a number of old Social Security systems like those of Germany – Germany has a Social security system that is about 110-115 years old – Bismark started it all – France, Italy, have had real problems in running the Social Security programmes. There is a political blockade in these countries; the partnership between employers and workers is not working as it did in the past, and they are finding it really difficult to go forward. They are struggling to reform their healthcare systems and their pension systems.

It is, however, not so everywhere. There are bright spots like Canada, Denmark, Switzerland and Sweden, which are some of the oldest Welfare States where people are not unduly critical of social security in these countries, major reforms have been carried out and the schemes have been put on a firm financial basis to face the future. So the situation is not all gloomy but unfortunately, it is gloomy in the big countries like Germany, France, and the U.S.

The US has not touched the social security programme since 1983, because of complete political paralysis; a country where there are 40 million people who are not covered by health protection. Although it is the richest country in the world it has done little in that direction.

There is a growing controversy between the public sector and the private sector. Does the private sector always do better? Now, if you were to be sitting in Chile, or Argentina, or Veneuzula, you would hear loud, and strong and passionate arguments in favour of private sector solutions and many other Latin American countries have moved towards cutting the public programmes in favour of introducing private programmes. The debate thee is loud and acrimonious, very bitter. The debate has been spreading across the world.

What we would like to see is that people should sit back and try to have a much calmer and a more informed debate because we are not getting anywhere with this kind of ideological exchange. We need to stand back and really think about what the public sector does best and what the private sector can do.

When we do this, we are going to come up against the biggest problem facing us for the future and that is this question of coverage because you know too many people in the world, in this country and also in many others, are outside of the systems. They have not been protected by the formal public Social security systems.

When I, as a young official, started working on Social Security, we were much more optimistic about this (extension of social security to the entire population), than perhaps we are today. We thought that with the growth of the economy, with the growth of industrialization, with the modernization of cities and with the growth of education, the programmes would gradually be extended to cover more and more people, something like what happened in Japan, or Germany, or France, over the course of a 100 years. Well, it has not happened really that way.

On the other hand, I think, we have seen a kind of a stagnation in the coverage of the population in many parts of the world and unfortunately, as I said earlier, we have even seen some progress in the opposite direction, which is not progress at all. It actually is the opposite.

Now we are struggling to find ways to solve this problem and one of the ways which we talked about at lunch the other day with Ms. Swaroop was to find out who really were the people who were not covered. We do not know enough in most countries about the composition of these people. We say the informal sector is covered, but in fact, they represent a vast complexity of people who were living either in the urban sector, or in the rural sector; some are in agriculture, some are in commerce, some are in small industry, they are very different kinds of people with different levels of informed education. So we really need to know much more about them before we can put forward credible solutions.

One idea that has taken root at the ILO, at the World Bank, and of course at the ESI, who are much interested in this as well, is the whole question of micro-insurance. Now India is a pioneer in this area – you probably have more self-help, community based protection systems than any other country in the world. I think you have a duty, and a challenge, if I could say so, to tell the world about the schemes that are operating at the local level. Do they work? How well do they work? What has been the experience? What is the limit to their growth? Why do these schemes sometimes work well for five years and then when you go back and look at them, they are not working well any more. What are the critical factors that allow these micro-insurance schemes to develop? Most of them have been able to provide primary healthcare for small populations like weavers.

The ILO is very much hoping that the Indian experience can be duplicated in other places like Latin America, Africa or Asia. But I will have to say that they were only in the very beginning of this new period of experimentation. There is a lot of skepticism about how far this can go, how much can you rely on people to help themselves. This is a very big question for the future and of course we need to adapt our existing programmes to fit these new economic and social realities. It is not possible for us to say that what we have got now has to remain and continue because it is the best and cannot be changed.

You know, as we look forward to the future we have to think about the fact that people are living longer than they did in the past. When Bismark set up the German pension system, people lived only about five or seven years after they reached retirement age. Now people are living for 15, and in some countries, even 20 years or more. So when you think of changing circumstances, we have to take such changes also into account.

One of the issues in the industrialized countries in the world is, of course, what we call the new self-employed and many of these new self-employed are Indian nationals who have emigrated to the U.S., Germany and so forth, and have set up companies, and who are now operating independently or with a small number of staff. The growth in the Labour market these days is not in the big companies in most countries it is in small enterprises of less than 20 persons and that is not what we thought when we created these Social Security schemes. We had quite different things in mind. So we need to tackle this reform issue, we need to find solutions.

To find technical solutions to a problem is not difficult. If you were to ask the experts of Social Security who are sitting in this room, we shall have a lot of technical solutions to these problems. We are not really at a loss for knowing the solutions to many of these problems or to fix them; the problem is bigger than that. I think it is a problem of political will, the inability to tackle the real issues, and most of all, I will have to say, since we are among friends, here in the Social Security Association, I think we have a real problem of public education and public understanding.

One of the biggest barriers to the spread of Social Security all over the world is the fact that the public, the citizen, the tax payer, the contributor, has such a poor idea about how the schemes work. One of the things that I often do when I travel to countries is, first to talk to the taxi driver on the way from the airport to the hotel. I always ask him about Social Security and what they think about their countries Social Security system. Well, I can tell your, I learnt the most amazing things in that short time between the airport and the hotel. One of the things that really disappoints me in many circumstances is how little people know about how the schemes work. Many of them think that the money they are contributing is being misused and that they really will not get the benefit when they reach old age or when they become sick. One of the reasons for this is, I think that we in the world of Social Security, the members of the ISSA, have not done a very good job about explaining and selling Social Security to the public. We have to do a much better job of telling the people about the positive contribution social Security has made to modern society.

A few years ago they did a survey in the U.S. about the U.S. pension system, and a shocking 50 per cent of the people who were surveyed did not know that widows were entitled to a benefit under the existing schemes. This is shocking because after all, widows' protection is an important part of a Social Security scheme. Now, why is it that the workers contributing to this programme do not know more about what protection is being offered? So I think we have a big challenge before us to really explain and to promote better public awareness about social security.

May be that requires hiring new people or new staff who have the necessary information and communicate the same to others. We have never done very much on this in the past. But I think, we have got to do a better job through the internet. T.V., good brochures, good posters and so forth, to explain to people what Social Security does for them. We are faced with another issue what is going to be the future mix, because, let us face it, the future is going to be a mix combination of schemes. Many national schemes are going to be made up in the future of public systems, private systems and individual systems.

When we sit around the table with the World Bank, and the IMF, and my colleagues from the ILO, there is no problem about that; we all shake our heads, and nod very friendly about the fact that we will be building mixed systems in the future but, as we sometimes say, the devil is in the fine print and the mix is not clear.

What will be the role of the state? There are a few things I contend that the State can do better than anybody else. The publicly administered social security pension systems, and healthcare systems, can provide cheaper, more efficient, more socially just benefits than any private insurance companies can do. When you look at the level of the miniscule costs of a well run pension system around the worked, under State supervision, you will see percentages such as 1 per cent, 2 per cent, 3 per cent, of the contribution go to meet administrative costs. If you were to ask the private insurance companies that are operating in the U.K., or in the U.S., or in Australia, how much of the contribution goes for administration? If they are honest, they will have to admit to you about those figures are probably more like 20 per cent, 23 per cent, 25 per cent. So this is a factor which, I think, has to be taken into account.

The private insurance companies are not interested in taking care of the middle class and the upper paid. There is no profit to be made in providing healthcare and pension benefits to people who are earning subsistence earnings. Therefore, we have to look to the State for much that needs to be done in the future and we also have to depend on the State, the public systems, to regulate and control the private schemes because I think this is going to be one of the big challenges for the future.

I see this in countries like Poland, the Czech Republic, in Russia, former Communist countries that are now transforming themselves into market economies, and they are setting up private insurance systems for healthcare, and for pensions, and they are setting up these private insurance companies in an environment where they have no regulatory framework. Now, a country as advanced with a long experience with pension policies is the U.K. suffered the maximal scandal.

The ISSA headquarters is in Switzerland and any of you who know Switzerland know that there are more rules and regulations about insurance in that country than probably in any other country in the world, but that does not prevent even a country like Switzerland from having a major bankruptcy and failure of a private insurance company.

It will happen in other places as well and in order to protect the population against this kind of misuse of monies, or from really quite unexpected events, the State has a role to play to control this private insurance sector and that is going to be such a difficult challenge for all of us to figure out, what that mix is going to be.

Unfortunately, some of you would like me to say that we are seeing a convergence now, that countries are all moving towards the same goal, but in fact, I will have to tell you that never in my experience have we seen such a divergence in the field of Social Security. Countries like Australia, New Zealand, Canada are moving in a very different direction from countries like France, Italy and Spain. The models are extremely varied and I do not see convergence at all.

I see in fact lot of divergence. So, for a country like India, I will have to say, "You really have an incredible choice now. If you look at the world, if you look at all the models, you have got everything from A to Z. there is no blueprint; there is no magic bullet you are going to have a big challenge in the future in deciding what your Indian mix will be between public and private.

Now one of the things that always gets in the way of this discussion when we talk about the new mix and the new systems, is the question of aging because those critics of Social Security will quickly tell you, "Well, we cannot afford it – we are going to have so many old people, that we will not be able to afford pensions or healthcare to be paid by the State. Everyone is going to have to take care of themselves". And I think this is a very specious argument, it is a dangerous argument, first of all because there is absolutely no evidence whatsoever, that if you shift the burden to the private sector, somehow, you will lighten the burden of the aging population. That is not possible. Taking care of the elderly is going to be a responsibility for all societies and the burden does not get lighter by just saying, "That is privatized". I think the burden will be lighter if we allow the older people themselves to work, to contribute, and that means that we have to really have to think differently in the future about retirement ages and about the whole course of their life.

One of the things that we ought to stop and think about for a moment is the fact that people in India are living much longer, many of them are living into their 70's and beyond. I do not know why we are moaning and groaning about this. Is this not an achievement? It is a fantastic achievement because all of us who are of a certain age can remember that it was quite unusual for family members to live into their 70s and 80s- there were a few of them and now that we have more and more of them, we seem to think it is a problem and a burden. I think we should congratulate ourselves and we should say, "Now let us figure out how we are all going to live together to have more older people in our society."

One of the thinks that I often quote when I given speeches outside of India, in Europe and elsewhere, is the statistics that the number of people who will be over age 60 in India by the year 2030 will equal to the entire population of the European Union today. We better think hard about what this means for the future. I am sure those in the room need not be told this, but some of our politicians and policy makers need to focus a little bit more on the future. So we need to open a debate and that in where you come in, the Social Security Association of India. I think you have a big role to play in this. You need to be active, you need to encourage people not to be lost in ideology but to engage in a really informed debate about the future of our programmes public and private, and how we are going to ensure the best kind of protection because the bottom line question, the bottom line issue is "What kind of society do we want our children to live in the future? Do we want them to live in a society where the better off have access to healthcare and pensions, and those who are not better off are just trying to cope as best as they can, or do we want to live in a society where there is the charming, the respect for aging and a form of intergenerational of solidarity."

We talk a lot about cost, investment, saving, about privatization, but I think it is high time that those of us who care about the future, start talking a little bit about social justice as well.

I am going to leave it there. I have had my little moment when I could say what I had in my mind. This is the kind of speech which I often do not get an opportunity to give. I am happy that I could give it in Delhi before this Association because I think that this Association is an important vehicle and it can play a major role in encouraging a debate on the future, about where India is going. I hope that there will be more such meetings leading to broader consultation about the shaping of the future, through your efforts.

12.

The Role of NHRC in Ensuring the Fulfilment of the Right to Social Security

Justice Sh. J.S. Verma
Former Chief Justice of India and Former Chairman, NHRC

JUNE 2002

As a matter of fact, in the present context, it assumes greater significance and there is greater need to appreciate and comprehend the full meaning of the expression Social Security.

Broadly stated, Social Security is a means or mechanism for protecting the human lives from the ill effects of social evils and economic dangers which they face in daily life and to provide adequate means for a life of dignity to every one. But that is easier said than done.

In the present context when you talk of any aspect of human dignity you cannot overlook what is happening around you. In a way I myself have been able to understand human dignity in its full sense viewed in the context of Gujarat. Only this morning a distinguished gentleman came to see me. He is involved in the relief and rehabilitation work in Gujarat. He was disturbed by the loss of property suffered by many people in Gujarat and he wanted to find some way to compensate them for the loss they had suffered. I told him, in the abstract, that it might not be possible to pay such compensation after the right to property had ceased to be a fundamental right and it had become only a legal right. I had earlier a dialogue with the Chief Secretaries of two States who had at different times put the same question to me and I had given the same answer.

Incidentally one of the topics with which you are concerned i.e., starvation deaths and the related issue of suicide committed by many people. Once a few years ago when I was in Bangalore, the then Chief Secretary of Karnataka asked me whether I would consider a suicide committed by a farmer for failure of crops a case of violation of human rights with all the attendant consequences. I told him that the answer would not be a simple yes or no. It would depend on which kind of farmer had committed suicide and why. I said that I was a professional and I had come to the bench from the bar. Many of my colleagues in the bar had large farms where without having sown a single seed they showed large income from agriculture for the purpose of income tax deduction. Similarly there were other professionals like doctors and architects. They belonged to one class. There was another class of big landlords who even after the abolition of property rights possessed large holdings in different names. In these cases if crops failed in one year it would only mean that a little less amount would go into their coffers and bank accounts. If such a person committed suicide it could not be for failure of crops but for some other reason and, therefore, it could be ignored.

But there are others who are marginal farmers entirely dependent on the crops they raise for their livelihood. If, in such a case, crops fail the option before the farmer would be either to see his family members and their children die of starvation or to commit suicide himself. Where a farmer is driven to commit suicide for being unable to feed ones family it would in my opinion be a case of serious violation of human rights. Not so in the first two types of cases.

This view has a Constitutional basis. One of the Directive Principles of State Policy in Part IV of the Constitution requires provision of reasonable means of livelihood to every citizen and that is the obligation of the State. If the State fails in that obligation and it leads to the person committing suicide the State would be answerable for it, especially because it claims to be a Welfare State. I would consider the failure of the state to provide livelihood in such cases to be a case of serious violation of human rights for which the State is not only answerable but also accountable and it should make amends for it. In other words, there is a paradigm shift in the nature of human rights which is very often not realized. It is time that each one of us fully appreciates the fact that the provision of the means of livelihood is not a matter of charity or a bounty; it is something more, it is a basic human right, inherent in human existence to which every human being is entitled.

We have had an occasion recently to spell out the State responsibility to protect the life, liberty and equality of all the citizens in the context of Gujarat. I shall read out a few sentences from the order the NHRC issued on the 1st of April 2002.

"It is the primary and inescapable responsibility of the State to protect the right to life, liberty, equality and dignity of all those who constitute it. It is also the responsibility of the State to ensure that such rights are not violated either through overt acts or through abetment or negligence. It is clear and emerging principle of human rights jurisprudence that the State is responsible not only for the acts of its own agents, but also for the acts of non State players acting within its jurisdiction. The State is, in addition responsible for any inaction that may cause or facilitate the violation of human rights".

This is how I appreciate, my Commission appreciates, the role and responsibility of the State in protecting human rights. This is not only our perception; it is the emerging principle of Human Rights jurisprudence. It is in that sense that what we said in our order of 1st April should be appreciated.

Dignity is the quintessence of human rights. Right to life, liberty and equality together constitute dignity. This is not what we have said for the first time. J.S. Mill said that these are the constituents of a State, the sum total of its worth.

It is also the responsibility of the State to ensure that such rights are not violated either through overt act or through abetment or negligence. It is an emerging principle of HR jurisprudence that the State is responsible not only for the acts of its own agents but also for the acts of non State players acting within its jurisdiction so that all human right violations within the jurisdiction of the State, whether by public servants or by anyone else, whether by direct acts of commission or omission, which result in the violation of human rights, the State is responsible for it. In addition, the State is responsible for any inaction that may cause or facilitate the violation of human rights.

This indicates the amplitude of the responsibility of the State, the full magnitude and extent of responsibility of the State. it implies that the State is responsible not merely for ensuring that it does not directly violate any one's human rights but also for ensuring that within its territory, its entire domain, there is no violation of any kind as a result of any act of omission or commission on the part of any one, whether a State player or a non State player. This is the Constitutional vision. It is in the preamble to the constitution which should be kept in mind while reading any provision of the Constitution that there is assurance of socio economic justice and all other rights. So that distributive justice and the dignity of the individual which are expressly mentioned there. These concepts were contextual when the Constitution was framed. Nowadays very often the alibi for disregarding these principles is that the dignity of the individual has to be bartered for national security. But those who put forth such an argument are trying to be wiser than the framers of the Constitution. I have not been able to find any flaw in the thinking of those great men who framed the Constitution. That was my experience every day in the courts when we used to hear matters relating to Constitutional validity of certain provisions and the relevant debates in the Constituent Assembly were being read to us. We always wondered at the vision, the depth of knowledge and the far sight of those people – how far ahead they were. The debates were of such high order. They had kept the dignity of the individual and the integrity of the nation as the core values which coexist. They would not name both of them in the same breath if they were incompatible. When the Preamble speaks of assuring justice, equality and fraternity, on the one hand, the dignity of the individual, unity and integrity of the nation, on the other, obviously, they are not inconsistent. They are certainly compatible. No one says that a situation will never arise when an individual interest may have to be forsaken for larger national interest. No one, not even that individual concerned himself will say "protect me at the cost of the nation". Such situations are, however, few. Most often one is able to balance those interests as they are not conflicting interests. After all where would the individual be if the nation is not there. what is the nation if the individuals are not there. That is the basic reasoning. There is, therefore, no difficulty in reconciling the interests of the individual with those of the nation. For the purpose of ensuring the achievement of these interests we have the guaranteed Fundamental Rights in Part 3 of the Constitution, the meaning of which has been widely expanded by reading them along with the Directive Principles. For example, Article 21 Right to Life, has been read to mean right to life with dignity and dignity means many things to many people. Otherwise, there would be no meaning in guaranteeing the right to life.

The Directive Principles in Part 4 of the Constitution starting from Article 36 to Article 51 set out the obligations of the State; they are a mandate to the State. They indicate the principles which are fundamental in governance; so that in policy making and in implementation of the policies and in all acts of governance all limbs of the State must bear the mandate in mind. Although if one reads the Articles literally, (that is how most often it is done) one gets the impression that they have to be kept in view only when enacting a legislation, they are not meant to be so limited in their application. Let me tell you that as a judge, I never limited the meaning of those Articles to legislation only. I always used to say and that is what I believed in, and that is what I tried to do. When I did so it might have appeared odd, but it has since been accepted as correct. What is the purpose of expecting only the legislature to keep the mandate in view while enacting a legislation? If those who are supposed to interpret the law are not influenced by that mandate? I, therefore, always believed that as a judge, we must read into the letter of the law, the mandate of the Directive principles. In that sense the concept of State must include all the wings and organs including the judiciary. It is through this process that the content of the Fundamental Rights has been expanded by the Supreme Court over the years, and that is considered to be the unique performance of the Indian judiciary universally accepted and widely acclaimed.

In the ultimate analysis, law is meant for public good. That is what Cicero had said. Law must be construed to ensure the larger public good. If that is the object and the Directive Principles are meant to indicate that India is a welfare State and that is what the State is mandated to do in framing its policies and enacting laws then in the implementation of the laws, the executive must have a similar psyche and in interpreting the laws the judiciary must have a similar psyche. Then only the circle would be complete.

If that happens then naturally the social security we are talking about would be automatic. If the individual dignity is taken care of and every individual's dignity, dignity understood in its widest sense to cover every aspect, the dignity of every individual or human dignity conceived as the quintessence of human relations. The circle would be complete. You do not have to look elsewhere. You do not have to look for a precise definition or meaning of social security. All that is necessary to protect human life not merely bare subsistence but a life with dignity should be ensured by social security mechanism and the social security schemes. That is the primary responsibility of the State.

When you talk of the State, you cannot keep the community or society away from it. Ultimately, what is a State? It includes the community.

When the Constitution was framed, the framers of the Constitution took care to make broadly a comprehensive provision for all that was needed in a Welfare State. Then they made a specific provision for the welfare of the disabled in the Directive Principles. Additionally provision was also made in Entry 9 in the State List of the 66 items in the Constitution. It indicates that even though by virtue of the Directive Principles, welfare of the disabled is the responsibility of both the Union and the States. There being only one entry in the 7th Schedule, that too in the State List, it is primarily the responsibility of the State Government to look after the disabled and not that of the Union. That is a restrictive reading of the Constitution. It is a different matter that so far as performance in this sphere is concerned, the combined efforts of both the Union and the States have been inadequate. Whatever has been done is by the Union and not the States. Even so I would say, that these provisions should not be read in isolation. They should be read in the broader context of the Constitutional Scheme.

We have construed Articles 14 and 21 widely, Article 14 containing the Right to Equality and Non-discrimination is a universally accepted basic Human Right. That itself ensures the requirement of equal opportunity for everything including development. If every human being, every individual has a basic right to development, every individual is entitled to full opportunity for development, which would be covered by Article 14, Article 21, Right to Life, covers the remaining aspects, if any. Between two of them, the entire field is covered. If there is a doubt that a particular area is not covered, we have gone further to deal with that eventuality.

A brief review of the available or existing legal provisions require us to see the provisions contained in the international instruments. Human dignity was emphasized in the U.N. Charter itself. The Universal Declaration followed, incidentally, at the same time at which our Constitution was being drawn up. The provisions in the Universal Declaration of Human Rights correspond to Parts 3 and 4 of our Constitution. So you do not need to go to the Universal Declaration for anything. Assuming there is any need, you will find parallel provisions there and in addition, there are the two Covenants of 1966, particularly the covenant on the Economic, Social and Cultural rights. These provisions are not required to be relied on because they are already incorporated in the Constitution Assuming that there is such a need you have the Visakha judgement.

Reference was made by Mr. Parduman Singh to the judgement in Visakha case. Earlier the accepted position was that domestic laws or the national laws must be construed in consonance with the existing international instruments or provisions therein. Visakha Judgement went further and said that provisions in international instruments, covenants or any other norm, can be relied on for the purpose of expanding the meaning of the existing rights guaranteed in the Domestic Law. If there is no inconsistency between the National laws and the International laws, the provisions of the international law can be relied on for filling the gaps, if any. So you can not only use them for the purpose of expanding the meaning of existing national laws, but also for filling the gaps. The Visakha Judgement says that it is not just permissible but it is the bounden duty. It is in this exercise of filling the gaps that the Visakha Judgement was passed because there was a legislative vacuum to cover the field of sexual harassment. We said, relying on the provisions of SIDA, the Beijing principles of the independence of judiciary, etc., reading those provisions into Article 14, Right to Equality, Article 19, Right to Work, Article 21 Right to Life with dignity, we said all this can be read into that and thereby through the judicial process, provision was made in the area to fill the gap and to say that by virtue of Article 141, which says that any decision of the Supreme court would have the effect of Law, which every authority is bound to implement. We said that the judgement would be the law till such time as Parliament chooses to enact a law to cover this field. Well, that time has not yet come but you do not have to wait for it.

So, all these methods have been used in our system to widen the means or mechanism for provision of social security – so that so far as rhetoric is concerned, so far as the text is concerned, so far as the theory is concerned, nothing is wanting. What is really needed is conversion of the rhetoric into action. That is the area where the community or the society comes in a large way-although it is the primary responsibility of the State. But then as I said, the State being found wanting to a great extent, the community through the organized system of NGOs, and you are one of them, have been playing an important role and it is this system which has got to be strengthened to ensure that the provision which exists is implemented, provision which is wanting is made and ultimately at ground level, where it matters, it is really translated into action.

I have been asked to speak about the role of the NHRC. Let me tell you how I visualize our role.

The role of the NHRC is primarily that of a facilitator or a catalyst to improve the quality of governance because ultimately the realization of all Human Rights depends on the quality of governance and it is good governance which is needed for the respect of human rights. As Mahbub ul Huq has said, humane governance is good governance because it has, for its focus, the public good at all times. That is what is needed now. We, in a way, act as a link between society and instruments of governance. Ultimately, it is the instruments of governance which have to deliver.

The NGOs of the society can also facilitate good governance. There are only a few things which they can do directly but they can facilitate good governance indirectly. That is where in a way we act as a bridge. Therefore, we have a dual role – the first is to act as a catalyst or a facilitator to either start a process where there is total inaction or inertia or to accelerate the process, where the process has begun but the speed or momentum is not what it ought to be, something which we are trying to do in Gujarat; that is one to monitor the performance. Unless we monitor, it will not be possible for us to identify the areas which need improvement.

Another role of the NHRC which we are trying to discharge is to help the mobilization of public opinion and help people discharge their participatory role through the medium of the NGOs so that they have a better impact on the minds of the people who are in charge of governance.

In a Republican democracy with a representative form of Government which we have, people have a very important participatory role in governance of the State. Peoples' role is not confined merely to voting sporadically at the elections, and then to wait for the next election (Elections have not become frequent but earlier they were meant to be only once in five years). People's role is to constantly monitor the functioning of the instruments of governance, or the governance as it is taking place, and that is the participatory role which is expected of every citizen and the people as a whole. This is something which is no longer in doubt.

One of the first persons who cautioned the people of the importance of their role was Joseph Story when the American Constitution was adopted. He said "Constitution is alright, but then the true keepers of the Constitution are the people". That caution was repeated at the inaugural session of the Constituent Assembly in our country by Dr. Sachidanand Sinha who was the provisional President of the Constituent Assembly. He quoted Joseph Story and said "We are going to make the Constitution but ultimately that responsibility will rest there. The people are the keepers of the Constitution". Dr. Rajendra Prasad reminded people of their responsibility at the concluding session of the Assembly. This is the participatory role which the people are required to discharge. How will they discharge that responsibility? As individuals, you may speak only once in a while. An individual is taken seriously when the instruments of governance or those in governance think that you deserve to be noticed. What is needed is to build up public opinion at that level where it cannot be ignored. That requires mobilization and that is where the institutions of NGOs have a responsibility and significance.

Another role which we are trying to discharge is to help the mobilization of public opinion and contribution of people's participatory role through the medium of NGOs so that the people are able better to discharge their participatory role and their mobilized and combined effort has a better impact on the minds of the people who are in charge of governance.

I may summarise our dual role in the NHRC:

(1) directly to facilitate the improvement in the quality of governance and to act as a catalyst to monitor directly-although for the purpose of monitoring also. We have the benefit of assistance of many NGOs as in Orissa and Gujarat; and
(2) the other is to help people discharge their participatory role.

So, this is, according to me, the broad role of the NHRC. Since the formal structure we have and the means provided to us are obviously too inadequate for the kind of role we visualize for ourselves, mobilization of the community effort helps us to expand our role and take on more responsibility.

This we have been trying to do in many ways. Apart from taking the assistance of the NGOs, we have constituted several core groups of experts. We have a core group of lawyers and a core group of doctors. For example, we are dealing with many public health issues but none of us in the Commission is an expert in public health. We may know a bit of law, that is alright, but not public health. We, therefore, have a core group of doctors to help us in dealing with issues of public health. That is how we were able to hold workshops relating to a maternal anaemia, nutritional deficiencies, access to healthcare, HIV-AIDs etc. It would interest you to know that the 2 days' consultation that we had on HIV-AIDs in November 2000, was even prior to the exercise performed by the U.N. so that when in Australia, after that, they held a Conference, our exercise, and the outcome thereof, including the recommendations which we had finalized and sent to the Government, were very much in demand at the Australian Conference. But that we are able to do only because we had the benefit of the voluntary service rendered by top experts. Similarly, in the core group of lawyers, consisting of top lawyers, we have the benefit of their service. I must acknowledge before all of you that all these experts have been rendering service and giving us assistance purely in honorary capacity. We have other similar core groups. We have special rapporteurs.

Recently, you will be happy to know, that we have appointed a very distinguished and visually impaired lady, Anuradha Mohit as a special rapporteur in the field of disability. She was earlier Deputy Chief Commissioner of Disabilities in the government of India. She is highly dedicated to the cause of the disabled and has offered her services to us.

It is in this manner that we are trying to expand our activities. We are able to do something because of the assistance of the informal structure which we have built up.

There are many other areas in which we are working relating to the rights of older persons and others. I would not like to trouble you with all those details.

Before I conclude, once again I must go back to Gujarat because that is always in my mind. One has only to go there and see the problems of the affected people to realize the myriad ways in which social security is needed and is required to be given. I must say, there also, my experience was that the community effort in providing relief and rehabilitation has far exceeded the State effort, which itself speaks volumes. Mind you, to begin with, it was only the community that came forward to provide relief. This is not the first time that has happened. When the earthquake struck it was the community that came to the rescue of the people affected by the earthquake before the State machinery could be awakened. I asked the Government, why, whenever such a calamity occurs, whether it is a natural disaster, or man-made, the unorganized community effort is spontaneous, effective, and very much in position within no time, whereas the institution of governance whose responsibility it is-they take time even to start thinking what they need to do. I said there must be something wrong. After all, those people also who man the institutions of governance come from the same society. Why is it that you are more sensitive when you do not have a direct responsibility and you act only as a human being? And why is it that you are not as sensitive when you do not cease to be a human being but you do not act as one? You act only as a public servant.

The significance of the role of the community in not merely performing the task but also activating the State machinery-that is our role and that is the participatory role in the governance of the people to see that the institutions function properly.

So social security aims are not difficult to achieve. If we are achieving to a great extent through the non-State Sector, through the informal Sector, if I may say so, than the formal Structure, then why should it not be possible to achieve all of it? You take any area; for instance, you take education. Article 45 requires free and compulsory education to be provided to all children up to age of 14. this was expected to be achieved within ten years of the commencement of the Constitution. 50 years have passed. The only thing they have done is to bring the 93rd Amendment which has shifted it from Part 4 Directive Principles to Part 3 Fundamental Rights. Instead of up to 14 years, it is now from 6 to 14 years. So children up to 6 go out of the State's responsibility. This is another subject of debate. At any rate, merely putting it in Part 3 of the Constitution is not going to help because there are already so many Fundamental Rights which have not been fully implemented. We have Article 23: we have Article 24 but we still have bonded labour and child labour, we still have human exploitation to a large extent. So merely shifting it from one part of the Constitution to another is not going to help unless it is translated into action and that is where the community comes in.

So I will end by saying you are involved in doing something which really is what is going to matter in the ultimate analysis. There is need for greater effort in this direction, greater realization of our responsibility, both to add directly and to monitor the functioning of the Government, institutions, because that is a part of our role as citizens. As a citizen, each of us is obliged to perform the Fundamental Duties which are mandated for us through Article 51A. The very first one is to abide by the constitution and if you read all of them, and if all of us do even half of them, I think there will be no problem. What is needed is networking of the effort because the mobilized effort is always going to make a much greater difference.

13.

Social Security for Migrant Workers

Prof. Jan Breman
Centre for Asian Studies,
Amsterdam School of Social Science Research

August 2002

I feel grateful for this opportunity to discuss some of the issues concerning migrant labour. I do that in the company of people who take the problems of labour seriously at a moment when they are not very popular. It has not been fashionable to talk of the problems of labour for the last decade or so. There is at present greater interest in matters relating to capital than those relating to labour which is looked upon more as a factor of production and as a commodity than as a collection of human beings. My lecture would address the problems of labour not only as a factor of production and as a commodity but as human beings who have a right to a decent life and a right to life of dignity, a right to get a wage which enables them to care for themselves and also those who live with them.

I am speaking among friends. I am pleased to see old friends whom I have known for a very long time. I am happy to see Sh. Sanat Mehta here. He has been carrying the torch for labour not only in Gujarat but also at the national and international levels for a long time.

I am not going to offer technical solutions for providing social security to migrant labour. I want to contextualise migrant labour in society and the economy and then explain why it seems so difficult to include them in programmes of social security.

Let me start by saying a few things about the time when I first came to India to involve myself in research at the beginning of the 1960s. I spent about two years in two villages in studying the conditions of agricultural labour in South Gujarat.

Agricultural labour is still the major working class in the world. Yet we know more about industrial labour and urban labour than about agricultural labour.

The conditions of agricultural labour anywhere in the world, particularly in South Asia and India are very pitiable. Most of the migrant labour come from that class. So I came to India to study the conditions of agricultural labour and the relations between landless agricultural labourers and the owners of land.

India is a country of villages. In most of the villages two thirds of agricultural capital namely land, is owned by ten per cent of the people. More than fifty per cent of the people have no access to land. They are landless agricultural labourers. They have to sell their labour power in order to make a living. In the beginning of the 1960s in South Gujarat there was also the institution of bonded labour. The system of bonded labour is still prevalent in many parts of the country. The system was called Kalthi which in Gujarati means to eat. when three was no work because of heavy rains or otherwise it was the duty of the landlord to feed the workers by providing the necessary provisions. Also when there were events in the family of the workers like marriages, birth, death etc. it was the duty of the landlords to support them by giving necessary assistance in cash or in kind.

That was a kind of social security system as it operated in the past in the peasant society, not only in South Gujarat but throughout South Asia.

Let us not glorify the system or idolize the system of social security of the past because it went together with inequality. There was a very unequal relationship between the landlord and the landless agricultural labourers. That was also expressed in the behaviour of the worker when he went to the house of the landlord in the evening to receive his wages. He had to approach the land lord humbly and deferentially. He had to bow his head, touch the feet of the master and beg him for his daily ration. It was also an expression of exploitation and an expression of patronage. Let us, therefore, not idealise the system.

The system collapsed around the middle of the century when a process of commercialization opened up the countryside signifying a change in the relationship between the landlord and the worker. The owners were no longer interested in providing social security to the people working for them. Their life style changed.

When I first came to the village where I worked there was just one shop for essential commodities like grain, vegetable oil etc. but not for fruits, soap, coco-cola or thums up. After commercialization of rural life the pattern of life changed and the pattern of consumption also changed. The inequality did not disappear. It became more articulated in a different way.

The land owners no longer invest in the people who work for them but in their own life style. If I go now to the same village where I worked previously, I will find that the land lords have bungalows with refrigerator, ceiling fans, some of them also have air conditioned car; their children go further for advanced education, the pattern of their expenditure has changed. They do not invest anymore in the village economy but in their own households. They may invest in agriculture but not in the household of their landless agricultural workers.

When I lived in the villages during the early years of the 1960s, I could not get out of the villages in the monsoon months. I used to be stuck there for three or four months, because there were no pucca roads and the country roads used to be flooded. If I go there now I will find that there are 23 buses going out of and coming into the villages everyday. That is a major change.

If you examine, as an anthropologist, which I am, who are sitting in those buses and where they are going, why they are going and then inevitably you encounter the phenomenon of migrant labour. This phenomenon changes the nature of the economy and of rural society.

People move out. The village has become accessible-but it has also become leavable. You can leave the village; you can go somewhere else and people of all social classes in the village go somewhere else.The people at the top of the village, Brahmins, Pattidars, and such others, they all go all the way to the West. They are also migrant workers. But when you talk of migrant workers, you do not have them in mind. They go to the West, with Green Card or illegally, without Green Card. Now a days you can go to the U.S. without Green card for Rs. 8 lakhs. For that amount an agent will take you wherever you want to go in the U.S. There are a lot of people at the top of the village willing to pay that money. They look up to it as an investment in the future. It is an investment for the family in the future.

In the middle range of the village, you find small persons, small farmers, small farming households. They also migrate. They go to the Gulf States to work as contract labour and come back. You see them at the airports. I am sure many of you who have been to the airport, would have seen them fairly often, carrying a video cassette recorder, or a rice cooker, or other kinds of household items. You see them coming back from the Gulf States. they bring back not only those gadgets but also money which they invest in housing, in land also and in improving agriculture.

The people at the bottom of the village society are also mobile, migrant. They are landless labourers. They do not have the money to go to the West and the West does not need them. They also do not have the money to go to the gulf, because to go to the Gulf you need a lot of money. You make more money once you go there but you need a lot more money to spend to go to the Gulf and they do not have that kind of money. So the people at the bottom of the village are migrant but they stay closer to home, that is to say, they stay in the same country.

People at the bottom of the village are both pushed out and pulled out of the local economy. They are pushed out because the farmers do not need them throughout the year any longer. There is no work for them in the village throughout the year. In that sense, they are pushed out of the village economy. But they are also pulled out because the diversification of the rural economy has made it look both possible and also attractive for them to leave the village economy. They escape from a closed labour market. They escape from a situation where they will be under the rule of the landowners and when they go out they escape the social control and the social power and economic power of the landowners. So to that extent, there is both a pushing out of labour of the village economy and a pulling out of labour of the village economy.

That has become possible because of the transport and communication system that came into being in the second half of the 20th century. Both in time and in cost, travel has become less cumbersome. When I was in the village in 1961, there were just two cycles (bicycles) in the village and mine was one of them. There were bullock carts; but bullock carts do not take you very far in terms of labour migration. As I said earlier there are 23 State Transport buses coming and going every day making it possible to leave the village. In terms of both time and cost, going out of the village is less cumbersome than it used to be.

The labour market has widened. The labour market has expanded and that has also to do with diversification of the rural economy. Agriculture has gone down in importance and certainly also in terms of employment. Agriculture is not any more the most important sector even in the countryside. We are not talking about urban economy; we are talking about the rural economy too. Agriculture is not the most important source of employment any more and that is how we see agricultural labour becoming rural labour.

I will not talk about the people higher up in the village in terms of their migration pattern. I will firmly focus on the people at the bottom of the village economy, the landless labour.

When do they leave the village in the first place? Here we come to a fairly important phenomenon. The labour migration is both cyclical and circular. Labour migration for a longtime was understood, in many studies, as leaving some place and settling down somewhere else; leaving the village and going to the city, that is the most dominant image of labour migration. People from the rural hinterland leave the countryside and go to the city, there they settle down and they become urban workers. Those who were rural workers become urban workers. It is not so in South Asia in the last half century and also, and it is not likely to be so in the immediate future. I think this is a very important point to note because the process of transformation which took place in the West in the 18th, 19th and 20th Century is not replicated at the moment in Asia. People leave the countryside, no doubt, but they come back. The migration is circular. People leave but they come back. It is cyclical. It happens at particular periods of the year. People do not leave indefinitely-they leave to work somewhere else, but they come back and that is very interesting because it shows that the pattern of transition which took place in the West, when the agrarian societies became industrialized societies, is not being repeated at the moment in large parts of Asia including India. That is because the process of urbanisation and industrialization in South Asia is different from the historical process in the West. But unfortunately that parallel is still very much in our mind. When we look at migration we think, "Ah, these people are leaving the countryside, they are settling down in the cities". But it is not so. They go to the cities to work no doubt. They are pulled to the cities but they are pushed back also, from the cities because the city does not need them indefinitely-does not need them throughout the year.

I can give you a very graphical example. When you came here to his building you would have seen outside, a gang of migrant workers making roads. I am sure you would not have given much thought to them but Delhi, Mumbai, Calcutta, Chennai, and many other cities are flooded with this type of people who come basically to work in a project and go back. You hardly see them. They are invisible. They are there but you do not know where they come from, why they have come, how they are staying here. Basically, they are not staying in the city. They are camping. For them, Delhi is a camp. A transient camp; they come here to work and then go back. That is remarkable. Many migrants come to the city not to settle down; to live here, to work here and to live here, to become urban citizens, but they come for a short period, remain in the cities as temporary arrivals. That is one of the great disillusions about the pattern of the Indian society as it has developed after Independence in India during the last half a century.

There was a grant design for bringing about social change in the country; it was worked out in a plan drawn up by the Indian National Congress before Independence. There was the idea that the agrarian society should be reconstructed. Capital had to be redistributed-capital in the form of land – through land reforms. But land reforms have not been a great success in India although they are more successful in India than elsewhere, for instance, in Pakistan, or in Bangladesh. You must have heard also recently that Operation Barga in Bengal carried out under tne Leftist

Government has only been able to redistribute not more than 15 per cent of total land. That was the best case. In many other states in India, the percentage of land distributed has been less. Redistribution of land was necessary to make agriculture more productive and also to promote equity among people in the countryside but, from the very beginning, landless labourers have been excluded from land distribution in India, except for a few exceptions, like Kerala; in Kerala too, not much land has been redistributed among landless labourers. But certainly, in no other State in India, not even in Gujarat, have landless labourers benefitted from land redistribution.

What was the future that Government of India had in mind for people in the bottom layer of society? There was a grand design India would become an industrial nation. These people who were redundant in the countryside would leave the countryside, go to the cities, settle down, become urban industrial workers but that has not happened.

Certainly, they left the countryside but not to settle down in the city. Certainly, cities have grown, but the city is a very unfavourable place for landless labourers to settle down. do you ever think that these people working downstairs in these trenches have the opportunity to settle down in Delhi to become industrial workers, to become eligible for housing and other urban amenities like health and education? No way. And to that extent, the Development Policy has failed.

These people, the landless labourers, are the biggest class of people in the country. We are not talking about a minor segment of the population. It is the biggest working class in the country. They were not included in the package that the Government had in mind for building a better society-with more equity. They come to the city as migrants and they stay as migrants. They go back when the work is over. The Mukkaddam or the Mistry or the Sardar or whatever he is called, takes them back. He is the contractor and he takes them back to wherever they came from.

One of the characteristic features of post-colonial India, is the lack of a Housing Policy for the labouring urban poor. There are some houses being built for them in the countryside but not in the urban environment.

At the beginning of the 20th Century, there were many housing societies in Europe. They were the products of the Labour Co-operative Movement. There were also public housing schemes, which took care of people leaving the countryside and coming to the industrialized cities in Europe. When we talk of housing co-operatives in urban India, we are talking of middle class housing-it may be the type of housing in which you are residing-but we are not talking of public housing schemes for the labouring poor. It shows that Government has not made any plan for shifting the rural poor to a new habitat.

They are migrant and remain migrant. That is not something that they like. Migration is very tiring. To remain a migrant throughout your life is very tiring. To leave your home, to go somewhere for a certain period of time, and then to go back again. That sort of labour migration is meant for a very poor life, not only in terms of income, but also in terms of a decency of life having access to the amenities that urban citizens usually have access to.

Labour migration has been mostly studied in terms of urbanization. But I have to point out that most labour migration is not rural to urban and rural to rural. Most migrants circulate around in the countryside. The perception that most migrants are coming to the cities or towns is based on an urban bias, is not true. Most migrants are moving around in the rural economy.

Doing what? Basically the same things that migrants in the lower echelons of the urban economy, fluctuating mobile labour, are doing in various kinds of employment which we have labeled together as informal sector employment-in building, road building, house construction, in the service sector, vending, (street vendors) etc. seasonally dwelling on the pavements. When the season is over, they go back home.

Home is an odd word to use in the context of the migrant labour, because year in and year out, they leave home and they make trips lasting from a couple of weeks to a couple of months, to a year, half a year, and then they go back. In that situation the term home loses all meaning.

I have seen also that households are split up on such occasions.

Part of my research was focused on brick kilns. Now you will find brick-kilns all over India. As a matter of fact, total employment in brick-kilns is much higher than total employment in factories. But we know much more about urban-based mill workers working in factories than we know about workers working in brick-kilns. It is season-bound. It starts around Diwali and it lasts until Holi when they go back to the village because rain is falling and bricks are not manufactured any more. They camp in the countryside like the sugarcane harvesters–in Gujarat and Maharashtra, Andhra, Tamil Nadu, U.P. and Bihar.

Millions of people are footloose, have become footloose in India in what you call the development process. Millions of Indians are footloose in the sense that they are driven out of their habitat for varying periods of the year but they are bound to come back again because it is a type of migration which does not allow you to settle down at a point of destination-you are driven back again.

The sugarcane harvesters in South Gujarat, who come from Maharashtra-Khandesh, they are recruited by a Mukaddam-a labour contractor who gives them a form to sign; they cannot read the form.

They are illiterate but what they sign is that they go back home at the end of the season; they are not allowed to stay on. In the same way, brick-kiln workers have to go back to their home once the season is over. When they go, how they go, and what they do after they go back consist of a range of possibilities. Some of them go off as individuals. Sometimes the whole household moves, men, women and children. If you are a child of a migrant labourers, you are bound to remain illiterate all your life and you are bound to become a migrant worker yourself. There are no future prospects for children of migrants.

Think of the millions of people in South Asia, especially in India, who are at the moment footloose. They are all recruited by a labour contactor called by various names Mukaddam, Sardar, Mistry, etc, who hire them on a gang basis. He brings the gang. He is himself a jobber, but he also supervises the work of the members of the gang wherever they go-in a quarry, in a road construction, in the salt pans, in the brick kilns, in the sugarcane fields.

I have seen households being split at the time of recruitment. You are sitting in the village. It is monsoon - rain is falling - no work - no income – no food in the house. Then the jobber comes along and he hands out an advance of Rs. 500 or Rs. 600, asks them to come with him. They have no other option but to accept the advance and they are bound to go wherever he takes them. There is a new bondage that has emerged after Independence in India. This is the bondage of contract labourers. It is a bondage which is different from the bondage between the landowners and the landless labourers. It is a new type of commercial bondage which keeps the people under the control of the Mukaddam (the labour contractor). He comes around Diwali. They go with him. If they do not want to go he has the power to make them go; if necessary, he uses physical violence. That is the system of bondage. We are not talking of free labour who take their own decision.

I have also seen the households being split because different Mukaddams come to hire the men, their wives and children. They accept money from different Mukaddams and they split and go in different directions.

One of the things that has rarely been studied is the loneliness of the migrant workers – being away from those who are close to their family, their spouses, children and parents. We do not know about the loneliness of these migrant workers.

Why are they going? Why this enormous mass of migrant labour? They become migrants because they have no options. There is no local employment available throughout the year and that is why they go off to work wherever work is available, in the city, in the town, or also in the countryside, for shorter or longer periods of time.

We should not only look at labour migration as a drama that is enacted. Labour migration is also an assertion of equality to get out of the system, to get out of a situation which is very much determined by inequality.

How much do they earn? Rs. 25,35 or 40 a day, it is not time wage, it is the amount paid for a job done. You are not working for a wage from 8 to 5 or from 7-6. You are working on the basis of the volume of work done, or goods produced, paid at piece rate. They do not earn much more than the agricultural workers; may be a few rupees more but not much more.

If you look at these labourers and if you share their company, they feel free and easy. They go around. They are part of a modern scene. Standing on a truck, at the back of a truck. They go to places. They see things. They leave the village. They encounter new situations. So labour migration is not only a drama. It is also liberation; basically it is an assertion of equality.

Now I come to the Social Security part.

Why do employers make use of migrant workers? Why do they use them at all? There is a very conventional and a very simple idea which you find in many labour studies. In these studies on labour migration, it is said that people move from one place to the other because there is no work at the place where they live and there is work at the place where they go to. That is a very simple, a very convincing and a very persuasive explanation. But I am afraid it is not so simple; it is a bit more complicated than that.

Nowadays, employers prefer temporary labour to permanent labour. They prefer to hire and also fire labour instantly and not involve themselves in permanent relationship with them. It is very interesting to observe that in places where there are many migrant workers coming from outside, there is no dearth of local labour. Local labour is available but employers prefer outside labour for two reasons because, basically, outside labour, as a rule of thumb, is cheaper than local labour and outside labour is more pliable. Local labourers are not only workers, they also have their social life. They have a house to go back to in the evening. They have dependents around them. A family to care for. They have events in the family like marriage, birth, death. They are not only a commodity, but they are also human beings who have a social life and they cannot be totally and completely controlled by employers in the way that outside labourers can be controlled. Outside labour is a commodity. You do not know them, you have no personal relationship with them, you hire them when there is work, in the fields, in the salt pans, in the brick kilns or you fire them if there is no need for them any more. You cannot do that to local labour. Local labour also has social power. Local labour has also social capital in the village, in the habitat where they live. They have a kind of bargaining power. The bargaining power of migrant workers is next to nil, yes, they can run away and they do that. If you talk to employers, they complain about migrant labour – who are not faithful, who are not loyal; they talk to you, pretending that the migrant labourers are unreliable and irresponsible. They say – "yesterday, they were at work and today they have gone, I do not know where, I do not know why". They do not understand that absconding, running away, leaving the worksite is also an expression of protest. Yet, employers prefer outside labour.

I will give you one example. In the village to which I still go, where I did my research in South Gujarat in 1960-61, the landless labourers would go to the brick kilns at far off places in Gujarat or Maharashtra; they would go after Diwali and return after Holi. Then they would work in agriculture for some time and after Diwali they would go again to another place. I went with them to the brickfields and asked the employers 'Why do you employ these labourers? Are they not available locally?' They said 'Yes, they are available, but these outside labourers are working hard and we are satisfied with them and they have been coming here every year and so we go on employing them'. That was in 1961. In 1971, after ten years, I did a re-study of the same village and I found that a brick-kiln had come up at the outskirts of the village. Someone had opened a brick-kiln outside the village. I thought that it was very convenient for the local labour and they do not have to go to Bombay any more because they can be employed in the brick-kiln in their own village. They know the work. They are skilled. But I was wrong. I found that in the brick-kiln outside the village, the employer had employed outside labourers. They had come all the way from Saurashtra, or from Kathiawar. So I asked the owner of the brick-kiln, 'why do you employ outside labour? There are many labourers who can work in brick-kilns in your own village; why do you employ outsider labour? He said, 'No, outside labourers are much better. They work much harder. They are more faithful'. So the same explanation was given which I had heard before. You must be familiar with this kind of explanation. It says something about the stereotypes and it hides the real reasons of the employer. Outside labour is cheaper and outside labour is more docile. Outside labour has no bargaining power. If the owner of the brick-kiln tells outside labourers to come at 2 O'clock at night to start the work, they do that. They work up to 10 O'clock in the morning. They go for a few hours of rest, they come back in the afternoon and again work till the evening. They work about 14-16 hours a day. local labour is not willing to do that. Local labour is having a life of his own. They would want to go back to the house/hut, at the end of the day. they want to sit with the family, have a meal with the family. They want to see their children. Migrant labour have no social relationships. It is a commodity. You do not invest in personal relationship with that sort of labour. You even avoid personal relationship. It is a commodity which you can hire and fire.

Then what is the Social Security of these migrant labourers? That is what I am expected to focus on. Let me say at the outset that there is no Social Security for them. The process of migration is itself a form of Social Security for them. Labour migration is Social Security. They go away because locally they do not get enough work throughout the year to make a living and to reproduce their labour power for the next generation. The employer has no interest in investing in Social Security for the migrant workers.

There are three dimensions of migration of workers which I would like to bring to your attention.

In the first place, they are mobilized from far away, but always time bound; they are not mobilized indefinitely; they are mobilized for a particular period of the year, and they have to get out again. Mobilization is the first dimension.

The second dimension is compensation for their work. The payment for their work, is not based on time rate-is not based on the hours of work say, they do not work for a fixed period of time from 8 O'clock in the morning till 4-5 O'clock in the evening like many of us do the modality of payment is different. It is based on piece rate for the job work done. That is why it becomes necessary for a labour migrant to involve other members of his household-wife and children. It is only by involving other members of the household in the labour process that he can make a living. Compensation is the second part.

The third dimension is casualisation. Migrant labour is essentially casual labour. They are not permanent labour. They can be hired and dismissed within a couple of hours and the employer does not accept further obligations. Even the cost of travel has to be borne by the labour migrant himself. The employer does not pay for that. The labourer has to pay for his or her own mobility. The pattern of migration and the income the migrant workers earn does not have a margin which can be used for their protection in times of crisis.

Social Security is meant to help a worker during periods of unemployment, sickness or old age. These basically are the reasons why people require Social Security. Migrant labourers are not able to make any provision for these purposes. They cannot put aside any savings for bad days. Bad days in terms of unemployment, bad days in terms of ill health, bad days when they cannot work anymore because of old age. The wages paid to migrant labourers and the large masses of them are unskilled, poorly educated, the wages paid to migrant labourers are so abominably low that they cannot afford to invest in Social Security. As a matter of fact, on days when they have no income, they have to sell their labour power in advance in order to get some money to buy food or meet any other expenditure they have necessarily to incur. That is the Social Security for them. Social Security is being tied to credit. Very often, migrant labourers are indebted to the Mukaddam, the labour contractor, the employer, the shopkeepers or money lenders in the village.

The report of the Second Labour Commission is due to be published shortly and it is already being discussed. If you go through the report, it is very fat (more than 1000 pages) you will find hardly any mention of migrant labour as if it does not exist. We are talking of millions of people in India beign footloose and in a major report on labour like this, that issue is hardly discussed. But at least they have been forthright in providing social security for the workers of the informal sector of the economy. That at least has been accepted and a whole apparatus is going to be established. And I think the Chairman and other friends here will know more about it. But I must confess and I will be very frank – I have no faith at all in the recommendations of that Report. I have no confidence that they will take care of social security of the migrant workers or any category of informal sector workers.

I say this on the basis of what I have been seen of the implementation of the Minimum Wage Legislation in the informal sector of the economy. On paper it is all there – minimum wages – and if you then go and position yourself in the milieu of the informal sector workers, it becomes very clear that they have no access to minimum wages. In the same way they will have no access to the social security provisions which have now been formulated. That is due to several factors, political as well as social factors.

When we talk about the sub-human conditions in which migrant labour finds itself, it is not only an expression of the fact that the supply of labour is much higher than the demand for labour at the bottom of the economy. We cannot explain it in only economic terms. We should also explain it in social terms.

All said and done, India is still a society dominated by social inequality and a rather callous, careless, indifferent attitude towards people at the bottom of the economy and society. The idea that they have a right to dignity is basically denied by the powers that be. That is because society is structured in terms of hierarchy and not in terms of equality. If there is no counter veiling power in the society to improve the condition of those who are at the bottom, then all you write on paper will be meaningless and will only be a means for officials to make money at the cost of the poor just as they make money out of the minimum wage legislation – not by implementing it but by using it for their own purposes, to line their own pockets. This is the economic factor.

The political factor has to do with social inequality. If there is no more counterveiling power in society to assert the rights and also the dignity of the labouring pool, then social security co-efficients will not work. They give a lip service by which mainstream politicians and policymakers say that they are doing something for them but in fact, the will to implement it is lacking. There is a stark contrast between the democratic fabric of Indian Society – praise be to that democratic quality of Indian society from Independence onwards – and it is an enormous tool for assertion, for the downtrodden in the society of India, the democratic quality of society, but, in contrast, there is the Government which is not giving to the poor what they have a right to ask for.

14.

Social Security and the Right to Food

Jean Dreze

Hony. Professor, Delhi School of Economics and
Visiting Professor GB Pant Social Science Institute, Allahabad.

April 2003

Today (It is Dr. B.R. Ambedkar Jayanti day) is a very appropriate day for this occasion because we are celebrating Ambedkar Jayanti and no one has done more than Dr. Ambedkar to put Social Security at the centre of India's Development Strategy and political agenda. Dr. Ambedkar had revolutionary vision for India's future which included Participatory Democracy, Social Equality, a Welfare State and the realization of a wide range of economic and social rights including the right to Social Security. We would do well to remember and revive this vision today as we consider the prospects of achieving social security for all in the near future.

Before I proceed, I would like to clarify what I mean by Social Security because it goes a little beyond the standard interpretation you may be used to. I am not thinking of Social Security in the narrow sense of guaranteeing a minimum level of income, or at least not only in that sense, let alone thinking of Social Security in the sense of doing it for a privileged minority of citizens who happen to belong to the organized sector. I am thinking more broadly of Social Security as a set of social arrangements that protect all citizens from poverty, hunger, illness, illiteracy, violence and deprivation of other basic needs. Social Security in this broad sense can be seen as one of the concerns of Dr. Ambedkar's life and thoughts.

In his vision of India's future, as I understand it, Social Security rested on three pillars-Participatory Democracy, Constitutional Rights and the Welfare State. So I will comment briefly on each of these, because I think they are really still very relevant today.

The central role of Participatory Democracy in this context arises from the fact that democratic practice is ultimately the only non-violent means we have of bringing about the far-reaching economic and social changes that are required for the realization of Social Security in the full sense of the term. There are many ways of defining Democracy and Dr. Ambedkar himself proposed several interesting definitions. One of the most inspiring ones, is the following: "Democracy", he said, "is a form and method of Government, whereby revolutionary changes in the economic and social life of the people are brought about without bloodshed." I think it is a very interesting definition and as this statement illustrates Dr. Ambedkar's vision of Democracy went far beyond the basic institutions of Parliamentary Democracy as they exist today. In fact, I doubt that Democracy, as we know it in India today, would be recognized by Dr. Ambedkar as Democracy in his own far-reaching sense of the term, even though, of course, he played a major role in putting these institutions in place. It is worth noting, in particular, that Dr. Ambedkar's conception of democracy included a substantial degree of economic and social equality. His notion of equality as a requirement of democracy and his fear that this requirement may not be met in Independent India was eloquently expressed in his concluding comments to the Constituent Assembly, which I am sure some of you are familiar with. He said on the 26th of January, 1950, "We are going to enter a life of contradictions. In politics, we will have equality, and in social and economic life, we will have inequality. In politics we will be recognizing the principle of one man, one vote, and one vote, one value. In our social and economic life, we shall by reason of our economic and social structure, continue to deny the principle of one man, one value. How long shall we continue to deny equality in our social and economic life? If we continue to deny it for long, we will do so, only putting our political democracy in peril." I think this fundamental tension of Indian Democracy, the tension between political equality and social and economic inequality is still with us today and it is one of the major preoccupations of this lecture.

This brings me to the second pillar of Social Security in Dr. Ambedkar's framework, which is Constitutional Rights. As I understand it, Dr. Ambedkar's own answer to this tension of political equality and economic and social inequality was the progressive realization of a wide range of economic and social rights, such as the Right to Food, the Right to Work, the Right to Education, the Right to Equality all of which are in the Indian Constitution. Some of these Rights are among the so called Fundamental Rights but most of them are in fact mentioned in the Directive Principles of State Policy. The Directive Principles are not meant to be justiciable in a Court of Law (enforceable). Or at least they were not meant to be justiciable in Dr. Ambedkar's scheme of things even though today there is a different judicial interpretation. I am looking at things as they looked to him at that time and he recognized that it was explicitly the way he had envisaged that these rights were not justiciable. Some times it is argued that if the Directive Principles are not justiciable, then they have no teeth; what is the value of having the Right to Food if it is just a Directive Principle which is not enforceable in a court of law. Dr. Ambedkar's response to that was that in a democracy, there are different means of holding the State accountable to its responsibilities of which legal action is only one and therefore even if the Directive Principles are not justiciable, the State can, in principle, be held accountable to them through other means such as public criticism, electoral competition, grassroots agitation, even, for that matter, civil disobedience. In other words, through democratic practice. So, in Dr. Ambedkar's vision, as I understand it, the expansion of democracy and the realization of constitutional rights went hand in hand in a kind of virtual circle. Democratic practice, on the one hand, expands the reach of constitutional rights just as the realisation of constitutional rights helps to bring about greater equity in the society and, therefore, enhances the quality of democracy. It is another matter that this complementary expansion of democratic pace, and constitutional rights have turned out to proceed at a much slower pace than Dr. Ambedkar had hoped and even to suffer occasional reversals. As I said, Dr. Ambedkar's dreams for Indian Democracy are yet to come true.

The third pillar of Social Security in Dr. Ambedkar's perspective was the Welfare State. As the Constitution makes it clear, he expected that the State would take direct responsibility for protecting and promoting peoples' entitlements to basic facilities such as elementary education, health care and Social Security. In this respect, he was in tune with the times, writing as he was in the period of accelerated expansion of the Welfare State in Europe that followed the end of the Second World War. That was the time when the National Health Scheme was set up in Britain, following the publication of a report which laid the foundation of the infrastructure of Social Security in England and also many other countries of Europe. To-day there is widespread skepticism about continued relevance and viability of the Welfare State. Yet if we take a long view, it is worth noting that the expansion of the Welfare State around the world is one of the most remarkable achievements of the 20th century. Indeed, a hundred years ago the share of public expenditure in national income was typically of the order of 10 per cent in industrial countries, and very little of that had to do with Social Security or Health or Education or related things. Bulk of it was spent on military preparations and related pursuits. To day in the so called market economies of West Europe and North America, public expenditure typically accounts for 35-45 per cent of GDP, rising to a 50 or even 60 per cent in countries like Netherlands and Scandinavian countries. Furthermore, the share of health, education and Social Security alone in total Government expenditure in these economies, tends to range between one half and three quarters. These are fundamental areas of State involvement which account for a major share of overall economic activity. It is also worth noting in passing that welfare related public expenditure in those economies is still increasing year after year in many cases in spite of all the rhetoric about the rollback of the State. In the light of this historical experience indeed, of many development experiences around the world (including India itself), there is every reason to reaffirm the continued relevance of the Welfare State.

In short, I believe that Dr. Ambedkar's message is as relevant today as it was fifty years ago and in particular that the realization of Social Security for all in India depends crucially on the revival of his visions of participatory democracy, constitutional rights, and the Welfare State.

You may wonder why I began with this long preamble about rights, and Constitution, and so on; the answer is that it seems to me that the basic reason why Social Security in the sense in which I have defined it, is still so far from being realized in India today is that it is not much of a political priority. That is the bottom line and in fact this can be seen as one particular example of a more general pattern of massive neglect, if not invisibility of people's basic needs in Indian politics. That itself, in turn, can be seen as a reflection of the continued marginalization of disadvantaged groups in democratic politics, in contrast to the process of gradual expansion of participatory democracy that was envisaged by Dr. Ambedkar. In other words, because people are excluded most of the time from the democratic process and even have limited ability to exercise their right to vote, because they do not have adequate information about the different parties, sometimes may be even physically prevented from voting. Therefore, their concerns and basic social issues tend to count for very little.

I want to illustrate this point with reference to the coverage of social issues in the media which can be seen as one indicator of how much importance is given to these matters and for this purpose I recently did a survey of opinion articles that were published on the editorial page of the Hindu over a period of six months. The Hindu is one of the best English medium newspapers. In fact, if there is one newspaper in this country which has a little bit of social orientation, I think, it is the Hindu. So if you were to look for media attention to social issues such as Social Security or health or education, I think you would look for it in the Hindu. Now as it turned out, over this period of six months, some three hundred articles were published on the Editorial page-there are usually two every day. So in six months, it will be about three hundred articles and out of these three hundred articles, there were three articles concerned with elementary education, two articles on poverty, one on human rights, and not a single article about health or nutrition as if Indian population is perfectly healthy and well nourished and there was no need to talk about it. This is in contrast with more than twenty articles about nuclear weapons alone-so there were more articles on nuclear weapons over that period than there were about education, poverty, human rights, health, gender and the environment put together. This is one indication of the state of affairs.

It is in this context of very serious marginalization of peoples' basic concerns in the media and more broadly in democratic politics I think it is very important to put greater emphasis on economic and social rights. Economic and social rights can be seen as a kind of built-in safeguard against this insensitivity of the system towards peoples' basic needs. It is a way of elevating the importance of these issues in democratic politics. It strengthens the bargaining power of the underprivileged. The assertion of rights can also help to debunk the myth that public facilities like health, education are unaffordable and it also makes a clean sweep of the need to justify public intervention in these fields on a case by case basis.

To this you may object that we have been talking about rights for so many years, starting with the Universal Declaration of Human rights and the Indian Constitution, and in more recent years, a lot of literature on the right to development, the right approach to development and all sorts of International conventions and papers and consultancies and so on and so forth and you may wonder if it actually makes a difference. My sense is, sometimes it does, and India is one country where I think there are interesting examples involving economic and social rights which have made a difference or at least, it has been shown that it can make a difference. I want, therefore, to proceed with a couple of examples of that before coming to the right to food, specifically.

I think one example of productive invoking the rhetoric of rights is the right to education. I think there is much greater recognition today of elementary education as a Fundamental Right of all Indian children than there was as recently as ten years ago In fact, if you look at debates on education policy, you will see that ten years ago, there was hardly any discussion on the Right to Education. The main focus was on compulsory education, whether it was the right thing or not to compel parents to send their children to school. In 1991, a very influential book, called, 'The Child in the State in India' was published authored by a professor in MIT and that triggered a lot of debate on compulsory education. Over time, in the last ten years, there has been a very healthy shift of attention away from compulsory education towards the Right to Education. This is not to say that compulsory education is not important. It may be important, it may be a useful means of making the Right to Education a reality. Once the facilities are in place, you may argue that it is important to make education compulsory because it sends a clear message to the parents that it is not up to them to decide. They have a duty as Indian citizens to send their children to school. I am not dismissing the importance of compulsory education. But I do not think one can start from there. I think the Right to Education as a foundation for education policies is a much more useful concept and compulsory education can be derived from that but the Right to Education is much more important. As I said there is greater recognition of that today. In fact, the Right to Education recently has become a Fundamental Right. I think this recognition of elementary education as a Fundamental Right of all children has played a part in the comparatively rapid expansion of education in the '90s to an extent that would have been quite unexpected ten years ago There has been quite a rapid improvement in school attendance to the extent that something like 80 per cent of all 6–14 age group children are attending school, which is, of course, still far from 100 per cent. Nevertheless, much higher than the corresponding figure ten years ago and also higher than what most people would have expected to be the case today. There has been also quite a considerable increase in literacy in the younger age groups, a reduction of gender bias, a big expansion of school participation in the educationally backward States of North India. These are all positive developments which, I think, have something to do with this wider recognition of the Right to Education. For example, if we find a village today without a school, I think everyone will immediately agree that a school has to be provided without delay. We do not have to argue any more. We do not have to say it costs so much and the benefits will be so much. Is it worth it? Is it not worth it? I think it is accepted that it is something that has to be done and that there are certain minimum norms that have to be fulfilled.

Another example, which is, I think, perhaps more interesting, is the Right to Information which is very crucial for Participatory Democracy. Anyone who has worked in rural India would be familiar with the tremendous disempowerment that people feel in all kinds of contexts, because of the lack of information and lack of access to public records. For example, people may have a ration card, but do not know what they are supposed to get from the card They may borrow from the banks without knowing what interest they have to pay. They may have to vote without knowing what the different parties stand for. Even more extreme example which I recently came across both in UP and in MP was of people who had been given land but they did not know what rights they had on that land. They had recently received *Pattas* for land through some kind of land reforms programme. But they did not know where the land was because they did not have access to the land records. The local Gram Sevak or Tehsildar, or whoever it was, refused to tell them where their land was unless they paid a big bribe which they were unable to pay. There are many such examples of how the lack of information disempowers people.

One answer to this is to deal with the problem on a case by case approach. We may say that we shall insist that there is a board in the ration shop showing what articles are there and what articles the people can draw under the PDS. We shall take the people to the tehsildar and ask him to show us where the land allotted to a person is. We shall go to the bank and find out the rate of interest on the amount borrowed; and so on But that is not practical. I think the real inspiration for the Right to Information movement was to see that there is a kind of across the board solution whereby every citizen has, once and for all, a right of access to all public records. That was the inspiration of the Right to Information movement which started initially, mainly, in Rajasthan and is now spreading to many other parts of the country to the extent that there is now, if I am not mistaken, a proposal to have a legislation at the national level on the subject through the Right to Information Bill which is before Parliament. I think this it will have an impact.

Just to give you one small example. Two years ago, I was working in the drought affected areas of Rajasthan and I was very much interested to learn that by all accounts, corruption in relief works had not been completely eradicated but certainly considerably reduced. If we look back to the drought of 1987, which was of similar intensity in Rajasthan, there used to be a very widespread practice whereby the Sarpanch, the Gram Sewak and /or the BDO would put fake names in the muster rolls and misappropriate the wages that were due to the fake labourers. That practice now seems to have ended. That is so for two reasons: one is that people now have a right of access to the muster rolls; you can see them; everyone can see them-in complete contrast with the earlier situation where it would have been a crime to see the same records. Ten years ago if you had been in possession of these muster rolls, you would have been actually breaking the law. Now it is the reverse. Everyone has a right to consult these records and it is not that everyone does it. It is not that in every village there are people who are busy scrutinizing the records; but it does happen in sufficiently large number of places that the officials who are running these programmes have to be careful about what they are doing; so one thing that has made the difference is this law on Right to Information. The other thing is that through the Right to Information movement, a culture of public vigilance has evolved so that people know that there is a law, they can use the law and occasionally they do use it and, therefore, it has become extremely risky now for the officials to continue with the practice of putting fake names in the muster rolls. That does not mean that corruption in Rajasthan has been eradicated. That is not the case at all. But it does show the kind of possibility that would have been hard to imagine ten years ago and that also indicates that much more can be done in that direction.

Right to Food

As you all know, we live in a very strange and shocking situation today in India which may be called hunger amidst plenty, where on the one hand, India is one of the most undernourished countries in the world and on the other hand this is happening under the shadow of enormous food stocks. According to recent data published in the World Development Report and the Human Development Report, no country has higher levels of undernourishment than India except possibly Bangladesh. I shall just mention a few statistics for those of you who are not familiar with the situation. According to the National Family Survey of 1998-99, 47 per cent of Indian children were undernourished in terms of weight per age criteria, 34 per cent of Indian babies were born with low birth weight, 52 per cent of adult women in India suffered from anaemia going up to 80 per cent. If you looked at pregnant women, 36 per cent of adult women had a body mass below 18.5 per cent. I am told that the WHO considers 40 per cent BMI as a famine situation. So it is almost like the Indian population is in a permanent state of famine according to the WHO criteria. There is also some interesting data from the same survey, though; somewhat less known, data on morbidity among young children which indicates, for instance, that at the time of the survey, 30 per cent of young children had fever, 20 per cent had diarrhea and another 20 per cent were suffering from severe cough. So something like at least half of Indian children are suffering from fever, or cough or diarrhea and of course much of it is due to undernourishment. So that is one side of the situation. On the other side we have the gigantic foodstocks which went up to something like 65 million tonnes not so long ago. They have come down a little bit now because of the drought that has prevailed in large parts of the country. Today it is about 40 million tonnes, it is going to go up again to 55 may be 60 million tonnes after the Rabi harvest because the Government is all set to procure another 20 million tonnes in Punjab and Haryana and Western U.P. during the next few weeks. It is so large and sometimes difficult to realize what is involved. One way to think about it is something like one tonne of food for every poor family. So it is like every poor family has one tonne of food locked in their backyard and they were not able to access it because Government is keeping it under lock and key. It is also worth remembering that the food subsidy today is close to Rs. 30,000 crores which represents about Rs. 20 a day per poor family. Incredible expenditure which is unfortunately achieving very little, in terms of protecting people from hunger. So there is a colossal failure of the food security system, which is, of course, integral, and a very important component of the Social Security system in the broad sense of the term. It is in this context that I think it is important to invoke the Right to Food because in an obvious sense the situation is a violation of Right to Food which is a part of the Directive Principles of the Constitution. In fact the Constitution talks nothing about the Right to Food but about the Right to Nutrition which is an even more interesting and advanced concept. I think it is by highlighting this aspect of the situation-this massive violation of the Right to Food - that we can hope to ensure that the problem receives the attention that it deserves-as has been happening. I think, to some extent, in the last two years.

What exactly do we mean by the Right to Food and how is it to be realized? These questions are not easy to answer and I think there is a fundamental sense in which the Right to Food is a more complex kind of right than, let us say, the Right to Education, or the Right to Information. The main reason for this is that in the case of Right to Food, the relevant entitlements and responsibilities are less clearly defined. In the case of the Right to Information, for instance, the entitlements are reasonably clear that every citizen should have a right of access to public records; may be there might be some exceptions like records relating to National Security and so on but the basic entitlements are reasonably clear and so are the corresponding responsibilities. We are saying that every government office has a duty to part with these public records if they are asked to do so by any citizen and if they do not do that, then there can be some kind of legal action or sanction. In other words, from the fact that the entitlements and responsibilities are well defined, it also follows that the Right to Information is largely justiciable, namely, enforceable in a Court of Law. And to some extent the scene applies also to the Right to Education. Of course, one can argue about what the precise reach and boundaries of the Right to Education are but there are certain basic aspects of it that are fairly uncontroversial. For example, we would all agree that if there were a Right to Education, then there should be a school within reasonable distance of every village and so on and again these entitlements are well defined; so are the responsibilities, and therefore the rights to a large extent, are justiciable.

In the case of the Right to Food, the situation is more complex. Broadly speaking, the Right to Food can be thought of as a right to be free from hunger. It is a claim of the individual on Society. That means the right to Food is an assertion that society has enough resources, both physical and institutional, to prevent hunger and to ensure that nobody goes hungry. The responsibility for protecting this Right is primarily the responsibility of the State, since the State commands the required resources and is generally responsible for the welfare of the citizens. However, the Right to Food is not only the responsibility of the State. For example, if we believe that there is such a thing as the Right to Food, and if, for example, we see somebody in the street who is starving I do not think we can just walk away and say, "Well, this is the responsibility of the State. It has nothing to do with me." I think if you are in a position to do something, you would have to do that. Similarly, if a girl is undernourished because she does not get a fair share of food within the family, I think that would be a situation where her Right to Food is violated. but the main responsibility for that may not be with the State, it may be with her parents. This example also brings out that the Right to Food is not always justiciable, is not always enforceable in a court of law because in this case, if a girl is neglected within the family, I doubt if the best answer would be to take her parents to court or even threaten them with legal action.

So then does the Right to Food have any teeth? If it is not enforceable in a court of law, does it really help us to do something about the problem of endemic hunger in India? My answer on the whole is, " Yes". I would like to conclude with some illustrations of how the Right to Food can make a difference even though it would be a mistake to think that the whole problem of endemic hunger in India can be addressed through the Rights based approach. There are certain aspects of it which are not easily answerable by invoking the law. Some examples of what I mean here.

Firstly, I think that some aspects of Right to Food are justiciable and some aspects are not. It is important to seek legal enforcements where it is possible. In fact, there has been some interesting demonstration of the justiciability of some aspects of the Right to Food in the context of the recent Supreme Court hearing in this matter which began in April 2001 with a petition by the PUCL in Rajasthan. The hearings have been going on for a couple of years and they may continue for a while before a judgement is reached. In the meantime there have been useful interim orders. For example, there is an order dated 28th of November, 2001, which directs all the State Governments to provide cooked mid-day meals in all primary schools. Now that seems to me to be an interesting case where an aspect of food has been incorporated in the Law. Some people feel uncomfortable about judicial intervention in these matters. They say, "Well, this is really a matter of policy; it is not for the courts to tell the Government whether there should be mid-day meals in schools or not". I can understand the skepticism. I have seen the court process from fairly close quarters in the last two years and I think it does have important limitations. But I think this is a case where judicial intervention was actually justified because this was a case where fundamental Rights of Children, of the Right to Education, Right to Food were involved. This was a case where it was a really obvious way of redressing a bad situation of poor attendance in schools. If providing a meal in the school could really have a big effect on school attendance and it could also ensure that the children could have some protection against hunger, or at least that they were not forced to study on an empty stomach., the case was reasonably clear, that the Court was justified in intervening even though it put a certain financial burden on the State governments. So I think this is one interesting case where it seems that it has been possible to protect the Right to Food.

The second example I would like to mention is the case of the Antyodaya Anna(dana) Yojana programme of Food Based Social Security for the destitute which I hope you are familiar with. It is essentially a scheme which involves identifying destitute households in rural areas through Gram Panchayats and Gram Sabhas and such other institutions and giving them special ration cards which entitles them to, at the moment, 35 kilos of grain per month from the PDS at very low prices, Rs. 2 per kilo for wheat and Rs. 3 per kilo for rice. These are fairly substantial entitlements, the coverage of the scheme at the moment is something like 10 million families or about 5 crore persons. It is not negligible by any means and I think it is an interesting initiative in the field of Social Security in India today. We did an evaluation of this programme almost a year ago in five states and we found that, on the whole, the programme was doing quite well especially in contrast with the PDS as a whole in the same States. We found that most of the households that had these cards were indeed destitute households; in other words, the community-based identification of beneficiaries had worked reasonably well. We found that there was comparatively little corruption in the programme and most of the households were getting the rations they were entitled to. Having said that there is one important limitation which is that the coverage of the programme is much smaller than it should be. We should be aiming at protecting all destitute households from destitution and one answer to that or at least one partial answer to that would be to give certain categories of people an entitlement to this programme as a matter of right. For example, we know that widows in rural India are among the most deprived.

If there is a household headed by a widow, it is almost certainly a very poor household. It is not always the case but we know from a fair amount of evidence that a large majority of households headed by widows are facing acute poverty and deprivation. So why not give all these households Antyodaya cards as a matter of right? Similarly, we know that among the so-called primitive tribes like the Sahariyas, there are enormous levels of poverty and deprivation. Most households, in these communities live in conditions of extreme poverty. So why not give all these households within these pre-specified groups a legal entitlement to access to the Antyodaya programme? I think that will be one way of using the problem of exclusion of some households from the coverage of the programme

Finally I want to say a few words about the Right to Work because the Right to Work is very closely linked with the Right to Food. Ultimately, I think, the best guarantee of protecting people from hunger would be some sort of guaranteed employment as has been done to some extent to the State of Maharashtra with the introduction of the Employment Guarantee Scheme almost 30 years ago. It is interesting to contrast the experience of the Employment Guarantee Scheme or more accurately we should say the Employment Guarantee Act because the Scheme is defined by an Act which is legally in force with that of employment programmes like the Sampurna Gramin Swarozgar Yojana which are of a more ad hoc nature. The Sampurna Gramin Swarozgar Yojana was introduced in the context of the Supreme Court hearing on the Right to Food. It was a kind of quick response from the Central Government to the petition in an attempt to preempt, further action in the Court by pointing out that the government was doing something about it and that hunger was going to be prevented. Unfortunately, the record of this programme of the Sampurna Gramin Swarozgar Yojana is very poor; the main flaw is that it is not any kind of guarantee; it is just a kind of ad hoc programme which comes from above; there are no incentives for the State Governments to co-operate with it. It has not given people any bargaining power. It has nothing to ensure predictability and availability of employment. It leaves the allocation of work in different districts or different areas completely arbitrary. And all this contrasts very much with what happens with the Employment Guarantee Scheme; because if there is an employment guarantee, then the people have bargaining power; the work is generated where it is most needed because that is where people will come out and demand for work. It also means that there is more predictability, people know what their rights are and, therefore, for example, there is less migration. If the people do not know whether they will get employment or not; then the temptation is to migrate and look for work elsewhere and that is what we are seeing now on a massive scale in drought affected areas of Rajasthan, Madhya Pradesh and elsewhere. People are not sure whether they will get work or not and, therefore, they tend not to take a chance and migrate to urban areas to look for whatever employment they can get there. So I think there is a strong case for extending the Employment Guarantee approach to all States. Of course, that will involve a fairly substantial financial burden. In Maharashtra, if I am not mistaken, the Employment Guarantee Scheme costs something like 15 per cent of the State Domestic Product. A corresponding scheme at the All India level would cost probably something like 1.2–2 per cent of India's GDP which is not a small amount at all. But it is not more than, in fact, it is much less than what is being spent today on the food subsidy and fertilizer subsidy, not to speak of the power subsidy. So I think it is a question of reallocation of priorities and of making the resources available. For a programme which is so important in terms of providing Social Security to all and protecting everybody from deprivation the price tag is not excessive.

In other words, recent experience shows that some useful steps can be taken to make the Right to Food a reality. If we are serious about freedom from hunger, which is a basic right of all citizens, then a number of basic steps would immediately suggest themselves which are not being taken today. For instance, if we really believe in food being a right of all citizens, then we would want to ensure that all citizens are well informed of their entitlements which is far from the case today. We would want to give these entitlements a legal backing wherever possible, which again is not being done except in some confined instances like the mid-day meal programme. We would put in place strong accountability mechanisms that protect the social security system from corruption and abuse which again is not being done. There is rampant corruption, for example, in the PDS. We would give people the means of seeking redress when their entitlements are violated and we would even arrange for compensation in situations where they have not received their due. As it stands, none of these safeguards is in place and therefore the Right to Food is out of reach of a large section of the population.

On a more positive note, because I would like to end my talk on a positive note, it seems to me that the situation in which we find ourselves today, of hunger amidst plenty and of endemic hunger with massive food stocks – aside from being a massive violation of the Right to Food, it can also be seen as an unprecedented opportunity to create lasting food entitlements. The absurdity of the situation has created a new awareness of the problem of endemic hunger in India as we can see for instance on the dramatic increase of media coverage on this issue in the last few years. The massive costs of excess food stocks have also created a new willingness on the part of the Government, to make use of these food stocks to prevent hunger through programmes like mid-day meals, Antyodaya, Food for Work. All these programmes have increased quite considerably in the last two years and there is an important opportunity here to convert these short-term initiatives into permanent entitlements, as has already been done in the case of the mid-day meal programme.

By way of conclusion, let me simply reiterate the need to remember and revive Dr. Ambedkar's ambitious dreams for India's future. More than 50 years after the Constitution he drafted came into effect, it is clear that his revolutionary vision of democracy has not been realized. Even the basic Constitutional rights he saw as a pre-condition for genuine democracy are yet to be fulfilled, but as I have tried to illustrate, the situation is not immutable and it belongs to all of us to change it.

15.

Revamping of ESI Scheme

SEPTEMBER 2004

Dr. Ajay Dua

Director General, Employees State Insurance Corporation

Revamping has, to my mind, two distinct elements: one is making the present scheme more effective, improving its productivity, efficiency, etc; and second, extending the coverage of the scheme because today we are covering only about 70 lakh persons in a country which has a workforce of 370-380 million (37-38 crore). While we address today in this seminar various issues I would think that these two elements will be at the back of our minds. When we talk about revamping, very briefly, what we have been concerned about are these two issues. As we move towards universal coverage of Social Security, we think it is possible to bring more people under the ESIC fold itself

The first step in that direction, would be to reduce the threshold limit from twenty workers which is there today, or ten workers in the case of factories using power, to five workers uniformly

Secondly, more and more sectors of establishments should be brought under the fold of the ESI scheme. Today, the scheme is applicable to shops, cinema houses, hotels and restaurants, newspapers and motor transport undertakings, apart from factories. Lately the Services Sector have expanded very widely. The ESIC and the Government have recently approved a proposal to extend the scheme to educational institutions which constitute an important constituent of the service sector. We have been following this matter with the State Governments. Two or three State Governments have agreed so far. The others are still considering it. There is another proposal to extend the scheme to workers of medical institutions. There may be a large number of hospitals, private nursing homes, etc., but the workers employed there are not at all entitled to medical care for themselves and their families in those establishments where they are

A symposium was organised by the Association.

employed. So we think that more and more such classes of establishments need to be covered. We should get to a stage where there is no distinction today among manufacturing industries. Anybody who undertakes a manufacturing process with the specified number of employees should be covered under the ESI Scheme. Similarly, all shops, all establishments, all services, irrespective of our having to name them, need to be brought under the coverage of the ESIC.

> An Annual Conference was held on the 24th of September 2004 to coincide with the Annual General meeting of the Association when a Symposium was held on "Revamping of the ESI Scheme". Sh. Sanat Mehta presided. Dr. Ajay Dua, DG, ESIC, delivered the key not address Dr. P.D.Shenoy delivered the valedictory address. There was lively discussion following the presentation of the papers. The addresses by Dr. Ajay Dua, Dr. P.D.Shenoy and the remarks made by Sh. Sanat Mehta, Sh. Parduman Singh and others in their intervention are reproduced below.

Third, which is a more fundamental proposal I am making today, relates to the geographical coverage of the coverage. Today, the ESI scheme is applicable only to identified geographical pockets. Every pocket where ESI scheme can be brought into force, has to be notified in the Gazette of India and the State Government Gazette. We are at present covering about seven hundred geographical pockets but many more are left out. The areas not covered are larger than the areas covered. I think the time has come to make the Scheme applicable to all urban areas of the country. We have done a very quick exercise about the impact of such a proposal There are at present one thousand six hundred and sixty three municipalities in the country. Of these, only three hundred and eighty five municipalities are covered under the Scheme; the remaining one thousand three hundred odd municipalities are left out of our fold. There are one hundred and seventy nine municipal corporations of which only one hundred and twenty two are covered. So in fifty seven corporations, ESI scheme is not applicable. (Bigger towns have Corporations and smaller towns have municipalities of different classes – A class, B Class and C Class.) I think instead of going through the whole exercise of identifying the geographical areas to be covered, getting the approval of the Central and the State Governments, calling for objections and finally issuing notifications making the Scheme applicable in each area separately, we should, by law, make the scheme applicable to all the urban areas, municipal towns of the country and then the ESIC and the State Governments will be enjoined to make necessary arrangements for providing medical benefit to all the people who will be brought under the Scheme. Rural areas may be left out for the present unless some major activity is taken up. There are many growth centers, known as focal points in North India and as growth centers in West and South India, where although they may not be in urban areas, the Scheme may be made applicable after making arrangements for providing medical benefit. If in the Municipal towns, the ESIC has not been able to create its own facilities for providing medical care, it should arrange to provide medical care to the insured persons through other agencies, private or otherwise, that may be in existence there.

A quick estimate is that if action is taken on the lines proposed by me the coverage will go up from 70 lakhs to 1crore 70 lakh workers with an additional coverage of 1 crore persons. So far as medical benefit is concerned, the Scheme is applicable to the insured persons and their families. Assuming an average family size of four persons the total number of beneficiaries will be over 7 crores (1.70 × 4) as against 3 crores at present. Thus these measures would help in providing Social Security coverage to a large number of persons.

Corresponding changes may be made under the EPF Act also. Today, luckily, coverage under the EPF Act is not limited on geographical basis. So that restriction is not there. But there is a threshold limit which is the same as under the ESI Act. When the threshold limit under the ESI Act is reduced, a similar reduction may be made under the EPF Act also so as to retain the uniformity between the EPF and ESIC in this regard.

Another change I propose, and in doing so, I may be moving away from ESIC briefly, is in respect of cess funds under which Social Security is provided. The cess funds (Welfare funds?) have been set up for certain industries. There is no reason why we should not consider covering all hazardous industries under such funds. The fact of the matter is that the workers employed in those industries are exposed to certain risks. and they need to be provided social security and it should necessarily come from those who are engaging them, or the people who are buying their products. Today cess funds exist in respect of about twelve industries; they could easily be extended to all the fifty four hazardous industries which have been notified by the Government of India in the Ministry of Labour. All of them could have Social Security Schemes which are cess funded and this would also promote much larger coverage than what we have today.

What happens if threshold limit is kept below 5? I think a time has come that wherever there is an employer employee relationship, the employer should be enjoined to provide social security to his employee. It need not be ESIC, it need not be EPF, it need not be a cess fund, unless it is a hazardous industry. It could be any agency which has the facilities to provide the benefits; the principal aim being that every employee should have social security. The law needs to be revised to make it mandatory for every employer to provide Social Security, not necessarily through the ESIC or the EPFO.

We have been debating this proposition in the Task Force which the Ministry of Labour has set up. The Task force includes the Director General, Labour Welfare and CPFC. I am also there in addition to two officials of the Ministry. The Task force is toying with the idea that whoever there is an employer he should be required to buy a social security insurance for every one of his employees. That insurance should provide (i) medical care up to Rs. 30,000 per annum and (ii) accident insurance for Rs. 1 lakh. The premium should be paid by the employer to the insurance agency which provides this cover. The workers should be free to have medical care any where of their choice subject to a limit of the cost to Rs. 30,000. It may be an ESIC hospital, or a Government hospital or a private hospital which honours such type of Social Security insurance. We have had a discussion with GIPSA the Association of Public Sector General Insurance Companies whether such a scheme is feasible. The first response was that it would require many more insurance companies than the existing four or five in the public sector. But then they also thought that this was a good opportunity and a market for development of insurance business. The employer would be free to go and scout around for an insurance policy which provides Rs. 30,000 to 1 lakh insurance cover at the cheapest cost from the cheapest source. There would be competition among the insurance companies. One insurance company may quote a premium of Rs. 300, another may quote Rs. 250, and a third one for Rs. 200. He buys the policy from the company quoting the lowest price of Rs. 200. Similarly the worker with that policy goes to any provider and seeks health cover up to Rs. 30,000. So that Rs. 200 becomes the cost of engaging a worker which the employer necessarily builds into his own scheme of things. A very large number of persons could get covered under this arrangement only by a legal provision being made.

ESIC, EPF would not be concerned, but certainly the Labour Inspectorate will be concerned. When they go for an inspection of an establishment they may also check whether every worker employed by an employer has a Social Security insurance cover

Markets will bring about efficiency in the insurance business and also health care arrangements, Coming to the question of making the ESIC Scheme more effective, I shall mention one or two proposals which we are looking at.

One is developing greater synergy between the ESIC and the EPFO. There is no reason why the two organizations should be working in parallel. Each of these organizations has a separate set of inspectors. EPF Inspector goes to check one thing, ESIC Inspector goes to check another. A time has come to integrate this function of the two organizations. After all both these agencies are under the same Ministry. The responsibility of checking whether dues have been paid or not are common to both EPFO and the ESIC. A greater synergy can, therefore, be developed between the two agencies. It will ultimately lead to a single contribution being paid by each employer for social security of his employees which may after receipt be divided between ESIC and EPFO. I think it is possible. There is a group exploring this possibilities with Mr. Chandrasekharan, former Insurance Commissioner, being a consultant for it. I think the efficiency of the Scheme would improve by such synergy, because the number of staff required would become less when the functions of the two organizations are integrated.

The Second Labour Commission has recommended the setting up of the Board of Social Security having two separate wings – one for all cash benefits including, pension benefits, currently administered by the EPFO and the cash benefits of the ESI and the second for medical benefit. ESIC's comparative advantage being in the medical side, it will deal with provision of medical care and the financial arrangements there for and the EPFO will deal with all the cash benefits.

Another issue which needs to be addressed is the duality in provision of medical control. Today, we are in a very happy situation where, if anybody tells us that our medical scheme is not running well, we say, "Look, we only provide the money, the State Governments are responsible. Section 58 of the ESI Act requires the State Governments to provide the medical care. We have given them the equipment and the money, but they are not running it well." They go to the State Government but the State Governments wash their hands, saying, 'We are only agents.' As a result, the workers are being tossed around and the medical care that needs to be provided is not being delivered satisfactorily despite a huge infrastructure, consisting of one hundred and forty four hospitals and three thousand dispensaries. Some quick surveys done through professional agencies show that the level of satisfaction on the medical side is rather low. There may be one or two hospitals whose ratings are high. (We are now getting our hospitals rated). But by and large, the Scheme does show that there is a high degree of dissatisfaction with them. This shows that the issue of duality of control needs to be addressed. There is only one way of addressing the issue. We should recognize that he who is taking money from the workers must also be squarely responsible for delivering the goods that means ESIC is squarely responsible for it. If a State Government is doing well and feels it can continue to do so the Corporation may use that State Government. If it cannot, the ESIC has to make other arrangements including direct provision for giving health care. In either event, the workers should not be tossed between two agencies, two highly impersonal agencies. Hitherto, it was alright. But we can no longer absolve ourselves of the responsibility to deliver by passing on the buck to the State Governments.

Finally, I think the time has come when we should not force anybody to accept the benefit package of the ESI Scheme, in its entirety. That means people should have the option to insure themselves for one or more cash benefits, or for medical benefit only or for a combination of benefits. Such a choice is necessary particularly when the quality of medical care which we provide has not shown over the years to be very satisfactory. If we keep on saying that we shall not extend the scheme to new areas or new classes of establishments till such time as medical care is improved, that time may never come. We should face this reality.

When the question came for raising the wage ceiling from Rs. 6,500 to Rs. 10,000 corresponding to the rise in the cost of living index (Rs. 9,700 was the equivalent of Rs. 6,500 on 1-4-2004). The Corporation and the Government decided to raise it only up to Rs. 7,500. They felt that since there was a great deal of dissatisfaction about the provision of medical care, people would not accept a higher rise in the wage ceiling. In the circumstances, if we were to unbundle the benefit package there will be greater flexibility in the administration of the Scheme. If in a particular area the medical scheme is not running well, the persons will have the choice not to come to us for medical care. If they think the cash benefits are good enough, let them have the cash benefits only. But today, the law does not allow such unbundling. So it needs to be amended to give option to the insured persons to select the benefits they insure for.

In the final analysis, I think, we need to move towards a stage where joining the ESIC Scheme itself becomes optional. All are agreed that social security has to be provided to the workers but they should have the option to get the social security cover from the ESIC, or from some one else.

In the year 1948 when the ESI Act was enacted probably there was no alternative to the State providing the services because the necessary infrastructure was not there outside the Government. But things have changed since then. Today, we no longer have the monopoly. The fact that the employers had no option but to insure themselves with the ESIC has affected our efficiency. It was bound to. Monopolies have that problem everywhere. Unless there is an element of competition things donot improve. We need to talk about how to introduce competition, but there can be no doubt that competition is necessary if the Scheme has to be revamped.

Sanat Mehta

Former Minister of Finance and Labour, Gujarat;
currently, President Social Security Association of India

I was very happy to hear Dr. Ajay Dua's unorthodox views.

Some twenty years back, when I was Labour Minister of Gujarat, I was very keen that the ESI Scheme should be decentralized. I was confident that if it was decentralized I could see that Gujarat became No. 1 in coverage and in the delivery of services of both medical as well as other benefits. But my proposal was not accepted. A committee was formed and then I do not know what happened. From there we have travelled far. The problems are becoming more difficult as far as the health services are concerned.

Health has always been considered as a key sector by all the Governments. The recent Common Minimum Programme has mentioned that Universal Health Insurance Scheme would be the main route for providing health care to the large masses of people. On the one hand, we are talking about the Universal Health Insurance Scheme, and on the other, as Mr. Dua said, we want the ESI Scheme to be extended down the line to the Unorganised Sector where the workers do not have enough income even for two meals a day; we want to offer them different packages of contributory schemes. How practical would it be?

The Common Minimum Programme focuses on development in the areas of education and health. I want to tell you about how such programmes work which may shock you.

I am staying in Baroda. Recently, I was working among the tribal people of Gujarat. I went to some tribal villages and found that the literacy level in those villages was zero. Then I looked into the statistics of growth in literacy. I selected forty three villages and compared the figures of development of literacy in those villages between 1990 and 2000. You will be shocked to know that within the period of ten years only one man had become literate! There is a primary school, there is a teacher and salary is being paid to him all along but only one man was made literate in ten years! I could not believe my eyes and I cursed myself that although I was the State Planning and Finance Minister for some time and though I was in Baroda, 120 km. from Ahmedabad, the situation was like this. So, to my mind, when we talk of any service to the people, the basic problem is how to take the service to the poor.

Services are there, the teacher is there, the school is there. Ten years passed, and if only one man is made literate in that village, whom should we blame? What are the ways? There are no shortcuts – I decided that I select a boy from the village, irrespective of his education and pay him

Rs. 500 per month. and make him the teacher. I told the villagers, 'You select the boy. Let him educate the village. He will work as a catalyst. He will not quarrel with the Government'. Within one year, I have got one hundred times more literate people in that village than a permanent teacher. So when I heard Mr. Dua saying that the packages will be voluntary, it will be optional, I think now we are understanding the right meaning of service. We should give service to the people in the manner in which they can avail of it.

I have my doubt if Mr. Chidambaram will be able collect 5000 crores for literacy and whether the programmes will make any dent in the rural areas. I am afraid that all those who are already educated will get further educated but those who are not, will remain illiterate.

So if you want to expand Social Security or Health Insurance or ESI, covering more and more workers, the real question we have to tackle is, how to take services to the poor.

I have some interesting figures relating to incidence of absenteeism among teachers and healthcare workers in public facilities. I shall quote some examples. In primary schools, the incidence of absenteeism of teachers is 15 per cent and in the case of health workers it is nearly 40 per cent. In India, 25 per cent of the teachers do not go to the school at all and 40 per cent of the health visitors do not go to the primary health centers at all. When I was Labour Minister I tried to make some improvement but it has not been of much avail.

So far as the ESI scheme I had never had any quarrel with the Corporation about money. I was more worried about the services provided by the Corporation. Hospitals were built – very large buildings – and when I visited them I found the conditions very bad. It was not the money, it was not the doctor, it was the facilities which they were providing, which were lacking. We had never planned properly as to how we were to go from one end to the other. So in my view, when you expand the services you have to think of how the services may be taken to the people – to the poor people.

Once I approached Rajiv Gandhi when he was the Prime Minister and I asked him 'Rajivji, you find out something that helps the poor very fast'. He said, 'You give me one suggestion' and I gave him. Let us have an insurance scheme for landless labour. He immediately on telephone asked the concerned Secretary to give Rs. 100 crores to the LIC, for the group insurance premium of the landless labour. But when I went to the ground level, years later, I found that the LIC was not interested at all in the insurance scheme for landless because the whole system was based on the insurance agent who would not get any commission. So he was not interested in the Scheme. That money could not be spent. Rajiv Gandhi gave Rs. 100 crores to the LIC for payment of the premium but it could not be spent. The service did not go to the poor.

The second point which is worrying me is, that along with the Minimum Common Programme having a Universal Health Insurance Scheme we are also talking now of promoting "Destination India" or "Health Destination" for the foreign clients. These are the exact words of the Tourism Minister. In Gujarat, our Chief Minister is toying with the idea of developing health tourism. What is this? We are pulling ourselves in another direction. It will increase the cost of medical care. We have faced this problem before. When we were providing medical benefit under the ESI. Scheme there were criticisms that our services were not good and that service in private hospitals was better. Now we are going in for a highly sophisticated, high technology based hospitals and more and more private people are coming in the health sector just to make profit. Now hospital is no more the work of a doctor. Now the builders have started going into the health sector. How will you compete with them? How will you protect your client from that aggression? It is going to be a very difficult problem. The Finance Ministry is giving a lot of concession for encouraging health tourism. To my mind it is adversely affecting the health service to the poor which you are trying to provide through your insurance scheme. This was not a problem in 1980-1985 when I was the Minister. At that time there were instances when I used to tell the private hospitals that the ESI hospitals were providing better services than they. Now it is doubtful whether within our limitations we will be able to say that. So this is a very challenging problem and that is worrying many people who are studying this Health Insurance Scheme under Social Security.

The third factor is that while promoting Health Tourism no thought has been given to the question of regulating it. In the health sector, we do not have adequate regulatory framework. Anybody can do anything. There is no regulation at all.

It is very good that we are trying to promote Social Security. I always believed in Social Security. I introduced the Group Insurance Scheme for Landless Labour. I had invited the then Chairman of the LIC, Mr. Joshi, to distribute the death compensation to the families of certain landless labourers who had died. He was not ready to believe whether it was possible to run a scheme of that kind. When he saw the poor widows taking Rs. 1000 or Rs. 2000 with tears in their eyes Mr. Joshi told me, 'Sir, I never understood the meaning of your Insurance Scheme for Landless Labour, giving Rs. 1000 or Rs. 2000 until I saw the beneficial effect on the poor today".

We are working in a very difficult situation. It is not important for me whether you are reducing the threshold limit from 20 to 10 and from

10 to 5 and. whether you are covering all the people. Once upon a time, that was our dream. On the Labour Day every year we used to make announcements about the extension of the ESI Scheme Today our worry is –when you talk of increasing the wage ceiling for coverage under the Scheme whether the people who are brought under cover will be benefited. Let us be very clear.

ONGC workers who are getting very large salaries do not want to be in the ESI Scheme. They are getting very good medical care under the facilities provided by the employer. They come to me and ask me and to get them exemption from the ESI Scheme. I am happy that the ESIC is becoming a little flexible. But you should consider, by becoming flexible, to what extent your economy and finances will be affected. That is going to be a very important factor.

These are the points which require a lot of work.

When we discuss the various aspects of coverage, decentralization and related matters we should not forget that we are working in an economy – what is called the market economy, the liberalized economy. As the current trend grows it is going to be increasingly difficult for public sector programmes to function. Already, talks are going on for dismantling many public services. Some time back a question was raised: why is there a Planning Commission? There is no need of Planning Commission at all. Tomorrow somebody may say, why ESI should exist at all. In this situation, when you express your views, kindly take into account the reality. Our target should be the last man, the lowest man; we should co-ordinate all our activities to see that the man who is in dire need and cannot provide for himself is taken care of. Perhaps ESI can render such a service but it has to find its own way to help him.

R.K.A. Subrahmanya

Former Additional Secretary, Government of India and
former Secretary General, Social Security Association of India

It is common knowledge that services in the ESI Hospitals have not been entirely to the satisfaction of the workers and the expression of dissatisfaction has been made in very strong terms in certain cases. In this context I would like to place before this audience one important development that has taken place in this country. Madhya Pradesh has developed a practice regarded as one of the best practices in the governance of public services-that is, the appointment of what they call Rogi Kalyan Samitis for each public hospital in Madhya Pradesh. This started some years ago when there was a threat of plague epidemic in Indore After Surat in Gujarat was hit by the epidemic it was apprehended it might spread to other states also. At that time, the General Hospital in Indore was in a very bad state. The Collector of the district took the initiative for appropriate action. He invited the citizens of the city for a discussion, took them into confidence and told them about the state of affairs and what was needed to be done to set things right. He also told them that the government had no money and requested them to make necessary contributions. The people realized what was at stake and made liberal contributions for carrying out necessary improvements in the hospital. They appointed a committee called the Rogi Kalyan Samiti to supervise the work. With that money and with the help of that committee, the hospital was spruced up and the condition of the hospital changed significantly. Services were improved and now it has become almost a model hospital for the entire State. Based on that experience, the Government of Madhya Pradesh adopted a resolution to appoint a people's committee to supervise the working of every public hospital in the State. Hospital management in the State has undergone a metamorphosis. This experiment is being extended to other areas of public administration. Other States have also adopted this practice. Karnataka is, I believe, thinking of appointing, or has already appointed, Arogya Kalyan Samiti for each hospital. I would like you to consider whether similar committees can be appointed for each of the hospitals of the ESIC making the insured persons or the beneficiaries share the responsibility of administering the hospitals. I would like this suggestion to be discussed here and if you all agree make a recommendation to the Corporation for necessary action

I have two other suggestions to make for making the ESI services to be available to the unorganised sector.

One is this: at present, there are a number of Welfare funds set up by the Central as well as the State Governments for the unorganized sector employments. There are proposals to set up more such Welfare Funds. In course of time, may be one or two welfare Funds will be set up. The practice so far has been, whenever it is set up, each Welfare Fund tries to set up its own hospitals and dispensaries- for example, beedi, mine workers- for all these they have their own hospitals. Establishments of such hospitals and dispensaries for each of these funds is not a desirable thing. They will never be able to provide the kind of service that is required by them. Actually the level of expenditure that is incurred on Beedi Workers in the hospitals run by the Beedi Welfare Fund is so low, it is hardly about Rs. 30 per capita or something like that, whereas in ESI you are spending something like Rs. 600 to Rs. 700 per capita on the average. So the kind of service provided by the Welfare Funds through their hospitals has not been satisfactory. Therefore, I have been advocating that the Welfare Funds should establish a linkage with the ESIC and the workers covered by them. Welfare Funds should provide medical care through the ESI hospitals and the cost should be met out of the Funds. The ESIC has worked out the average cost of medical care for purpose of reimbursing the expenditure incurred by the State governments. The Welfare funds may also be required to make payment at the same rates.

Another suggestion is: today you must have read in the newspapers that the National Advisory Council to the Prime Minister has made a recommendation that all the workers in the unorganized sector should be covered under the Health Insurance Scheme. There is already a Health Insurance Scheme called Universal Medical Insurance Scheme. I do not know whether the recommendation is to start a new scheme, or the same scheme will be modified or extended to the others. In either case, most probably, this scheme will be administered by the GIPSA i.e., the Public Sector General Insurance Companies. My suggestion is that the ESIC should join the Scheme. I have always wondered why the ESIC cannot undertake a general health insurance scheme in competition with other insurance companies It requires a measure of flexibility in your Legislative Cover. The ESIC is governed by the ESI Act, which limits its activities to the organized sector where there is an employer and an employee and both are required to make contributions at specified rates. The object clause of the Act needs to be widened to enable the ESIC to expand its activities to cover the self employed and others and to function as another Public Sector Health Insurance agency. This is one concrete way in which the ESIC may be able to extend its activities to the unorganized sector.

Parduman Singh

Vice-President, AITUC
Former President, Social Security Association of India

I have been a member of the Regional Committee for twenty to thirty years. I have an intimate knowledge of how the ESIC works. I am not happy with it at all. I shall mention a few points based on my personal experience.

One is the geographical coverage. I have been fighting for long that geographical coverage of municipal committees or corporations is not sufficient. If you go by road in any state there are a large number of industries, coming up between towns If the coverage is limited to municipal limits many of the units outside those limits will be left out. My suggestion is that coverage should be industry wise. All industries employing a specified number of workers should be covered.

The second point about coverage relates to the threshold limit. All political parties, talk about coverage of all people. My suggestion is that the threshold limit should be reduced from 20 to ten in the first instance and after some time it may be further reduced to five or less. You cannot suddenly reduce the limit from 20 to one. These remarks apply to the EPFO as well.

My third point is about Medical Benefit. All the complaints against the ESIC relate to the administration of the Medical Benefit. No one comes in time. In some cases the doctor comes earlier than the other staff. He opens the door of the dispensaries Service is very poor. The dichotomy between the state governments and the Corporation has been affecting the quality of service adversely It has to be done away with. The financial position of most State governments is not good. The money that the ESIC pays for providing medical care to the insured persons is utilised by the governments for other purposes and there would be no money for expenditure on providing medical benefit.

The fourth point is about the panel system. I remember when the ESI Scheme was started in 1952, there were only panel doctors that was called the panel system. Subsequently the ESIC established its own hospitals and dispensaries at several places. That was called the service system. Where these systems are working exclusively the insured persons are not satisfied with either system. My suggestion is to have a combination of both. If a worker does not get service from one he may go the other system I am against privatization of the medical care system of the ESIC entirely

All private hospitals are not like Escorts and Apollo. There are thousands of private hospitals now. Even in villages a private doctor would be available for a small fee. I, therefore, feel that the ESIC should utilize the services of these private doctors and hospitals for providing medical care under the Scheme.

And my next point is about the Universal Health Insurance Scheme introduced by the Union government. The Scheme has been drawn up by certain gentlemen sitting round a table who have prescribed that the persons insured under the Scheme should pay one rupee a day, that is, 365 rupees a year. Imagine this. Crores of people in this country who have no food to eat are required to make the contribution. How can they give you one rupee, even if they have it? In my opinion the Scheme should be financed by Public Funds. Just now it has been decided to levy a cess for education. I have been writing for over thirty years that a similar cess should be levied for social security. I, therefore, repeat that a similar cess should be levied on all types of products for financing the expenditure on health. Public expenditure on health in India is the lowest in the world. Pakistan spends more than India, not to speak about U.S., U.K., etc. The public expenditure on health in India is 0.9 per cent of the GDP. In Pakistan it is 1 per cent while advanced countries spend upto 6 per cent, of the GDP. It is obvious that the amount of public expenditure on health should be increased. The question will naturally arise where the money for the enhanced expenditure on health will come. I consider that the only way to raise funds for it is to levy a special cess on all direct and indirect taxes.

Finally, I would say that this threshold limit has to be brought down to 5 immediately and eventually to one.

One more thing. That relates to the ESIC and the EPFO functioning separately. Some time back the Additional Secretary in the Ministry of Labour asked me to prepare a paper for combining the two organizations. I prepared a paper and gave it to him. Well, like all papers, and all reports, no action was taken. Actually, there is no need to have a separate local office for the ESI and a separate sub-regional Office for the EPF. These two organizations should be combined immediately. That is my opinion.

Dr. Ajay Dua

(Interruption/Comments)

I think the six suggestions made by Mr. Parduman Singh, are exactly what I probably said and I fully endorse them. Sir, I think I did not clarify the geographical coverage point. All that I said was, that the scheme should continue to be extended from time to time as it is done today to the areas where clusters of economic activities are started with concentration of workers by notifying them. In addition, all the urban areas and cities should be notified at one stroke instead of covering them piecemeal. The moment we do that, all the municipalities numbering about 1660 and all the corporations numbering about 179, will get covered. If there are industrial or other economic activities outside these areas, they will also continue to be covered as at present. That means that the focal points in Punjab, the growth centers in Maharashtra etc. which may be outside the cities will be covered by issue of special notifications. Export Promotion Zones are also areas where economic activities take place and there is a concentration of workers who could be covered.

On all other suggestions made by Sh. Parduman Singh I am one with him.

Let us bring down the threshold limit from 20 to 10, 10 to 5.

We need to do away with the distinction between factories using power and not using power and make the limit common to all types of factories by reducing it to ten to begin with and then reduce it further to 5 and eventually, everybody may be covered under the scheme.

Finally, I agree with the point that has been made about using the ESIC infrastructure for unorganized sector and others absolutely. Wherever the ESIC infrastructure of medical care is there, for its proper utilistaion, it should be made available to the unorganized sector. Otherwise, to keep the infrastructure built up by the ESIC idle will be wasteful.

There is no reason why the cess funds should be running their separate hospitals-particularly when they do not have such a large infrastructure, advantages of scale, etc.

We have to work out the administrative mechanisms for allowing persons other than those who are insured with the ESIC to utilize the facilities available after considering who would is using them and how it is going to be paid for etc.

Dr. P.D. Shenoy

Secretary, Union Ministry of Labour

Firstly, I will take up coverage. When the ESIC tried to increase the coverage by raising wage ceiling from Rs. 6,500 to Rs. 10,000, we thought it was a very simple thing and that all Trade Union leaders would jump at it and accept it. But we found the Trade Union representatives in the ESIC were vehemently opposed to it, as much as the employer representatives. That made the job difficult. We thought that we could convince them. But we could not. I was surprised at their response After all, workers have to contribute only 1.75 per cent of the wages to the ESI Scheme, whereas the employers have to contribute 4.75 per cent. So I thought that workers should grab the proposal. but that was not the case. With a lot of persuasion, mediation and conciliation, it was ultimately agreed to raise the ceiling from Rs. 6,500 to Rs. 7,500. Those in the hall, who were witness to the discussions in the Corporation meeting would be aware of it.

Secondly, we wanted to expand the coverage to different types of institutions. So lot of bargaining took place before a decision could be taken to make the Scheme applicable to educational institutions. Many States have now come forward to extend the coverage to educational institutions.

I am with the DG when he says that we should cover all municipalities because that is an easier way for us to deal with the problem.

Unbundling of the benefits is also a right thing in today's world.

We need to have a National Social Security Authority or Council so that there is a synergy among all Social Security institutions and schemes, namely, EPFO, ESIC, Welfare Funds, Government Social Security schemes, Public Sector and Private Sector, Social Security schemes, Schemes administered by Social Justice Ministry, and others.

Sanat Mehtaji rightly mentioned about decentralization. Sir, while we want to expand ESIC, we should not try to go every where in rural areas or to cover the entire unorganized sector. I do not think we will be in a position to manage such a large expansion We are able to mange the Scheme with its current coverage because of the contributions we receive from employers and employees. Where the employers cannot be identified easily, it becomes very difficult to cover the workers under the ESI Scheme. An abortive attempt was made to introduce in fifty districts the Unorganized Sector Social Security Scheme. But it was not possible to implement the scheme because no employer would come forward to contribute to that Scheme. Unless there are contributions from both employers and workers, the employers making the larger contribution it would be very difficult for an organization like the ESIC to cover the unorganized sector.

Workers in the unorganized sector certainly need social security but we can evolve schemes for that sector step by step as has been done for beedi and building industries.

Beedi Workers Welfare Fund is there but their hospitals are not running properly and they cannot have hospitals wherever there are beedi workers. The way out is to permit the beedi workers who have been registered with the Welfare Fund, to utilize the facilities available with the ESIC on payment of a contribution at the same rate which we charge i.e., Rs. 750 per annum, or whatever, or if it is something more as R.K.A. Subrahmanya has already said. The same can be done to the construction workers and handloom workers They have Welfare funds for which money is collected by levying a cess. The money can be transferred to the ESIC and the synergy can be worked our. The Director General Labour Welfare, which is a wing of the Ministry, has already approached your organization. This has to come before your Board, and the board ahs to agree, of course. Without that, one cannot proceed further.

Now, Universal Health Issue Scheme is not easy to implement. The internal information amongst the four nationalized insurance schemes which are implementing the Universal Health Insurance Scheme currently in force – I am not talking about the modifications in the Scheme announced recently – is that it has failed. That is what all of them feel. They feel that it is very difficult to implement it and also very expensive The amount they are recovering will not be adequate to recover the cost; so, it is uneconomical. They are therefore not enthusiastic about it. So it has to be revisited and revised to make it viable.

I personally do not feel that Health Tourism and extending health benefits to the rural sector are opposed to each other. Not at all. We can have centers of excellence and we can attract money. Only Government need not give money to those 5 Star hospitals. Let them spread their network and attract tourists so that our country can be enriched by that.

We have taken over fifteen hospitals including those in Delhi which are meant to be Model Hospitals. I have seen a perceptible improvement in the service provided in the Model Hospitals which have been taken over by us. It is an irreversible step. The decision to taken them over has been after discussion at several Board meetings The decision cannot be reversed. We now require competent doctors to go and work there in a spirit of service. Without doctors, it is very difficult to run them. Some, at least a couple of ESIC doctors have to be there in every Model Hospital, along with the State level doctors.

At the same time, what ESIC requires today is consolidation first and then expansion later. Optimal utilization of the facilities, by whatever method, is one. Welfare Funds. may utilize the facilities available with the ESIC for providing medical care The CGHS card holders may also use them. Government can pay to ESIC the prescribed amount per employee or otherwise for utilizing the services. It is easy to collect the contributions from Government or government agencies. The employees may be identified by the cards issued to them. I am a retired person. I have a CGHS card now. After paying Rs. 18,000, it covers me and my wife throughout our lives – it is insurance. I will be going to stay in Bangalore – so I will not have difficulty of utilizing CGHS facilities. But many other card holders cannot get these benefits, ESIC hospitals may be there and ESIC can recover the money from the Government and you can have a linkage. This matter can be taken up with the CGHS through the Director General or an Additional Director General of CGHS who is on our Board. State government servants may also utilize the facilities by a similar arrangement.

The ESIC employees themselves are not covered by ESIC; EPFO employees are also not covered under the ESI Scheme. Whether it is feasible to cover them and whether they can get this benefit, if they are willing to pay for it at least after their retirement needs to be examined.

So you must try and get more and more assured clientele, paying clientele-not free clientele-so that you may be able to utilize the facilities available optimally by extension of the services to them.

There is another thing in the health sector which I wish to mention. There is a gap in the health sector, compared to the engineering sector or other technical sectors. For example, on the engineering sector, there are different levels of qualification for employment such as the Certificate Course in ITI's, and ITC's. Diplomas, Graduate degrees, Post Graduate degrees, Doctorates and so on. But on the Medical side, Allopathic Sector in particular, we have demolished everything below MBBS. One of the main reasons why the Rural Health Scheme is not succeeding is, that it is very difficult to make MBBS doctors go to the grass root levels. Many go, but not all go. We do not have those LMP's – Licentiate Medical Practitioners who would be found in or may be interested in going to rural areas.

I know, the MBBS doctors look down upon them but they are the barefoot doctors, Licentiates in Medicine and Surgery – LMP, LMS. We need to have some scheme under which with – proper education of say, 10 + 2 + 2 years, or 10 + 3 years, or some diploma course we can employ persons who are prepared to go to rural areas and take care of the rural. patients.

For preventive care, as you rightly pointed out, we need to expand Yoga, Naturopathy and other indigenous systems of medicine of which I am myself a great beneficiary.

Now, coming to Rogi Kalyan Samitis, it is a very good suggestion and we need to utilize this.

The practice of producing false medical certificates for sickness benefit should be curbed. There is one State, I do not want to mention the name-where there the incidence of sickness is shown to be 2.5 times the National average. Such false claims have to be curbed by a vigorous drive. A team of doctors and officers should go and camp in some of these places where the utilization of the hospital beds is very poor but the sickness benefit claims are high. For example Patna: not a single bed is utilized in the 50 bedded hospital that has been established there. I think some improvement might have taken place since I saw the report last. We have to ensure that utilization rate is brought up to 75 per cent, to begin with. Today, the average occupancy is just about 50-55 per cent. We should then aim at 100 per cent occupancy; Incomplete buildings should be completed. No more hospitals should be built.

Kerala has a large number of welfare fund schemes for the unorganized sector. ESIC can establish linkage with those schemes so that they can make use of the medical infrastructure built by the ESIC to provide medical care to their members and that can become the model for other States to follow. Many States like Madhya Pradesh, West Bengal and Karnataka, are starting several Welfare funds. and they may establish linkage with the ESIC for providing medical care to the members of those welfare funds.

Duality in the administration of medical care has been there for the last fifty years. If you want to take over the administration of medical benefit under the scheme entirely and have all the doctors under you it may be difficult at least in the initial stages. We have a culture of finding unity in diversity. That is the Indian culture and that is an art of management-getting things done through other agencies. When some Companies in U.S. can outsource their work through some Indian Companies, can we not outsource some of our work through the State Governments? It should be possible. I think it is an art of management. It depends upon the managerial skills to utilize optimally, their services also. Of course, the panel system is working in one or two cities like Mumbai but that is not also free from complaints There are some lacunae in that system and they require to be rectified.

16.

Democracy and Employment Guarantee

Aruna Roy
Member, Advisory Council, SSAI
Recipient of Magsaysay Award, Founder of Mazdoor Kisan Shakthi Sanghatana, Leader of the Right to Information Movement and Member National Advisory Council

July 2005

Basically, no social action is the work of one individual. I firmly believe that what I see today or what comes as a process of thinking of mine has been conditioned and contributed to by innumerable people, not only by members of the middle class, who are teachers, friends, colleagues, intellectuals, but also by large numbers of people who are called the working class.

The number of people who have influenced my thinking, who told me when I am wrong, made me understand the nature of politics, the nature of economics, the nature of social relations, are people who are to most of us just numbers on a fact sheet, people who beg on the streets, people who are a nuisance because they build and construct and obstruct our beautiful landscape in cities, people who are a problem because they produce too many children, because they are on the wrong side of the border. They practise the wrong religion, or they practise something we may not agree with. They may have child marriage, they may believe in caste, they may believe in untouchability. So we think, at least notionally that we are superior to them.

The first thing I had to learn, and unlearn, when I left the IAS and went to rural Rajasthan, was that Aristotelian logic is not everything, that I had not the only claim to logical thinking, that people in the villages have logic, they think and they survive and I tell myself today that were I in their position, I would have died long ago.

The skills that are enumerated as skills are skills that are primary to our lives. We give them high value and so we call them unskilled labour. I tried for two weeks to work as an unskilled labourer and I can tell you that it is very tough and it is a highly skilled job. The person- a woman or man- digging the earth, filling in the Tagari, lifting stones on his/her head, lifting mud is called an unskilled labourer. We are making a gross mistake in saying so and it is a violation of my understanding of all logic, because it requires tremendous technique to understand how to lift the Tagari of mud to the head; you have to know how to shovel the mud to the Tagari, you have to know and how to lift the Tagari.

So my life has been a series of learning experiences, and even in the IAS, while I was there, I learnt many things. It gave me a great opportunity to go and see rural India for the first time; I saw how very often when we went to the village, we never really met the poor people, how the power brokers in village always intervened between us and the poor, how people who appeared to be poor are not necessarily the poor, that the poor may dress better than the very rich peasant. The very rich peasant who looks like a poor person, in fact, may be the richest Lambardar of that village, that the Dalit who does not want to pass off as something unseemly will always come neatly dressed to meet you. So there were a number of things that one learns and in this process, I have redefined Democracy for myself and in the MKSS, we have tried to see democracy as an extremely important tool for peoples' empowerment.

There are large debates that go on today in the middle class homes and in drawing rooms, blaming democracy for all that is not O.K. with India. We say we are too naïve to use democracy, we are illiterate, so we cannot use democracy; we have casteism, therefore, we cannot use democracy. Therefore democracy is not a system for this country. What else do we have, and what else do we want? That is the question that has not been answered. Many arguments have been preferred as to why democracy is not the right system for this country. But if you sit with me as I do in a small village with the MKSS, you will understand better.

MKSS is a non-party peoples' organization. We are non-party political workers. We do not take institutional funds. We take money, we do not take donations, from individuals and people who support the ideology and the work we do. MKSS consists of a small number of people; there are only ten full time workers in the MKSS. We do not have a large campus, we live in two mud huts in a small village called Devdungri, which falls on NH No.8, between Ajmer and Udaipur.

When we first went there, in the year 1977, people dismissed us as very romantic. They said "All you will do is to pack your bags and come back again. It is all very well to live in a mud hut because all you do is to dream, dreams like Gandhiji. But you are not Gandhi-you cannot achieve any thing that Gandhiji did and you will come back; because how can you start a revolution, how can you start a class war, how can you start working things for the rural working class, living in an idyllic state, having a goat-we also had a goat, by the way. But one thing that we have firmly understood now, that if you live along with poor people, more or less the way they do, I will never be poor. So long as I speak English, so long as I have a mind which has been conditioned by Western Liberal Education, so long as I can read, write and listen and cogitate, yes, I certainly have great advantages over my women friends in the village, but they have tremendous advantages over me, as I said earlier. So, living with them was both an ideal and a very practical decision because if you look at Gandhiji again, and as we grow older, there are many lessons for people like us, even though many of us may disagree with some of his statements or ideas. Nevertheless, unless you live with the people, and feel the burden they bear, you do not think of the practical solutions to their problems. So we went and stayed in Devdungri. Living in Devdungri and looking at the way things work, you will start to dislike the way democracy works but there is nothing else but democracy. At least once in five years, you are made to feel important, everybody comes to you, asking for your vote, everybody makes much of you, at least once in five years. The Collector, if he comes or she comes, we sit on the roadside waiting for the Collector to come, for hours and hours we sit under a tree and wait, and the we see the red light, the Lal Bathi is so important and to see the Lal Bathi on the car is itself an assurance that the administration has come to us. So the democratic process- the system of electoral politics is important for the poor. But the point is, it has been co-opted, distorted and taken away from us. How do we bring the democratic process back to where it should belong, not necessarily stand for elections, but engage with electoral politics to make electoral politics deliver for the poor is a primary preoccupation of the MKSS and many other peoples' movements in this country. In fact, we have come together to form a Peoples' Political Front just to examine as to how we can engage with peoples' politics. As a result of many deliberations in the National Alliance of Peoples' Movements and many other such formations-. we have realized that unless we engage with electoral politics and democratic institutions, whatever there is for us will soon be completely taken away. So we will have what seems like a democracy, that means we all go to vote, we will cast a vote, but what happens out of the ballot box, will be completely unrelated to us; as it is, even today, whether it is National level politics or State level politics, you have to fight for every inch for peoples' concerns.

Previously, and this was also continuing tradition of Gandhiji, Vinoba Bhave and J.P. Narayan, there was a feeling that if one occupied any position of power, one gave up on one's ethics. There was this false hiatus in the mind but which is a real hiatus-that power corrupts and absolute power corrupts absolutely; so anyone whoever becomes a minister, a chief minister or prime minister or occupies a position of a pradhan or sarpanch must be corrupt. In fact, the onus now is on people to prove their honesty. So those who believe in ethics and honesty have tried to keep away from what appears to be one of the most unethical institutions in the country, which is politics, I would say electoral politics.

Politics is a very large issue for me, which defines any tussle for power between two groups, one which is deprived and one which benefits from power; whether it is a women's issue, whether it is a Dalit issue, there is politics. Electoral politics is really seen as dirty business. Unless we address this issue, there is nothing for us. So how do we do it?

One of the fallouts of this big debate, and an important fallout, is the Right to Information campaign. Every time we went to Government and demanded payment of minimum wage, we were told that we were lying. So we had to demand to see the records,. Many of our friends in the IAS and outside, lots of politicians who are honest, lots of lawyers, judges, journalists and all sorts of people joined the campaign because no single group had any claim to an ethical view of life today. NGOs are corrupt, social institutions are corrupt, politicians are corrupt, civil servants are corrupt, wherever you see, there is corruption and I do not think there is any group of people whom you can see today, is corruption-free. So the coming together of all people who wanted ethics in civil society and decent administrative system and who wanted the poor to have the right to know and right to live was important. Because, for us, the right to know is connected to the right to live.

Whether the hospital functions properly, whether you get medicines, whether you get the school building properly constructed, whether the Indira Awas Yojana is built in such a manner that it does not collapse on your head and break your head, and such other issues are all livelihood issues, life-related issues. So the demand for the Right to Information led to the Right to Food campaign.

In the Right to Food campaign we demanded to have food. The officials would say that there was no food although the godowns were full of foodgrains. Now they say the godowns are empty and that there was no money to procure it. So the poor people realized that if they wanted food, life and livelihood, or health and education, their battles had to go beyond the narrow confines of their villages. They had to ask larger questions and to confront the system with questions that were uncomfortable.

I remember once, that was in 1996, we sat in a forty-day Dharna in Byavar, a place called Changet. People came and joined this Dharna, slowly and gradually, so that in the end we were quite surprised at the numbers. Slowly and gradually, they understood that we were asking for the right to transparency and the right to know, which related to everything in life. That place became the hub of all political activity in Byavar for forty days.

I remember one lawyer coming to us and saying, 'This is a very good issue, but you will never win this. In your lifetime, you are not going to get transparency and the Right to Information, because you are asking for the heart of the system to be taken out, but it is not possible". All political parties supported us, some officially and some unofficially. All other organizations-white collar, blue collar organizations supported us and we found that India was ready for a genuine democratic struggle – may be not in urban centers, may be not in moffussil towns, but certainly at the grassroots level – people were ready for the battle.

After our fight for the Right to Food, and for our right to proper wage, the next step was obviously the demand for the Right to Work. The Right to Work is a major question which calls for amendment of the Constitution involving the enlargement of the scope of Constitutional Rights. The Employment Guarantee Act is a sub-set of the Right to Work.

In Maharashtra there is a EGA which has been functioning well for the last twenty five to thirty years.

In this country, there are many wonderful innovative ideas which are being implemented successfully in one place or the other. EGA is one such idea. If there can be an EGA in Maharashtra, why cant there be one for the whole country? When this question was raised in a series of discussions lasting for over twenty years ago the answer was that the EGA in Maharashtra was fraught with a variety of problems. Subsequently, the EGA was evaluated by many studies and it was found that, though there were reservations on certain issues, the EGA on the whole was successful in improving the livelihood and economic status of workers. It has also given a strong bargaining strength to the workers in negotiating the terms of employment with other industries in the State. It has, by and large, given an entitlement to the poor.

The EGA in Maharashtra has accepted, notionally, that if the Tahsil or the Panchayat does not give work to the poor person, he or she will get an unemployment dole. That means that the onus of providing employment squarely rests with the State. The State must provide employment.

I remember, fifteen years ago, in Rajasthan, there was severe drought in one district. Planning Commission had deputed a team to study the situation. The team consisted of Prof. C.H. Hanumantha Rao and many other specialists. Three hundred people stopped them on the main road and said to them, 'We do not want your dole, we do not want a hand out. What we want is work. We want to earn and live with dignity. The people of this country are very dignified people. Just because there are some poor people who beg on the streets in the big cities, it does not mean that the people lie to beg. We are people with dignity, we have the skills, and we have tremendous human potential'. So they said to the team 'You give us work." Many of them were starving – they had had no food for months and were suffering from endemic poverty – yet had the courage to tell the team that they did not want dole what they wanted was employment. "You give us a wage and we will buy what we want and eat what we can afford to buy. In the past there were famines for lack of food grains. The situation has changed. There is now no dearth of food. What we do not have is the money to but the food'. So they asked for employment.

As a result of many of these things, in the last three or four years, an increasing number of people are demanding the enactment of a national EGA.

One of them is Prof. Jean Dreze, who has written many economics books with Prof. Amartya Sen. He is not a professional or a Gandhian committed to any ideology, but who lives an extremely simple life. He actually lives in Timarpur in Sanjay Basti, which is a basti. He has very few sets of clothes. He has very few personal belongings, but he is an academic of the highest order – an extremely committed human being. He, along with several other academicians in this country, started thinking of the economic arguments and justifications for an EGA.

We came together three or four years ago. We traveled extensively. In the Rozgar Yatra, which has just concluded, we went round fifty of India's poorest districts, I have personally traveled all round Rajasthan, representing the MKSS, West to East of Rajasthan, South West to North East Rajasthan, as well as Central Rajasthan. We have gone to villages which are divided on party lines, villages which are divided on caste lines, as well as villages which are divided on communal lines. Wherever we went we found that the one issue on which they were all united was on the need for employment. A few years ago, some people had coined the slogan that India was shining. The people wondered what was shining? They said that there was a feel good factor in Rajasthan, with our limited knowledge of English, we thought we would get some new type of gud, jaggery, which had come into the market. Ultimately we decided that the only real thing we wanted was the guarantee to provide work.

We have no Social Security now, we have no subsidy, subsidies are being removed, all the laws that protected our rights in the villages are going. The New Economic Policy is taking away all the benefits we enjoyed before. The notion of Global Markets makes us so small as if we do not exist. Huge mechanization process has begun. In the past we used to work by our hands on the construction of roads; today there are machines. Our future is bleak.

In this context, the EGA is the only means by which we can have livelihood security, assured future for our children, for education, for health, for access to any of the resources, even to stay in the villages, to mobilize, to fight for our demands. Otherwise, because of lack of employment there will be an increase in migration to cities. They come to Delhi and go to other places as construction workers without any rights; they do not have ration cards, they do not have living rights, they do not have any other rights, adding to their own problems as well as those of the State.

So, overall, if you look at this country, employment is a vital issue.

We therefore lobbied with every political party before the recent elections including the UPA to have the EGA included in their legislative programme, When this new party came into power, the UPA, we were not hopeful that they would give us an assurance on our demand, but when they brought out the National Common Minimum Programme, and wrote as the first item on the Programme, that they would bring forward a National EGA immediately we were happy. They made the promise that one person in every household would be provided hundred days of assured employment. They set up the National Advisory Council, to monitor the CMP. One of the reasons that some of us joined the National Advisory Council was our interest in the EGA, apart from other things which they had promised but this was of crucial importance.

We worked very hard to ensure that the promise was fulfilled. A large number of peoples' organizations looked at the draft bill which the Government had drawn up. We had a huge meeting in Bhopal in which several hundreds of people got together and many hundreds of organizations were represented. We drew up our own Bill, and presented it in the NAC. The NAC trimmed it and pruned it to fit it into its own agenda. We wanted guarantee of work for three hundred and sixty five days; they said only one hundred days. We wanted every adult, male or female, who was in need of employment to be provided wit work, but they made it one person per household. We accepted what they offered, as a beginning, in the hope that we could fight for the rest later. The draft then went from the NAC to the Government of India where it was cut down further. They proposed to begin with one hundred and fifty poorest districts and to extend the Act to other districts in the course of five years.

Well, we all know how the Government functions. The moment it went in, the Government of India raised all sorts of arguments about lack of money – it will cost four lakhs crores of rupees, we cannot raise that amount, we cannot do this, we cannot do that. The cost of the programme was not more than 1 per cent of the GDP. It was not much to provide livelihood to 60 per cent of India's population which is on starvation. There was no political will to push it through.

There is a difference between a political statement and a political will. We feel that if you make a public commitment as a nationally elected leader, and as a member of the ruling party, you just have to keep to it. So how far we can push for this depends on our collective struggle. One of the ways of embarrassing them is to organize, from time to time, various kinds of protests. We should fight them on the streets, we should fight within the NAC; we should fight with the economists, we should fight with political parties. We should fight to see that there is justice, In an elected democracy, people who come to power cannot dishonour their word.

We wanted a Universal EGA, that is for every adult in this country. They first restricted the application of the Act to certain States. We said that the Act should be made applicable to the whole of India within five years. They said that it would be an off and on progress. We said that a guarantee once given is irreversible. One cannot say to you today, 'You have a right of expression', and take it away tomorrow. One cannot say to you, 'You have a right to practise religion today' and take away that right tomorrow. These are all Fundamental Rights. You cannot say today, 'You have a Right to Guarantee of Employment' and tomorrow 'no, no, I am going to switch it from your district to the next because of political reasons, because of economic reasons. "Whatever reasons, you cannot do that. So reversibility was totally unacceptable to us and that is what they did. They also said the one hundred days. We did not agree. We said 365 days.

About the minimum wage, they were quiet. The minimum wage, as you all know, as people who are involved with Social Security, is a very important issue on which systematically, every Government has come to power. We said that at least the Statutory Minimum wage in the State where a person works must be paid. We also said that there should be equal participation by women., it should be extended to the whole country in the manner we want.

The Government referred the Bill to the Standing Committee. We lobbied with the Standing Committee. We gave testimony in the Standing Committee. In doing so we hoped that that the Standing Committee would give a report substantially supporting what we were saying. To strengthen our case with peoples' voices, we organized the Rozgar Yatra which round fifty districts mobilizing public opinion. The yatra ends today. Tomorrow we will have a Jan Manch.

Today we know that there is a Food for Work Programme in certain districts applicable to persons below the poverty line. The Employment Guarantee Scheme is expected to replace that Scheme. That scheme is fraught with several problems.

First, the problem of identifying persons below the poverty line.

I do not know how many of you are interested in things like the Below Poverty line list. There is a saying in English that the devil lies in the details. So if you look at how the below poverty line is determined, there are thirteen criteria. They assign points in an ascending order for each criterion. First, your economic level will be determined by the nature of your toilet. It is a major preoccupation in our country. So the toilet will determine your economic status. Do you have a toilet or not? If you do not have a toilet, you get zero. That means you are on top of the list. If you have access to a community toilet, which is dry, then you get one point. If you have access to a community toilet with water, you get two points. If you have a personal toilet, with water, you get four points. So, what happens? You have an Indira Awas Yojana programme which is for the poorest of the poor. The houses built under the Yojana have toilets with a sceptic tank. So it is technically a toilet with water. So the poor person, to whom you give a house under the Indira Awas Yojana gets four points. An extremely rich farmer, who has thousands of Bighas in Rajasthan does not have a toilet because to build a toilet in the house is not part of their cultural tradition. So he gets a zero. Now he will get on top of the list of persons below the poverty line and the person who is allotted a house under the Awas Yojana goes below.

Then, of course, there is this whole question of ownership of land. Fathers die, grandfathers die but land is not partitioned and titles are not made. So though a person actually owns twenty or thirty bighas of land he is shown as landless because the land is not in his name and he is shown below the poverty line.

The last question, that is the thirteenth criterion, is the most amazing question. It asks you what you dream of becoming, it is a dream, it is not even reality; what do you want to be? A labourer, a worker, an engineer, a doctor, what is my dream? And on that you are given marks. If you say that your son or daughter will remain poor, you are given zero point. If you say that you would like your son or daughter to be an architect or an engineer, you would be given four points.

The list of persons below the poverty line will be drawn up on this abysmally irrational basis. The Government proposes to use the basis for allocation of work under the Employment Guarantee Act. How can we accept it?

If you look, apart from the criteria, at the selection process, you find very rich people in the Below Poverty Line list. Because the Below Poverty

Line list is an entry ticket for not only the Indira Awas Yojana, but all kinds of other benefits which Government offers, it is badly misused which.

Having regard to these facts we have made it known that the criterion of Below Poverty Line classification is totally unacceptable to us.

The most horrendous thing for me is that the perspective plans are being now contracted to NGOs who may or may not consult the Panchayats. The Scheme requires that perspective plans should be drawn up for a district, or for a whole division and they will be in force for five years. They cannot be changed within that period. So leaving out the Panchayats in drawing ups such perspective plans is wrong. The panchayats are the primary institutions for the welfare of the people. The proposal to entrust the making of perspective plans to NGOs, who may or may not consult the Panchayat is totally wrong. On the one hand, we are talking about Panchayats and empowering of Panchayats. On the other hand, we are doing everything possible to disenfranchise the Panchayats. I would say that it is a fundamental struggle for democracy that the Panchayat should be the basis. However bad we are, we must make the Panchayats accountable. As we are doing in Rajasthan, where we have Ward Sabhas, Gram Sabhas, in which they display their accounts, and are accountable to the people. As it has happened in Kerala, as it has happened in many other parts of India-may be in Karnataka also where we make them accountable to the people. We certainly do not want that the Panchayats should be bypassed and the work is given to NGOs whose main interest is to perpetuate themselves, who are unaccountable to the people, but only to their funders, through a small balance sheet and a statement of account that they give to them.

So I would argue that the Employment Guarantee Act is a fundamental Right of every individual who is poor in this country. It is wrong to say that there will be floods of people demanding employment under the Act. Only those who are prepared to do unskilled work in the heat of the day will ask for work under the Act. That number would not be large. At any rate it is their Fundamental Right to a decent living in this country. For those who believe in democratic processes and in the Fundamental Right to Life and Livelihood the Employment Guarantee Act is extremely important.

So tomorrow when this Yatra comes back after having travelled in fifty districts, with lots of slogans and releasing lots of energy, hundreds and hundreds of people from different parts of the country, from different parties and organisations will be coming to Delhi tonight.

Tomorrow we have what we call a Jan Manch. I have distributed invitations to all of you, we invite you to the Jan Manch. The Jan Manch will be where people from all over India, and particularly those from these fifty districts will come. The former President, K.R.Narayanan, will be at the Jan Manch, former P.M. V.P. Singh, will chair the Jan Manch. All the political party members have said they will come and it is a process which strengthens my belief and our belief in Democracy. Ten years ago, if we had a Jan Manch, and invited political leaders, I am sure none would have come because they would have considered us non-entities. But today, somehow, the process has been somewhat reversed. It has been established that every voter has a right, every citizen has a right, and every group of members who come together to fight for democracy has a right. So tomorrow in the Jan-Manch we will see what happens, we will see what each party has to say. We will see how many absent themselves and how many come because that is also a gamble. One cannot ensure attendance. We will see how many of them come tomorrow. As people are concerned with issues that concern me as well as Social Security Association of India, I would appeal to you that some of you come to the Jan Manch tomorrow and also pledge support to the enactment of the Employment Guarantee Act which will benefit hundreds and thousands of Indians. Crores of unorganized people will have a fall back security in employment and a wage. And I think without that this country is doomed because today the biggest problem in rural India is employment.

So I come to you with a plea to take a pledge to support the Employment Guarantee Act and support the peoples' movements in their big battle. However you can, I do not know how you function. You are all individual members who have come together to form this organization. You lend us the support of this organization through your own struggles, or through writing to the Prime Minister, writing to the President, writing to the Parliament, however you think fit.

We have a website; you can access it. There are many Research Associations and people who are doing research or studying for PhD in sociology, economics, anthropology, and so on come and help us with all the data. So please come and join us. This is really a national issue of tremendous importance for all of us if we want to live in peace.

I think as the last election has shown we cannot shine without everybody shining with us; if we shine alone, then we are doomed. So if all of India has to get a share of the cake, or a piece of bread, the Employee Guarantee Act is terribly important.

17.

Social Security Development in Asia and the Pacific

Corazon S. De La Paz

President, International Social Security Association (ISSA)

NOVEMBER 2006

Social security discussions in the 1990s were dominated by issues on the advantages and drawbacks of publicly managed defined benefit versus privately managed defined contribution old-age pension schemes.

Happily, the discussion of the 1990s have since given way to more balanced and less polarized views on social security reform, especially with the knowledge that reforms must be more adapted and calibrated to a country's unique circumstances.

Thus, from the heated debates of the 1990s, the social security agenda has refocused itself on four of the long-standing challenges confronting it, namely, coverage, programme adequacy, sustainability and governance.

The refocusing of the social security agenda serves as a reminder that the basic purpose of social security is to offer people income security over the course of their lives. I, for one, have always believed that work or a job is the bet form of security and that the role of social security is to ensure that if an unexpected occurrence disrupts the income stream provided by employment, then there are mechanisms in place to meet these unforeseen contingencies.

Three Cross-cutting Issues

There are three global factors driving this refocused social security agenda: the globalization of markets and its consequences; the agening of the population; and the dramatic implications of public health threats such as SARS and HIV/AIDS, particularly in developing countries.

Let me take these three factors in turn.

Developing world, and the less developed countries in relative terms will face an even more serious ageing problem between 2000 and 2050, and would thus have to build stronger social security systems to prepare for this challenge.

Population ageing has already started in the Asia and Pacific region. This is true in Eastern Asia which includes Japan, the Republic of Korea and China.

This is also true for South Central Asia which includes India, Iran, Nepal, Kyrgyzstan, Pakistan and Sh. Lanka.

And for Southeast Asia which includes Indonesia, Malaysia, Myanmar, Philippines and Thailand.

And in Oceanic which includes Australia, New Zealand, Fiji, Samoa and the Solomon islands.

It is only in western Asia where after 50 years, the population pyramid would still look like a pyramid, Albeit, with a noticeably narrower base. Western Asia includes Bahrain, Jordan, Kuwait, Lebanon, Palestine, Qatar, Saudi Arabia, Syria, Turkey, United Arab Emirates and Yemen.

In 2005, the ISSA regional office for Asia and the Pacific conducted a survey on developments in public old age benefit schemes in Asia and the Pacific. The results of the ISSA survey show that many of the public pension systems in the Asia and Pacific region are in various stages of reform. The efforts are largely focused on strengthening the schemes through various parametric and institutional reform measures, with some countries exploring the feasibility of unifying existing schemes. A critical factor that prompts most of these pension reform efforts is the length of the actuarial life of the fund. The trend of reform is thus towards the use of conventional measures such as increasing the contribution rate, raising the retirement age, and tightening entitlement conditions for benefits.

Developed countries have also adopted a wide range of reforms in response to the ageing of their populations. These policy responses include adjusting pension schemes to curb the "generosity" of public pensions. Parameters such as retirement age and required number of years for which contributions are paid have been raised, and formulas used to calculate pensions have been tightened.

Measures to curb early departure from the work force have also been introduced. Over the past 25 years, it has been the experience of OECD labour markets that people start to work later and retire earlier such that the working life span has become shorter. Consequently, stricter policies on early retirement as well as for disability and unemployment have been implemented. Back-to-work schemes have also been adopted.

Population, at the other extreme, social security coverage in sub-saharan Africa and South Asia is around 10 per cent of the population.

These figures serve to emphasize how far formal contributory approaches to social security have fallen short of providing universal and adequate coverage to all, especially those in the developing countries. Extension of coverage must therefore be treated as a priority. Advancing on this goal requires strong political commitment and innovative strategies that would improve the reach of social security programmes to also better include women, those in the agricultural and urban informal sector and migrant workers. This was one of the major conclusions at the fourth ISSA meeting of Directors of social security organizations in Asia and Pacific held in November 2005.

In the Asia and Pacific region, only a few countries have met the challenge of reaching universal coverage for their populations, and these are the more industrialized countries in the region such as Australia, Japan, the Republic of Korea and Singapore.

Two important lessons we have from these countries are that first, there is a close connection between the level of economic development and social security coverage. In fact, in a recently completed ISSA study, 15 countries were classified into per capita GDP, and the correlation between per capita GDP and social security coverage is strongly positive. This is a clear indication that affordability of the contributions is a key determinant of coverage.

The second lesson is that there must be strong Government commitment to extend coverage. The experience of the National Health Insurance Corporation of the Republic of Korea is very instructive. Because of the Government's priority on rapid extension of health insurance, it took Korea only twelve years to extend its social health insurance to the entire population since its first introduction to employees in large corporations in 1977. It helped immensely, of course, that Korea had the economic resources for this expansion owing to this rapid economic development.

Our coverage experience with formal social security programmes, particularly in developing countries, is inconsistent with what we have been theoretically expecting. Classical development theory assumes that as economies grow, most of the labour force will eventually be employed in the formal sector, with regular wage employment.

This has not been happening.

Extending Social Security Coverage

The question is, how do we provide social security in an environment that has traditionally been difficult for conventional, formal economy style social security programmes?

There is growing policy interest in smaller scale, voluntary mechanisms tailored more closely to the needs and contributory capacities of individuals. Micro insurance and area-based schemes, particularly for health care, are seen as an important first step in cases where coverage in a more comprehensive programme is not yet possible. Micro finance, on the other hand, is seen as providing workers with opportunities to increase productivity and earn decent incomes which, it is hoped, would allow them to provide for more than just daily subsistence needs.

India is achieving a number of important innovations in this area. In a recent social health insurance conference held in Manila last month, participants found out more about the Yeshavini Cooperative Farmers Health Scheme of the Karnataka, the Indore Municipal corporation Health Insurance Scheme of the Madhya Pradesh, the Naandi Foundation School health programmes of the Andhra Pradesh and the health protection programme in Jharkhand.

In the Philippines, the social security system offers a comprehensive, range of cash benefits as insurance for retirement, death, disability, maternity, sickness, old age, death and work-related injuries. In addition, low interest loans are also made available to SSS members, efforts have been made over the years to make SSS more accessible to the informal sector. But so far, of the 26 million registered SSS members, only about 5 million are informal sector workers.

A number of informal social security schemes have also evolved in the Philippines. These schemes are rooted in the traditional forms of family and community support. As it is in most developing countries, Filipinos look to their families, relatives, friends and community for financial support during contingencies such as calamities, illnesses and death, or during major social events such as marriage and religious celebrations.

Many of these schemes begin as savings-based loan schemes wherein members borrow money to support productive, providential and emergency needs. To some extent, these community-based efforts attain a certain measure of success because they offer members affordable contributions, flexible terms of payment, simple procedures and speedy access to benefits.

In closing, let me quote Mr. Alistar Darling, the Former Secretary of State of Social Security of United Kingdom.

"The problems of poverty and social exclusion have built up over a long period, it will take a long time to put this right. We must continue to listen to people on the ground, especially those who are themselves living in poverty, to make sure our policies are having the right effect".

18.

Pension Reform in India – A Social Security Need

D. Swaroop

Chairman, Pension Fund Regulatory and Development Authority

March 2008

This gives me an opportunity to show-case an important reform being undertaken in India and to inter-act with a very knowledgeable audience. Let me begin by sharing with you, in brief, the background under which the National Pension Scheme (NPS) was introduced and then take you through he current status of implementation of the NPS structure.

India has nearly eighty million elderly people, which is one eighth of world's elderly population. This segment of population is growing at a rate of 3.8 per cent per annum as against a rate of 1.8 per cent for the overall population. A vast majority of this population is not covered by any formal old age income scheme and are dependent on their earnings and transfer from their children or other family members. These informal systems of old age income support are imperfect and are becoming increasingly strained.

Poverty and unemployment may have acted as deterrents to provide a tax financed state pension arrangement for each and every citizen attaining old age. Therefore, in the organized sector (excluding the Government servants) a pension policy has been adopted based on financing through employer and employee participating. This has, however, denied the vast majority of the workforce in the unorganized sector access to formal channels of old age economic support.

As all of you already know, a comprehensive pension system has 3 basic pillars. Pillar 1 covers every citizen of the country through a standardized, state-run pension system, which offers basic coverage and is primarily focused on reducing poverty. Pillar 2 is mandatory occupational pension system where employee and employer contribute towards their pension. Pillar 3 is a voluntary, private funded system, including individual savings plans, insurance, etc. let us now see where India is placed vis-à-vis this internationally accepted principle of providing income security after retirement. Pillar 1 i.e. State-financed pension has very limited coverage in our country – it covers indigent persons above 65 years through the NSAP for poor and elderly and persons employed by the Government through the traditional PAYG scheme or the defined benefit scheme. Pillar 2 covers workers in the organized sector through a DC-cum-DB scheme. Pillar 3, i.e., purely voluntary schemes, is present in a very restrictive form through PPF, superannuation schemes and personal pension plans through annuity providers.

Pension Policy in India has primarily and traditionally been based on financing through employer and employee participation. As a result, the coverage has been restricted to the organized sector and a vast majority of the workforce in the unorganized sector has been denied access to formal channels of old age financial support. Only about 12 per cent of the working population in India is covered by some form of retirement benefit scheme. Besides the problem of limited coverage, the existing mandatory and voluntary private pension system is characterized by limitations like fragmented regulatory framework, lack of individual choice and portability and lack of uniform standards. High incidence of administrative cost and low real rate of returns characterize the existing system, which has become unsustainable.

Non-sustainability of the existing pension system is accentuated by the sharp increase in financial burden on the Government and the other employers on account of pension liabilities. While the total pension liability on account of the Central Government employees has increased at a compound annual growth rate of more than 21 per cent during the 1990s, the comparable rate for the State Government was 27 per cent per annum.

As all of you would be knowing, Civil Servants' Pension (CSP) is a traditional defined benefit scheme which runs on the basis of pay-as-you-go-system, for employees of Central Government who were recruited up to 31st December, 2003 and employees of State Governments recruited up to the effective date mentioned in notifications issued by those governments. CSP is an unfounded scheme and there has been no attempt at building up pension assets through contribution or any other provisions.

CSP schemes is indexed to wages and inflation. A modified one rank one-wage principle applies to it wherein all retired employees of a certain rank get the same pension. Pension payments are revised periodically to reflect the growth in wages and consumer price index. Growth in pension benefits in old age is typically higher than inflation.

The main problem under CSP is that of fiscal stress. CSP was designed at a time when going by the pattern of life expectancy most of the employees who retired at the age of 60 were expected to live up to the age of 68 or so. The value of the annuity embedded in the CSP has gone up due to elongation of mortality in the recent years. The mortality characteristics of Government employees, who belong to the higher income group than the average, are more or less in line with the OECD populations. The fiscal stress at the sub-national level has been more acute. Some of the State governments have not made timely payment of pension benefits. One State government chose to cut benefits by reversing recent increases in the pension benefits due to hikes in the wages of existing employees.

For the organized sector employees, excluding the Government employees, the basis structure of pension and other retirement benefits has been outlines in the EPF and MP Act, 1952. The provisions of this Act are applicable to all defined establishments, employing more than 20 workers and cover about 40 million employees in the organized sector. This Act remained virtually unquestioned and there were virtually no changes in the contribution, administration and benefits being provided under this Act for almost four decades. First major change occurred in 1995, with the conversion of part of defined contribution EPF Scheme to a defined benefit scheme in the form of Employees' Pension Scheme. This change in the EPF and MP Act, 1952 marked an important break from the existing policy of the Employees Provident Fund Organization in two ways:

(a) With this amendment, the concept of a mandated annuity to the employees of private sector was introduced for the first time.
(b) It added a new pension liability (since the scheme is not fully funded) to the existing liability with regard to the civil servants of Central and State Governments.

The EPF & MP Act, 1952 is administered by the Employees Provident Fund Organization (EPFO). At present, EPFO administers the following two old age income schemes, which are mandatory for all employees in the organized sector, earning a monthly salary of less than Rs. 6,500:

(a) The Employees Provident Fund (EPF); and
(b) The Employees Pension Schemes (EPS).

All the functions/processes of EPF and EPS are handled by the EPFO, except fund management, which has been outsourced to one external agency (State Bank of India). However, some establishments, which are under the purview of EPFO are allowed to manage their own funds. EPFO treats them as exempted funds. These exempted funds are, however, required to follow the same investment pattern as being followed by EPFO and are required to match the returns of the EPFO.

The Employees Provident Fund (EPF) Scheme is an individual account defined contribution scheme wherein both the employee and employer contribute to the fund at the rate of 12 per cent of the employee's pay. There are a number of provisions under the scheme for pre-mature withdrawal of accumulation. This pre-mature withdrawal provision is frequently used by the members of the scheme which leads to small balances at the time of their superannuation. Because of low balance in individual account of the members', old age income benefit is negligible. The EPFO scheme enjoys an 'EEE' tax structure which constitutes a major tax bases subsidy.

The Employees Pension Scheme (EPS) is a defined benefit scheme, based on a contribution rate of 8.33 per cent from the employees to which government makes an additional contribution of 1.16 per cent. EPS was introduced in 1995, and is applicable to the workers who entered into employment after 1995. In case of death of a member the scheme provides for a pension to the spouse for his/her remaining life.

There are other voluntary pension schemes available for general public but these schemes cover a very small segment of the total population. Life Insurance Companies and Mutual funds are offering these plans. These are essentially defined contribution schemes. Personal Pension Plans and Group Pension Products offered by the life insurers are being supervised by the Insurance Regulatory and Development Authority (IRDA). Scheme offered by the Mutual Funds are regulated/supervised by the Security Exchange Board of India (SEBI). Tax benefits up to a specific amount are being offered to investors buying these pension plans. Total coverage under these pension plans is about 1.6 million.

The other popular scheme is Public Provident Fund (PPF) which is also a defined contribution scheme. Government is managing this scheme. A fixed rate of return is offered under the scheme. In addition, tax benefits are being offered for making investment in the Public Provident Fund account. Coverage under the Public Provident Fund is about 3.5 million.

Pension Market in India

The existing system of pensions which leaves more than 88 per cent of Indian workforce uncovered is unlikely to act as a social security umbrella for the ageing Indians. Even for those that the system covers, the defined benefit is strictly not guaranteed as most DB schemes are either wholly unfounded for under-funded schemes. Improvement in healthcare facilities leading to increase in life expectancy, evolution of nuclear family systems and rising expectations due to increase in per capital income, education etc. are some of the factors likely to compound the problem in future. The new pension system, based on defined contribution and funded liability is a significant step in the direction of addressing this problem. Spread of NPS is seen by many as the direction in which the pension reforms need to move to find a viable and sustainable solution to the problem of old-age income security.

In 2001, Government of India appointed a group for experts to study the various aspects of extending an organized system of pension to the unorganized sector. The group submitted its report in October 2001. According to this report, the pension market (which includes pensions, provident funds and other small savings i.e. NSC, NSS) would grow to about Rs. 4064 billion by 2025. The growth would largely be due to normal growth of economy in terms of growth in income and population and does not consider the significant increase in coverage that would arise because of reforms in the insurance and pension sectors. A more conservative estimate is that the pension market will be worth about Rs. 1808 billion by 2025.

The New Pension System

During the last seven years, from 2000 to 2007, a market shift in pension policy in India was witnessed which culminated in introduction of a new pension system. A High level Expert Group (HLEG) and the Old Age Social and Income Security (OASIS) Project commissioned by the Government were the two initial milestones on the road to pension reforms for the Government employees and the unorganized sector respectively. These efforts culminated in setting up of the Pension Fund Regulatory and Development authority (October 2003), introduction of a New Pension System (December 2003), and introduction of the PFRDA Bill in Parliament (March 2005).

HLEG suggested a new hybrid scheme that combines contributions from employees and the Union Government matching basis, on the one hand, while committing to the employees a defined benefit as pension. The objective of the Government was to design a scheme for new entrants in Central Government service where the contribution is defined, where no extra infrastructure is sought to be created in Government and which is capable of serving other groups like State Government employees, middle class self-employed people and even those in the lower income bracket amongst the unorganized sector subsequently.

OASIS report recommended a scheme based on individual Retirement Accounts to be opened anywhere in India. It was envisaged that Banks, Post Offices etc., could serve as "Points of Presence" (POPs) where the accounts could be opened or contributions deposited. Their electronic interconnectivity will ensure "portability" as the worker moves from one place/employment to another. There will be a depository for centralized record keeping, fund managers to manage the funds and annuity providers to provide the benefit after the age of 60.

The New Pension System (NPS) which has its origin in the two reports mentioned above, was made operational through a notification dated 22nd December, 2003. it has been made mandatory for new recruits in the Central Government (except Armed Forces) from 1st January 2004. it marks a shift from the defined benefit to a defined contribution regime. It is based on the principles of defining upfront the liability of Government, giving choice to subscribers, facilitation portability of labour force and ensuring transparency and fair-play in the industry. About 100,000 Central Government employees (excluding employees of autonomous organizations) are already covered under the new pension system and contribute 10 per cent of their salary and dearness allowance towards pension with a matching contribution from the government. Nineteen States have also notified and implemented a defined contribution pension system for new employees. Many other State Governments have made significant strides in this direction. NPS will also be available to all individuals in the unorganized sector on a voluntary basis.

Under the NPS, for all subscribers, at the time of retirement there will be compulsory annuitisation of at least 40 per cent of the accumulated pension wealth and the balance will be paid as a lump sum. There will be multiple pension fund managers licensed by PFRDA and the choice would be with the individual subscriber to decide which fund manager to go with. There would be four broad categories of pension schemes offering investment options with varying ratio of equity and fixed income instruments. The choice of a scheme would rest with the subscriber. Full transparency and disclosure of information regarding investments will have to be provided by the intermediaries. Portability will be provided to the participants along with the option to transfer accumulations from one fund manager to another.

To bring the new pension system within a statutory regulatory jurisdiction, an ordinance was promulgated on 29 December 2004 setting up a statutory Pension Fund Regulatory and Development Authority. Subsequently, a Bill was introduced in the Parliament to replace the ordinance. The Bill provides for establishing a statutory Authority to promote old age income security by establishing, developing and regulating pension funds and protecting the interest of subscribers to schemes of pension funds. Once the Act comes into force the Authority shall regulate all intermediaries under the new pension system including pension funds, central record keeper, points of presence, etc. It will approve the terms and condition of the schemes, lay down norms for the management of the corpus of the pension funds including investment guidelines under such schemes. The Bill envisages that the pension supervisor will provide robust regulatory umbrella essential to sustain member confidence and to protect the interests of the participants and to develop the pension system by inculcating saving habits for long term. The Bill also provides adequate safeguards to take care of the subscribers to the NPS and stringent penalties for contravention of the provisions of the proposed Act and the Rules and Regulations framed there under.

In accordance with Parliamentary conventions in India, on introduction in the Lower House the Bill was referred to the Parliamentary Standing Committee on Finance. The Committee, having considered the evidence and clarifications placed before it, opined that "...the reform process in the pension sector involving the setting up of the PFRDA as a Statutory regulatory body for managing the NPS is an urgent necessity mainly on account of burgeoning fiscal stress of pension payments on the Central and State revenues and the need to provide a viable alternative to the populace at large to save for old age income security". The Committee approved the PFRDA Bill for enactment subject to certain modifications, which are under consideration of the Ministry of Finance, Government of India.

The Bill is yet to be taken up for further consideration by Parliament. Meanwhile, in view of one of the recommendations of the Standing committee that the initial or broad contours of the regulations governing the implementation of the NPS under the infrastructure of PFRDA be framed and put in public domain. PFRDA has prepared the broad contours of Regulations on registration of intermediaries and put them in public domain for comments of stakeholders.

The NPS has been mainly designed to fill the gap of old age income security to the unorganized sector. The scheme is envisaged to be a voluntary one for this segment of the population. Given a high savings rate of 35 per cent of GDP, Indian workers are encouraged in respect of their capability to contribute towards a self financed old age income security scheme. In this framework, the New Pension System will provide them with the opportunity to fulfil their needs of old age income support in the most productive way. Further, the system will also be capable of providing a delivery mechanism for the other segments of population viz. Pillar-I (population vide mandatory pension system) and Pillar-II (mandatory occupational pension system). The low cost structure of the architecture will enable Government to utilize this infrastructure to deliver any scheme of old age income support to any segment of the population in the most efficient manner.

While the introduction of the New Pension System for new recruits of the Central Government/State Governments is a positive step in the direction of reforming the pension sector in India, the road ahead has many challenges.

The level of financial literary and preponderance of rural aged make the task daunting. Sex ratio of the workforce and economic status of women pose special problems in the design of pension systems. Designing an effective, efficient and accessible system, which caters to the requirement of a heterogeneous work force, nearly 88 per cent of which is not covered by any pension of old age security scheme, is the immediate priority of those concerned with pension reform process in India. The challenges of translating the design into reality will arise thereafter and will take a while to overcome.

The new pension scheme is an attempt to move away from the defined benefit pension plans to defined contribution based schemes. But, this change would be applicable only to the new entrants. The problem of financing the pension liability of those already under unfounded or partially funded schemes is like to cause fiscal stress for the next two or three decades. Some parametric changes will, therefore, become necessary for effective and efficient discharge of this liability. Thus, apart from spread of the new pension scheme, introduction of parametric changes in the existing defined benefit mandatory pension systems is equally necessary for reducing the fiscal stress. Attempts to estimate the future pension liability arising out of the existing unfounded pension plans are at a nascent stage in India. Recently, some private researchers have tried to undertake a limited exercise in respect of the defined civil service pension scheme. One such study puts the implicit pension debt liability of the Central and State Governments arising out of three components of civil servants pensions at Rs. 20034 billion or 64.51 per cent of GDP. While the methodology and/or the results can be questioned, the magnitude of the problem that this estimate suggests cannot be ignored. The enormity of the problem becomes even more apparent when this liability is compared with the explicit internal public debt of Government of India, which is 84.86 per cent of GDP (2004-05).

Empirical evidence collected through a nation-side survey suggests that India is in transition from old age support systems based on the family to a new reality where for the generation of workers now aged 40, the balance between family support and self support in retirement is likely to fall heavily in the latter direction. It is, therefore, essential that policymakers correctly anticipate the course of the transition so that adequate counter measures are in place at the appropriate time. The survey also indicates that without guidance, encouragement and support, most

Indian workers will not save sufficiently for their old age and the capacity of the State and the labour market to face the challenges is likely to become even more limited than is the case now. Recognizing the fact that pension reforms are an urgent social priority, policymakers in India are working hard to evolve suitable pension systems.

A major challenge of the New Pension System is to provide the individual subscriber with an adequate retirement income. Public sector pension schemes involve 'policy risk' in as much as the Government of the day may not be able to accommodate required pension outlays leading to delays in pension payments or defaults in some cases. On the other hand, private pension schemes are less subject to this 'policy risk' because Governments are less prone to confiscate private property. However, DC funds do involve 'market risk' during the accumulations phase when contributions and returns on investment build up in the fund. The risk is that the pension funds' performance may be insufficient to give reasonable retirement income to the pension subscribers. Our draft Regulations have addressed this issue by providing prudential investment rules and ensuring that Pension Fund Managers diversify their portfolios. Also, these Regulations aim to promote competition by requiring standardized reporting and disclosure.

One issue which needs attention for making the new pension scheme equitable is the tax treatment. Pension savings in general and the NPS in particular is a very long term saving instrument having a time horizon of 30-35 years. Therefore, the treatment of this instrument from a tax perspective, if not the most preferential, should at least be at par with other medium or short term financial instruments. This is especially important at the nascent stage of the new pension system development. In this context, example of Public Provident Fund (PPF) and other such instruments are worth mentioning. PPF having a life cycle of 15 years is under an EEE (exempt-exempt-exempt) tax regime and is not taxed at exit. Therefore, subscribers to NPS are at a disadvantage compared to the PPF especially when seen in the context that NPS is a mandatory scheme whereas PPF is a voluntary scheme. The Government employees appointed before 1.1.2004 participate in the GPF scheme which is again an EEE tax regime whereas NPS is subject to EET regime and the withdrawable tier-II account of NPS (a substitute of GPF) is envisaged to get no preferential tax treatment. Further, a common ceiling for contributions of both the employees and Government under the Income Tax Act, 1961 may be a disadvantage for the subscribers of NPS. Accordingly, a need is felt to treat all long term savings instruments equitably and provide the same tax treatment to NPS as being given to PPF and other similar schemes. The tax treatment merits a review so as to take care of the distortions across financial instruments and giving right fiscal incentives for the development of the pension sector.

Current Status

Pending passage of the PFRDA Bill and establishment of full architecture of the new pension system (NPS), the contributions received under NPS are being kept in the Public Account of the government concerned. While a fixed return of 8 per cent per annum is given by the Union Government on total pension contributions, (both employee as well as the matching contribution by the Government), the actual return would have been in the range of 14-29 per cent per annum if the proposed investment options were given to employees. Delay in the passage of the PFRDA Bill has thus resulted in lost opportunities to Government employees.

In order to address the issue of investment of pension contributions under the NPS through a mechanism of consensus, a Conference of Chief Ministers' on Pension reform was held on 22nd January 2007, which was chaired by the Prime Minister. All the State Governments, except West Bengal, Tripura and Kerala, were in favour of the proposal to adopt the guidelines applicable to the non-Government provident fund prescribed by Ministry of Finance for investing the accumulations under NPS till the Bill is passed by Parliament.

Consequent upon the consensus arrived at the Chief Ministers' Conference, Government has authorized PFRDA to appoint a Central Record-Keeping Agency (CRA) and three Fund Managers from the Public Sector to manage the accumulated funds of Central Government employees. The services of the CRA and the Fund Managers have also been offered to the State Governments to manage the funds of their employees.

PFRDA has identified National Securities Depository Limited (NSDL) as the CRA and is in the process of finalizing a contract with it. Three sponsors of Pension Fund Managers have also been appointed; they are SBI, LIC, UTI-AMC. All the three sponsors have incorporated Pension Fund as separate entities and registered as new companies under the Companies Act, 1956. The selection process for the Trustee Bank and Custodian are also in the final phase of completion. An NPS Trust has also been registered which will be the registered owner of assets under the NPS. Thus, all the inter-mediaries under the NOS have been identified and the system is now ready to be rolled out by 1st June 2008. As regards the cost structure of the NPS, the fund management charges are to be in the range of 3-5 basis points (3.03 per cent-0.05 per cent) of assets under management. The record keeping costs are low compared to the low volume at present. This cost will decline further once the volume increases under the system. The total cost of the NPS is estimated to be around 1 per cent of the total assets under management (AUM) in the initial years and expected to decline to less than 0.5 per cent of AUM within few years of its operation.

Till the PFDRA Bill is passed, there will be two investment options: (i) as per investment guidelines issued by the Ministry of Finance for non-government provident funds (wherein upto 5 per cent can be invested in equity and upto another 10 per cent in equity linked mutual funds, remaining 85 per cent in debt instruments) and (ii) in government securities exclusively.

At conclusion, I would like to emphasise that pension reforms which have been set into motion in the last five years need to be taken forward immediately if India wishes to take advantage of the edge that its demographics offer over similarly placed economies. Average age of Indians in 2005 was about 26 years with 31 per cent of Indians being younger than 15 years, and nearly 64 per cent of Indians in the working population. Thus, the time for undertaking the reforms in the pension sector could not be more appropriate, but the end of the hour is to push the reforms further without delay in terms of offering this system to the unorganized sector workers. The demographic advantage is not going to last forever because India's elderly are growing at a much higher rate than the total population, as a consequence of which the current dependency ratio of 15 is likely to shoot to 40 in the next four decades (dependency ratio here defined as the number of persons over age 60 years to number of persons between 20-59 years). The implications of demographic dynamics for pension planning in India become more evident when one takes into account the fact that average life expectancy at age 60, which is currently 17 years, is likely to rise to more than 20 years in the next three decades and that the population over 60 years of age will approach 200 million in 2030. However, India is still at an early stage of the demographic transition. This is the right time, therefore, to roll out the NPS to all segments of workers. The New Pension System is designed to use the 21st century Information Technology so as to achieve portability, competition and coverage. In contrast to the traditional approach of mandating participation and contributions from the workers for old age income support coupled with tax incentives and guaranteed returns, the voluntary nature of the NPS for unorganized sector is expected to succeed. However, poor financial literacy and the attitude of the households towards financial savings, risk and retirement planning, post a challenge to achieving optimum coverage of NPS. Creating awareness about these reforms and gaining the confidence of the people to encourage them to be a part of this movement is the single most important challenge faced by policymakers today.

19.

Corporate Social Responsibility

Dr. A.K. Balyan
Director (HR) ONGC

OCTOBER 2009

I feel honoured to have been given this opportunity to share the corporate philosophy of ONGC and also my personal ideas and convictions on the social responsibility for betterment of the unorganized workers at workplace. The subject of discussion, I have been asked to talk about — corporate social responsibility and the betterment of lot of unorganized workers for protection of their means of livelihood in terms of income security and availability of goods for daily consumption, are most contemporaneous issues for debate and dialogue. The Association deserves my personal thanks for initiating such a dialogue for the good of the working class.

To open the discussion, I would like to quote from our Hon'ble Prime Minister, Dr. Manmohan Singh's independence day speech delivered on 15th August 2007 from the rampart of Lal Quilla:-

> i. "While we have moved ahead for the last three years on many fronts, there is an area where considerable works needs to be done. Millions of our fellow citizens are not engaged in any formal employment in the organized sector. They work in small establishments, run their own little shops or offer their services on daily basis. They have neither a social security net nor a sense of economic security. They become destitute or indebted when they fall sick or suffer accident."

Nothing could have been a better spotlight to start my discussion. Because the Prime Minister in his speech has succinctly put the basic issue confronting the unorganized workers – the workers in small establishments or those who are self employed or those who earn their wages on daily basis bereft of a social security net or any economic security. They constitute the most hapless, the most venerable segment of our society and the preponderate section of our national workforce. In the ONGC, a large number of workers are employed on daily basis through outside agencies. You would be happy to know and I am very proud to inform you that we have taken the responsibility to protect the economic as well as social security interest of this group of workers in the very best way. Our objective is to protect them from deprivation and destitution and thus to protect them from lapsing into poverty. Before I go into the details of our various social security initiatives, I beg your leave to say a few words on our corporate social responsibility philosophy.

As I had mentioned at the outset that I am beholden to SSAI to have given me an opportunity to talk on social issues before this august assembly of social security experts and administrators. This makes my task both worthy and also professionally satisfying. Today, the issue of CSR has become the guiding principle of corporate excellence and we in ONGC take pride in stating that we have devised a fully enlightened and all pervasive social responsibility policy.

Corporate social responsibility (CSR) has been around for some decades now; the expression came into currency in early 70's of the last century. It evolved out of the corporate recognition of ethics in business – the philosophy to give back to the society what it has derived from the latter. The other view is that it was a consequence of the pressure from the developing countries protesting against exploitation by the big entrepreneurs. Be that as it may, the fact of the matter is that the birth of CSR is unerringly traced to the philanthropic feeling of an entrepreneur and an exhibition of his commitment to the social cause. Corporate social responsibility had a silent start. Earlier CSR was an option. Today, it is a must.

It is well accepted that corporate social responsibility denotes "operating a business in a manner which meets or excels the ethical, legal, commercial and public expectations that a society has from business." World Business Council for Sustainable Development has defined CSR to mean "commitment by business to behave ethically and contribute economic development while improving the quality of life of the work force and their families as well as of local community and society at large. In the words of one of the pioneers in industrial development of our country, viz, Sh. Jamshedji N. Tata, "in a free enterprise, the community is not just another stake holder but is, in fact, the very purpose of its existence."

By definition, therefore, the corporate social responsibility has both ethical and social commitment so as to meet public expectations, because an enterprise exists and flourishes only if the society exists and flourishes. The World Business Council is very emphatic that a corporate should behave ethically and must contribute to the improvement not only of the quality of life of the workforce and their families but also of local community and society at large and in the words of Sh. Jamshedji N. Tata, as quoted above, a free enterprise is just another stake holder in any given society. In ONGC, our philosophy is to do business and earn enough to give back to the society as much as possible for its sustenance and development. Under the corporate policy, we have developed a highly focused policy, called, Corporate Citizenship Policy (CCP) which may be more meaningfully described as follows:

(a) Under this policy ONGC group of companies shall promote, as a responsible Corporate Citizen, the following:

(i) Education.
(ii) Health Care.
(iii) Entrepreneurship in the community and support.
(iv) Water Management.
(v) Disaster Relief in the country.

Environment

(a) Our CSR activities started during the year 2001-02 when ONGC Board approved allocation of 0.75 per cent of net profit for CSR activities. In 2002-03, we became one of the founder members of Global Compact Society – on vision of Mr. Kafi Annan, Secretary General, United Nations to bring industry and UN bodies together to work for a better world. It was in 2003-04 that we adopted the above stated corporate citizenship policy making budgetary provisions for performing corporate social responsibility. In 2004-05, we initiated ONGC Pure Trust with a corpus of Rs. 10 crore for providing urban amenities in rural areas translating the vision of our former President of India, Dr. A.P.J. Abdul Kalam. In 2008-09, ONGC Board enhanced the allocation to 2 per cent of our profit after tax for our social responsibility activities. In 2009-10, we took another step forward by setting up a more formal organizational structure for empowerment and identifying additional focal areas.

The CSR approach in ONGC has a distinct stakeholder participation model. I would like to say a few words in describing this model which distinguishes our approach with that of others. Our CSR activities are undertaken based on project concept. We first identify stakeholders (society) and the intended beneficiaries. After initiation of the project, we continuously measure the impact of that particular project/activity to assess as to how it has benefited the society leading to increase in social bottom lines. Finally, the impact study should bring out quality of corporate social performance.

The project activities are reported in a systematic manner. The report is three dimensional. The report analyses the inputs for the project. This is basically an analysis of the funding of the activities/programmes including adequacy of the funds used. Then the second dimension is the outputs assessment, say, if it is an educational programme what material support has been given to the children, what scholarship support has been provided etc. And the third dimension is the outcome analysis, such as, how many children have been benefited, whether literacy level has gone up and, if so, to what extent, how the life style of the people have changed resulting from the activity undertaken by us.

As I have mentioned earlier that we have already identified our focus areas in the field of education including professional courses, health care, development of self help groups and livelihood generation schemes, infrastructure support in professional areas, environment protection, ecological conservation, protection of heritage sites, promotion of artisans, craftsmen, musicians, women empowerment, girl child development, gender sensitive projects, promoting sports, supporting sports persons, supporting agencies promoting sports, water management including ground water, helping the physically and mentally challenged persons and sponsorship of seminars, workshops and conferences.

Besides the focused areas, we have also taken up projects with immense social and economic impact. One such action area is Project Saraswati. The other area of concern is developing disaster relief system to come to the help of the society in the face of natural calamities faced by the society particularly around our work centers. In the area of education, we have set up nine Shishu Vihars in different work centers with our full financial and administrative support. We have also invited Kendriya Vidyalaya Sansthan and DPS Society and other reputed schools to open their branches at our work centers so that high quality school education is available to the students even in remote areas also. I am happy to mention here that the B.S. Negi Mahila Pravidhik Prakasan Sansthan, Dehradun, a woman polytechnic for technical education of women, is running with full administrative and financial support from our organization. We are supporting one institution, called, Himjyoti Foundation, Dehradun, for development of infrastructure and support for 50 under privileged girls every year for last eight years. We are supporting Akshay Patra Foundation for providing modern kitchen facility to provide mid-day meals to school children in Mangalore. We are offering scholarships to the students who are children of widows of Uttarakhand through one institution, called, Loomba Trust. We have set up one institute, called, the Energy Research Institute for development of a centre for study of energy security. It is a joint venture of ours with TERI. We have set up another institute on JV, called, ONGC-TERI Biotech Limited for development of oil zappers for bio remediation. For differently abled children we have organized a workshop on film making on these unfortunate children. In this regard, we have set up what we have named, Auroville Language Laboratory at Pondichery for development of Tomatis Language for the visually impaired people. For the physically disabled children, we have set up a computer centre at Tamanna Special School. For abolition of child labour, we have set up Mobile Creches in New Delhi, where we are educating the children, providing nutrition food to them and taking care of them at the construction sites. We are providing support to 150 Anganwadis in Western sector of ONGC. We have set up Computerised Braille Machine to meet the Braille printing requirement of blind students of East and North-Eastern States, at Ramakrishna Mission, Narendrapur, West Bengal.

In the health care area, we have developed medical facilities at various locations, by means of setting up primary health centers or consulting hospitals. We are also patronizing development of super specialty hospitals. In addition to the above institutional approach, we are also organizing medical camps at regular intervals. We are distributing medicines, including spectacles, providing reliefs, organizing eye camps, providing ambulances, running mobile medical units, distributing artificial limbs. We are supporting projects for setting up information technology (IT) linkages with health care systems. For these activities, we are encouraging NGOs and other civil societies involved in health care by providing them financial support. We have supported establishing C.T. Scan and MRI facilities at Government hospitals at Mumbai, Silchar and Uttarakhand. We have introduced a mobile cancer detection unit in Dibrugarh. We have supported Shankara Netralaya, Chennai for setting up a genetic and molecular biology diagnostic department. We are supporting one charitable hospital in Kolkata run by Ramkrishna Mission Sevashram. We have provided aid to the Cancer Institute, Chennai for setting up of an intensive care unit. We have provided support to Sh. Shridi Sai Rural Welfare Trust, Nellore for running a mobile medical unit. We have given support for construction/upgradation of a burn ward in the Government hospital at Karaikal. We have supported polio eradication programme through Rotary International. We have also given institutional support to HIV-AIDS through NACO and population stabilisation through Jana sankhya Sthirta Kosh. We have given support for establishing a blood bank by the Rotarians in Uttarakhand. We have assisted setting up AAKHA, 'Boat of Hope', a mobile medical unit for providing medical care for people living in and around in Majula islands near Jorhat, Assam. We supported the venture of Life Care Society set up by the ex-employees of ONGC for organizing medical check ups in remote villages in Uttarakhand and had provided them a mobile medical unit to facilitate their work. Similarly, we are supporting Bharatiya Kusttha Niwarak Sangha working in the tribal district of Bastar, Chattisgarh for work on sickle cell anemia and malnutrition amongst the tribal. One retired General Manager of our ONGC family is working with this Sangha for taking their work forward. We have set up Life Line Foundation for Trauma care of accident victims on the highways of Gujarat & Uttarakhand. We have provided artificial limb to orthopedically challenged in Chennai and in Sudan. We have also supported international community through our subsidiary Oversees Venture Limited.

I would again refer to our beloved Prime Minister's speech on the independent day of 2007 that millions of our citizens have neither a social security net nor a sense of economic security. In ONGC, we are conscious of this problem in our society and we, therefore, have resolved to give back to our society in our limited way to alleviate the aforesaid social problems and be socially useful. In our country as we look at the employment scenario, we find that in the year 1999-2000, about 93 per cent of the work force was in the unorganized sector and only 7 per cent in the organized sector. The annual rate of growth in employment was in the horizon of 1.25 per cent in the unorganized sector and 0.34 per cent in the organized sector. Again, the majority of the unorganized workforce was employed in agriculture and when we analyse the incidence of employment in the unorganized sector and employment across industries, we find that unorganized workforce in agriculture, hunting, forestry and fishery as also in construction, hotel and restaurants constitutes 98.8 per cent, in transport and communication sector it is about 78.5 per cent and in the services sector about 65.2 per cent. The incidence of unorganized employment was least in electricity, gas and in water sector, to the tune of 21 per cent. The situation, therefore, calls for effective measures to provide social security for the multitude of unorganized workforce not only by the Government but by other civil societies in the country. Although the government has introduced large number of social security initiatives, like, Mid Day Meal Scheme, 1995, Community Gramin Bank Scheme, 1996, Targeted PDS, 1998, Annapurna Scheme, 2000, Antyodaya Scheme, 2000, several social and pension Schemes, like, Janashree Bima Yojana, Krishi Samajik Surakshya, 2001, Varishta Pension Bima 2003, but these are not enough. The enactment of the Unorganized Workers Social Security Act, 2008 has for the first time underpinned the responsibility of the government to protect the interest of the unorganized sector workers. It has highlighted the issue of social security in the unorganized sector and the need for involvement of other stake-holders and the social partners.

For responsible corporate, it is an opportunity to partner with government to come to the aid of the workers in the unorganized sector by offering social protection.

In ONGC we have made detailed analysis of the problems of the unorganized workers who are called contract workmen and the social security concerns of those group of workers. Our findings are as follows:

(a) Firstly, they are not paid minimum wages in all cases. They are paid less than the prescribed rate of wages or if paid according to the notified rate, it is paid late.
(b) Secondly, they receive nothing or minimal medical facilities and health care.
(c) Thirdly, there is no training for their skilled enhancement. So their employability is hindered and limited.
(d) Fourthly, there is no payment of bonus in recognition of the work done by them. They have got inadequate or sometimes no retrial benefit. There is no allocation of kits and liveries at the workplace.
(e) Lastly, their employers are not committed to their cause and show little sense of responsibility in tackling their issues.

For providing social security for the unorganized workers, we have developed multipronged approaches which I would like to describe in details. We have made them part of a trust, called, Sahayog Trust. We have prepared model system to ensure that they are paid fair wages and wages are paid always in time. The objectives of Sahayog Yojana are fourfold. Firstly, to extend financial aid to the family of workforce in service of ONGC. Secondly, to meet the expenditure of medical care requiring substantial expenditure. Thirdly, to promote higher education of their children. Lastly, any other specific purpose which may be decided by the trustees dependent on the circumstances and the state of distress and hardship. The CMD of ONGC is the Chairman of the Trust. There are five other trustees including the Director, (HR) and Director, (Finance) of ONGC in this Trust. An official of the ONGC nominated by the Board acts as the Chief Executive Officer of the Trust and manages its working on behalf of the trustees. It is the endeavour of the trustees to manage the various social security schemes for the employees and their families, to address the problem of attrition, to deal with the issues related to employment and the dependants of the deceased and to inculcate of a sense of bondage and commitment.

We have formulated a model tender document taking into account all types of contracts relating to various ancillary job requirements of the organization, like, canteen, security, housekeeping, survey work, loading, unloading, horticulture, etc. We have decided to develop uniform approach across the board for outsourcing our labour intensive activities mainly to eliminate the variation of procedure for award of contract at work centers. Such a procedure, we believe to be an effective measure to avoid litigation in such activities. Currently, the organization is saddled with 25 labour conciliation cases, 47 adjudication cases and 40 High Court cases. By adopting the said model tender procedure we seek to ensure cent per cent licensing of contractors under the Contract Labour (Regulation and Abolition) Act, 1972. It also seeks to ensure that every contractor has an independent code number under the EPF and Miscellaneous Act, 1952 and ESI Code under the ESI Act, 1948 for health care. Those contractors who do not have ESI Code being located outside the covered area should have medical insurance for its workers. It also seeks to ensure that every contractor has an independent office/administrative set up. Every contractor shall also have either a gratuity trust or a group gratuity for its employees.

We have adopted a conscious policy to ensure that every one employed in connection to our work is paid minimum wage as per the statutory provision. We, therefore, maintain full information about the various statutory notifications regarding minimum wage payable to the skilled, unskilled and semi skilled workers. It is our commitment to ensure fair working conditions to all kinds/classes of labour. We feel that the need of the hour is to bring in uniformity in approach with regard to the role of contractors and compliance of statutory provisions to be ensured. We believe that the workers are entitled to fair wage and fair wage means his pay package shall consist of minimum wage, plus additional wage, like, dearness allowance plus provident fund plus bonus plus leave with wages plus ESI, where applicable. We have, therefore, laid down the rule that fair wages have to be incorporated in the tender itself. At the same time, we have streamlined the procedure to ensure payment of fair wages and other benefits by the contractors. We have also laid down condition that the contractors would be required to enter into settlement with workmen prior to the commencement of work.

I am happy to inform this august audience that ONGC is planning to launch the ONGC Bima Siksha Yojana and LIC Janashree Bima Yojana which aim at heralding a new era in providing social security for the unorganized workers. This insurance cover would be available to the unorganized workers who are working in our areas or living in the same location. Under the Janashree Bima Yojana, the beneficiaries are entitled to death benefit, permanent disability as well as partial disability benefit due to accident. We are planning to enroll BPL families for the purpose of these schemes and the estimated cost of the project is going to be to the tune of Rs. 130 crore. Under Siksha Yojana, the children of the workers studying between IX and XII standard would be given scholarship to the tune of Rs. 1200 per year per children in two installments. The benefit is to be restricted to two children per family.

In operationalising these two insurance schemes, we plan to select one village in every State to ensure uniform implementation of policy across the country and to guarantee equity in our CSR policy. Our objective is to show up corporate policy by uplifting a specific segment of people and for this purpose we are identifying specific occupations across the country. In selecting the areas for our operation, we will give priority to States with low literacy level because one of our CSR objective is to create a literate society. By adopting the aforesaid policy we are intending to synergies corporate responsibility with governing bodies and insurance companies.

In the area of sports, we have come to the help of the All India Football Federation in promoting football which is a very popular sports across the country. We have also been supporting individual players with talent and potential in all the fields of sports to increase the national stock of talented sportsmen. Our commitment for development of sports is unflinching.

To sum up, I would say that we have made a small beginning in discharging our corporate responsibility to the society. To conclude my talk, I would like to recall what one of our illustrious I.T. gurus, Dr. N. R. Narayana Murthy, Chairman, Infosys Technologies, has said as follows while addressing the students of New York University (Stern School of Business) recently:

> "I believe that we have all at some time eaten the fruit from trees that we did not plant. In the fullness of time, when it is our turn to give, it behooves us in turn to plant gardens that we may never eat the fruits of which will largely benefit generations to come......:"

We, in ONGC, have also faith in the same philosophy propounded by Dr. Narayan Murthy, If, we are acclaimed today as a giant in the oil industry and are counted among the top business entities across the globe, we have no doubt that we have derived that strength to become a giant amongst the giants in the world of business from your own society. It is our motherland, it is our people who have given us light and inspiration to develop into our present stature and it is our bounden duty to give back to the society whatever we can. As I have said earlier we have made a beginning. We have seen that our endeavours are bearing the fruits. Imbued by these successes we propose to move forward.

Social Security Association of India

A Profile

New Delhi

Social Security Association of India was established at the initiative of a prominent trade union leader Sh. Parduman Singh of AITUC, two retired senior civil servants, one, Sh. T.S. Sankaran, IAS, who was Additional Secretary in the Ministry of Labour for some time (retired as Member, Board of Revenue, Tamil Nadu) and the other Sh. R.K.A. Subrahmanya, IA&AS, who retired as Additional Secretary, Ministry of Labour and later became the Director General of the Mahatma Gandhi Labour Institute, Ahmedabad, and a member of the AP Administrative Tribunal, Sh. B.M. Sethi, an entrepreneur, management consultant, and Vice President of All India Organisation of Employers, and late Sh. P.B. Duggal, Industrialist and President, Small Scale Industries Employers' Association, Delhi. These enthusiasts were all social activists in labour related issues, covered in Delhi from various parts of the country and got to know each other as members of Central Board of Trustees, Employees Provident Fund Organisation or as members of National Labour Law Association. Irrespective of their individual professional affiliation, they shared one vision in common that social security movement in the country should be given a formal platform and in this endeavour all the partners and stake holders in the labour market should congregate and act together. These pioneers were joined by a few more illustrious persons of eminence in their profession as founding fathers of the Association, like, Late Sh. S.K.Wadhwan, retired Consultant, I.L.O., Sh. Har Mander Singh, former Director General, Employees State Insurance Corporation, Dr. L.D. Mishra, Civil Servant, Sh. A. Viswanathan, Administrator (Social Security) and Sh. S.P. Mehrotra, Consultant (Social Security). The collective contribution of these few individuals in structuring the social security movement in our country deserves to be written in letters of gold.

To start with, they had no tangible assets except their indomitable spirit to chart out new path for the good of the working class. However, they were fortunate enough to get patronage of the then Union Labour Minister Sh. P.A. Sangma who was himself an ardent supporter of the cause of labour and a statesman par excellence. He was convinced that the society needs to have a strong social security agenda to successfully weather the effects of opening of markets removing geographical boundaries for trade and commerce. He not only encouraged the idea of forming an association on social security, but went beyond the normal contours of his duty to help these enthusiasts to form an association to promote social security in India. Fortunately, the then Deputy Minister of Labour, Sh. Paban Kumar Ghatwar was drawn from the tea garden labour union of INTUC and he extended his full fledged support and help to overcome the teething problems of setting up an organization and to achieve their objective. Another personality, Sh. S. Gopalan, IAS, then Secretary, Ministry of Labour, who stood silently but solidly not only to provide momentum but also valuable counsel in shaping the formation of the Association. In fact, but for his unstinted support and encouragement the birth of this historic Association could have been stymied in the cauldron of bureaucracy. Another civil servant and a silent stalwart, Sh. P.C.Hota, then Additional Secretary, Ministry of Labour, who championed the cause of social security and contributed substantially in mastering the much needed support of the government in realizing the dream of those enthusiasts referred to earlier. It is also a streak of providence that two of the premier social security institutions of the country, viz., Employees State Insurance Corporation and Employees Provident Fund Organisation were at that point of time headed by two distinguished civil servants, Smt. Kusum Prasad, DG, ESIC, and Sh. B.N. Som, CPFC, who gave infrastructure support to this group to organize their movement. In fact, the birth of the Social Security Association of India took place in the chamber of Central Provident Fund Commissioner (CPFC), then at Mayur Bhawan, New Delhi where the founder members gathered together and signed the Memorandum of Association heralding the birth of the Association.

It is again a turn of history and great coincidence that the Association was inaugurated by the then Union Finance Minister (now Prime Minister of India), Dr. Manmohan Singh in December 1991. It was registered as a Society under the Societies Registration Act, in July 1992. The milieu of the membership of the Association covers all the segments of the society fulfilling its objective of promoting social security in India. It thus consists of social security institutions, public administrators, serving and retired trade union leaders, managers, management consultants, judges, lawyers, academicians, experts in social security and other persons interested in social security. Its membership is spread over the length and breadth of the country. As this Association is the only entity in the field of social security in our country it has received accreditation of the international bodies – it is affiliated to International Social Security Association (ISSA), Geneva and International Labour Organization (ILO), Geneva. The registered office of the Association is located in New Delhi. It has seven Chapters covering the states of Andhra Pradesh, Karnataka, Kerala, Orissa, Rajasthan, West Bengal (Kolkata Chapter) and Maharastra (Mumbai Chapter).

The Association has been formed with the primary objective of promoting social security in India. To achieve the aforesaid objective, the Association conducts studies and research into the existing laws and schemes of social security, their coverage, extension and implementation. It also provides a forum for free and frank discussion on the various aspects of social security particularly the need for and the feasibility of introducing new laws for providing social security to people outside the organised sector of employment through seminars, symposia, workshops and other forms of discussion and debate.

List of Abbreviations

AITUC = All India Trade Union Congress
ASSEFA = Association for Serve Sewa Sangathan Farms
CCP = Corporate Citizenship Policy
CRA = Computing Research Association
CSP = Civil Service Pension
DWCRA = Development of Women and Child in Rural Areas
ECD = Early Child Deployment
EET = Exemption Exemption Tax
EGA = Employment Guarantee Act
EPFO = Employees' Provident Fund Organisation
EPS = Employees Pension Scheme
ESIC = Employees Estate Insurance Corporation
FCI = Food Corporation of India
FOCUS = a NGO
GDP = Gross Domestic Product
GIPSA = General Insurance Public Association
HLEG = High Level Expert Group
IAS = Indian Administration Service
ILO = International Labour Organisation
IPEC = International Programme on the Elimination of Child Labour
ISSA = International Social Security Association
LPG = Liberalization, Privatization & Globalization
MIT = Massachusetts of Information Technology
MKSS = Mazdoor Kisan Sakti Sangathan
NAC = National Advisory Council
NACO = National Aids Control Organisation
NGO = Non Government Organization
NHRC = National Human Right Commission
NPS = National Pension Scheme
NSAP = National Social Assistance Programme
NSC = National Savings Scheme
NSDL = National Securities Depository Ltd. (Pension Fund)
OASIS = Old Age Service Social and Income Security
OHP = Overhead Project
ONGC = Oil and Natural Gas Corporation
PAYG = Pay As You Go
PDS = Public Distribution Systems
PFRDA = Pension Fund Regulatory & Development Authority
SEWA = Self Employees Women Association
SSAI = Social Security Association of India
STEP = Strategies and Tool against Social Exclusions
UNDP = United Nation Development Programme

Index